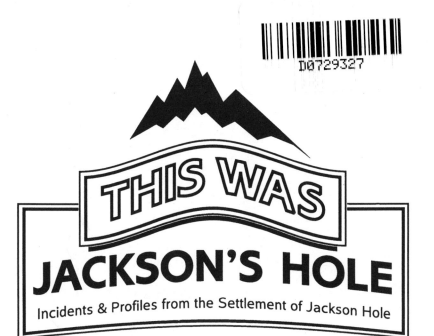

THIS WAS

JACKSON'S HOLE

Incidents & Profiles from the Settlement of Jackson Hole

Also by Fern K. Nelson

Soda for the Sourdoughs

Mountain Men of Jackson's Hole

THIS WAS
JACKSON'S HOLE

Incidents & Profiles from the Settlement of Jackson Hole

Fern K. Nelson

HIGH PLAINS PRESS

The cover art of the softcover edition
is titled "Seeking a Homestead Location."
The artist is Fern K. Nelson,
and it depicts the Martin Nelson family's ride over Teton Pass.

10   9   8   7   6   5   4   3   2

Library of Congress Cataloging-in-Publication Data

Nelson, Fern K.
This was Jackson's Hole/ Fern K. Nelson
p. cm.
Includes bibliographical references and index.
ISBN 0-931271-26-6 (hardback : acid free)
ISBN 0-931271-25-8 (soft : acid-free)
1. Jackson Hole (Wyo.)--History--Anecdotes.
2. Jackson Hole (Wyo.)--Biography--Anecdotes.
I. Title
F767.T28N45 1994
978.7'55--dc20   94-25082
                                                  CIP

HIGH PLAINS PRESS
539 CASSA ROAD
GLENDO, WYOMING 82213

*Dedicated to the memory of those hardy pioneers
who loved the Jackson's Hole country enough
to stay and "weather it out."*

$\mathcal{C}$ONTENTS

ꝼOREWORD

Fᴇʀɴ ɴᴇʟꜱᴏɴ ᴡᴀꜱ ʙᴏʀɴ May 4, 1911, in Vernal, Utah, as Fern Knutsen. Her father obtained the mail contract over Teton Pass in the fall of 1911. The family moved to Jackson either that fall or in the spring of 1912.

Before she was a year old, Fern lived in Jackson Hole. Always interested in fine detail, Fern has never claimed to be a native of Jackson Hole or of Wyoming. But if honorary credentials are ever given for Jackson Hole Native, Fern should be at the top of the list.

I have known Fern for about fourteen years. Since we first met, I've known of Fern's passion for Jackson Hole history. When I was first a volunteer at the Jackson Hole Museum, Fern was a part-time staff member. At that time I was spending long hours with Slim Lawrence documenting his wonderful historical collections. Fern and I struck up a conversation on valley history, and whenever I wanted to know something about early settlers, I went to Fern. I'm proud to say that our conversation about the valley's old timers is still ongoing.

For many years Fern Nelson contributed articles to the *Jackson Hole Guide* on early Jackson Hole. Fortunately, these articles are for the first time made available between the covers of this book. And Fern has also included additional articles which have not been published previously. Many readers will, however, be reading all of Fern's stories for the first time.

You will discover two things about Fern's writing. One is that Fern wants everything she writes to be as accurate as she can possibly make it. The other is that Fern loves a good story. What a great combination. Enjoy.

Rᴏʙᴇʀᴛ C. Rᴜᴅᴅ, Fᴏʀᴍᴇʀ Dɪʀᴇᴄᴛᴏʀ
Jᴀᴄᴋꜱᴏɴ Hᴏʟᴇ Mᴜꜱᴇᴜᴍ ᴀɴᴅ Tᴇᴛᴏɴ Cᴏᴜɴᴛʏ Hɪꜱᴛᴏʀɪᴄᴀʟ Cᴇɴᴛᴇʀ

THIS WAS JACKSON'S HOLE

THE FIRST HOMESTEADERS

JOHN R. AND MILLIE CARNES AND John Holland *were not* the first people to live in Jackson's Hole. Indians, mountain men, and explorers had preceded them, but these early visitors usually headed for more hospitable climates at the first sign of winter.

The Carneses and Holland *were not* the first people to stay in the valley through the winter. There is little doubt that some Indians stayed through the winter and that occasionally trappers, and maybe outlaws, spent a winter or so in Jackson's Hole when necessary. If so, their names are lost to history.

But John and Millie Carnes and John Holland *were* the valley's first settlers. They filed claims to homesteads in 1883, built cabins and stayed through the winter, intending to make Jackson's Hole their permanent home.

John R. Carnes was born in Steubenville, Ohio, in 1839, where he attended school for about two years. He was inducted into the Union Army and fought in the Civil War, then he drifted out to the west. He stopped in Wyoming in the area of La Barge, where he carried the mail for some time. He filed on a homestead in the area of Fontenelle Creek but must have relinquished this claim. On March 17, 1881, while in the Fontenelle area, he married Millie Frappe. John was about forty-two years old at this time.

Millie was the widow of Ike Frappe, a trapper who had died in 1874 or 1875. She was the daughter of a Ute Indian woman and a trapper of German-French descent named LeRose. As was the habit in the west, Johnny Carnes was referred to as a "squawman." But the marriage of John and Millie was legal and happy. Millie was quite a person in her own right.

Millie evidently had adopted and raised a boy named Charles Harmes, who later remembered her with an eighty-acre allotment in his will. She also finished raising her sister's boy, Jesse Barker, whose father had been killed in the Civil War. There is no record of John and Millie having children of their own, nor of children being with them in Jackson, so presumably Millie's foster children were old enough to be on their own when the Carneses moved to Jackson's Hole.

The other early settler, John Holland, was a fine-looking, strapping young man who had been a bullwhacker on the construction of the Oregon Short Line across Wyoming and Idaho. He was an expert woodsman and probably handy in all pioneering labors. He was active in the La Barge area and no doubt met John Carnes there. They became trapping buddies and had trapped in Jackson's Hole before 1883. In that year they decided to stake claims in that valley so alive with game and fur.

Holland and the Carneses came to Jackson's Hole on horseback, with their equipment on pack horses. They followed a well-established trapping route up the Green River and its tributaries to the divide now called Bacon Ridge, from there down Bacon Creek to the Gros Ventre River, then down that river to the valley floor of the Snake River. They selected a spot on the Little Gros Ventre (now called Flat Creek) where the wild hay promised good feed for the horses and where two sparkling streams tumbled off the mountain to join the Little Gros Ventre. They staked off their 160-acre homestead claims and, in due course, raised a cabin.

Next they set about digging a ditch to irrigate the natural grass in order to increase their hay production. The ditch came out of a headgate located two hundred feet below the confluence of Sheep Creek and Twin Creek, tributaries of Little Gros Ventre. It must have been Holland who made the long ride back out of the valley to a land office to file claim to water rights for the homesteads. Apparently both were filed by Holland in 1883, as Holland #1 and Holland #2. They were the first claims filed in Jackson's Hole. One was granted in 1886; the other in 1887.

The Homestead Law required that a dwelling be put on each one-hundred-sixty-acre allotment; also improvements had to be made to the land to the value of $1.25 per acre. Ditches and fences counted toward these improvements. As soon as they could, the

❧ *John Carnes and his wife Millie were the first settlers to file for a homestead in Jackson's Hole.* (Jackson Hole Museum & Historical Center)

men put up another log cabin. They had built the first cabin close to their joint property line. For convenience's sake, they put the next cabin on the other side of the line and joined the two with a dog-trot shed.

There is no record of how consistently the Carneses and Holland lived on their homesteads, but the Homestead Law required five years' residency for at least seven months of the year as part of the requirements to "prove up." As a means of supplementing their income, the two men also took out hunting parties. An incident related by Carnes' descendant Beatrice Edwards is illustrative of the harsh realities of the frontier condition.

It seems that one of the hunting parties included two surgeons from the east. Noticing that John Carnes had a skin cancer that had reached a dangerous state, the two offered to remove it. Carnes accepted. The operation was performed in the primitive conditions of the cabin. The surgeons did have their own instruments with them. Apparently the operation was a success because Johnny lived to be ninety-two years old.

According to the information gathered from relatives of John and Millie, the Carneses moved back to Fort Hall, where they lived on Millie's Indian allotment from 1895 until her death in 1923. The Carneses received their homestead patent for the Jackson land in 1897. (Sometimes the patents were held up in the land office quite some time after the final proofs were filed.) John Holland did not prove up but rather sold a relinquishment to his right—some say around 1890. Although John Holland was evidently in Jackson's Hole in 1898, old timers of the valley think he must have left before 1890, perhaps returning for visits.

Some of the early settlers had used the Carnes and Holland cabins for temporary quarters while putting up their own log cabins. The Carneses and Holland were very accommodating; they either moved over and shared their facilities, were gone temporarily from the valley, or moved out. We know that John and Millie Carnes loaned the use of their cabin to the Wilson family when they first came into the valley in the winter of 1889. In 1896, the Budge, Allen, and May families were able to use the cabins while the men went to the timber for logs, dressed them and built their own homestead cabins.

When Millie died in 1923, John was eighty-four years old and probably somewhat senile. At any rate he was sent to the Soldiers' Home at Boise. He had no use for that place and kept running—or walking—away and getting back to the reservation at Fort Hall, 260 miles to the south and east.

Harry Hutchinson, a friend living in Fort Hall, took him back to Boise a time or two, then struck a deal with the authorities. "Shucks, he doesn't want to go back there. Just leave him stay with us." So that is where John spent his last days. He died of cancer of the throat in 1931. He was ninety-two.

❧ *John Holland, younger than Carnes, is thought to have provided strength and vigor for the early homesteaders.* (JHM&HC)

In their joint venture at homesteading, it is easy to imagine that of the two men, John Holland was the mover and doer. He was a well-educated man for the time and place, a man of mature strength and vigor. He probably lined up the hunting parties and made the trips out for mail and supplies—a matter of some two hundred miles round trip the first few years.

Research indicates that Holland married a woman from Victor, Idaho—Maud Carpenter. Then they moved to Scio, Oregon. It is recorded that he sold a relinquishment to his homestead for five hundred dollars.

In 1898, Holland returned to Jackson to guide the Holmes party on a hunting trip in the vicinity of Black Rock, in the Togwotee Pass area. They discovered a cave and tried to explore it. They had to duck through two small waterfalls. A third one stopped them. Mr. Holmes didn't forget the adventure. In 1905 he returned with his son Edwin (Ned) to explore it further.

On that trip, he contacted Mr. Griggs, of Victor, Idaho, to guide him. Holmes asked John Holland, who had moved to Oregon by then and retired from guiding, to join the party. T.R. Wilson, another Victor resident, was also in the party. They went well equipped to explore, and it was late enough in the fall so that the stream of waterfalls (later named Holmes Creek) was nearly dry. They were able to get past the waterfall which had stopped them before.

They spent a week looking over and mapping the features of the cave. Holmes named the cave for his son and the Holland Chamber for the guide who had first led him to the place. Holmes sent a letter containing maps and information to the Honorable Bryant B. Brooks, then Governor of Wyoming, and was credited for the discovery of the cave.

This seems to be the only natural geographic feature in the valley named for either of the men who were its first white settlers. Their homesteads became the property of Dave Goe and his sons, Ben and George. The properties are now incorporated in the National Wildlife Preserve.

A WINTER ADVENTURE

WHEN ALBERT RICHARDS WAS a lad of eleven or twelve, growing up on a frontier ranch in the wilds of southwestern Wyoming early in the 1880s, he chanced to become acquainted with trapper John Holland. John was in his twenties or early thirties then—old enough to be smart and able, not so young as to be brash or lead a lad astray. Albert thought John could do just about anything. Especially was he entranced with John's tales of the country to the north called Jackson's Hole. There the mountains were the highest, the most rugged, the most beautiful of any seen anywhere in the world. And the trapping was the best.

Albert clamored to know all about this country, and John gradually told him all he knew. They finally made a pact when Albert was thirteen years old. If Albert could get a companion to go with him, they could come to Jackson's Hole, and John would meet them on the Buffalo Fork of the Snake River and show them the upper country. Albert thought of little else all summer as he helped with the farm work and chores.

It wasn't hard to talk his friend Will White into eager agreement to go along. The hard part was getting the parents to agree. Finally they did agree, knowing that the boys were as good in the mountains and as good in taking care of themselves as most men were. After the hay was put up and the cattle gathered, the boys made up their camp equipment. They took slabs of bacon, salt, sugar, flour, beans, dried peas, dried fruit and a start of sourdough. They each had a saddle horse and a pack horse, their bedrolls and a tipi.

Holland had given them a good description, and maybe a map, of their route and the boys had no trouble finding the trails. The fall weather was beautiful, they caught fish anytime they wanted them, and rabbits and grouse helped with their grubstake. It was yet too early to trap but signs of fur-bearing animals abounded.

On their way they came upon a camp of Indians who were making pemmican. The Indians grilled the meat on a grill made of green willows then pounded the cooked meat and berries together. The boys tried this and added pemmican to their camp supplies.

When they arrived at the Buffalo Fork, the boys made camp and looked around for their friend. Holland never did arrive at the rendezvous. The boys didn't worry much. They started setting traps, and, finding the fur prime, they set to their business of trapping. As the winter advanced, the valley received the usual amount of snow. They found a good campsite with high wild hay along the stream. The horses pawed down to feed and also browsed on the willows. The boys were doing so well with their trapping and skinning that they seldom noticed, nor cared, that the days rolled by. Finally they had about all the pelts they could pack, and the snow looked like it was about all their horses could buck. They decided they had better get out of the valley while they could.

They followed the river down the valley (we can imagine their snowy camps). The thing is, they neither panicked nor gave up their furs. They wallowed along as a matter of course. Arriving at Munger Mountain, they found two trappers who were holed up for the winter, Jack Davis and a man named Leland. These two fellows were familiar with the difficult trail down through the Snake River Canyon. They agreed to guide the boys down the canyon to the mouth of Greys River, where the canyon opened up. Here the boys gave the remainder of their grub to the trappers. On their own once again, they crossed Greys River onto the Salt River drainage, working their way south through Lower and Upper Star Valley, then up Salt Creek, over the pass, and down into the Bear River drainage. Considering the winter conditions, they had an easy ride on to Cokeville and home—arriving sometime in February.

The scope of the boys' undertaking becomes more evident if we keep in mind that the most direct route from the Buffalo Fork to Cokeville on today's highways is about 150 miles.

ℱIRST ᴡHITE ᴡOMAN & ℂHILD IN ᴠALLEY

ON JULY 3, 1888, Berthe Johanna Overlund Nelson, the first white woman to enter Jackson's Hole, came riding over Teton Pass horseback with her husband, John Martin Nelson. Behind her saddle rode her four-year-old daughter, Cora. The first white child to come to the valley, Cora said that the view wasn't so good from back there, but she remembered the ride well because her mother had tied two sad-irons to the back of the saddle which rubbed her legs the whole trip. Martin rode in the lead, followed by a pack-string carrying all their possessions.

Berthe had come to the United States from Norway in 1881, settling in Milford, Iowa, where she had uncles and cousins. She got a job in the mills, and it was there that she met Martin. They married in 1883, and after a few years, they traveled west, settling for a time in Teton Basin, Idaho. They already had two little daughters when they set out upon their journey from Iowa. The second little girl, born in Milford on August 21, 1886, died at the age of twenty-two months, in Idaho.

In 1886, Nelson visited Jackson's Hole on a hunting trip. He was determined to go back to settle. Two years later, he brought his wife to see how she liked the place.

During that first summer, the Nelsons camped and rode around in the valley, looking for just the place they wanted to make their own. They settled on a spot on the east side of the East Gros Ventre Butte where there was a nice spring, plenty of wild hay on the meadows of Flat Creek, and a good building site. (It was two miles north of the present town of Jackson.) They staked their claim and prepared to ride back out of the valley, leaving some of their things with Johnny Carnes because it would be some time before they could return and start work on the place.

By late fall, Mrs. Nelson knew she was expecting a new baby in May of 1889. It was decided that she should go back to her relatives in Iowa until after the birth. Nelson went to the land office in Evanston to file the claim for the Jackson's Hole homestead. He returned to the valley the next spring to work on the homestead and then traveled east to visit his family. His wife and children did not come West until the new baby boy, named Milliam Eng, was two years old. Alas, Milliam thus missed being the first white baby born in Jackson's Hole. His sister Grace was possibly the third child born in the valley. (Effie Jane Wilson, Joseph Howard Cheney, and Grace Cauline Nelson all arrived in March 1891.)

After the family settled in Jackson, five more children were born to the Nelsons; two of them died in childhood. Cora, Milliam, James, Mose and Pearl survived the diseases and perils of childhood and grew up in Jackson.

Berthe was what is known as "a good neighbor." She was always on hand to help new settlers as they came to make a home. Her good humor and good practical sense eased many a problem. She met the pioneering hardships with fortitude and good humor. When, in the "Indian Troubles" of 1895, a little Indian child was separated from his mother and picked up by the posse, it was to Berthe that he was taken to be cared for until he could be returned to the reservation and his parents. Eleven-year-old Cora assumed much of his care and became quite fond of him. She was sad when the army trooper came to get him to return him to Fort Hall and his Indian folks.

Since the ranch embraced a part of the Flat Creek Slough, Nelson was nicknamed Slough Grass Nelson. After that, hardly a person in the valley knew his real given names of John Martin—especially since he always signed himself Martin Nelson, never John, John M., or John Martin Nelson.

When William Owen's official survey of the valley in 1897 revealed that Martin's home was outside his property line, he simply moved the house within his own boundary.

Cora attended the first school in the valley, which was started in 1894 by the Sylvester Wilson family in South Park. Cora, who

❧ Berthe Nelson was the first white woman known to enter the valley. She is shown here with her children Milliam (left) and Cora. (JHM&HC)

would have been ten that year, didn't tell me how she traveled from two miles north of Jackson to five miles south of Jackson. Did she ride so far alone? Did someone take her every day? Maybe she boarded with some of the Wilsons from Monday until Friday. Fortunately, the Clubhouse was built in what would become the town of Jackson and a school was started in that building in 1900, according to Frances Deloney Clark. Cora, age sixteen, was among the first pupils. Now she was able to attend school much closer to home. Cora grew as the town grew. In her teen years she enjoyed all the things the valley had to offer — riding, fishing, huckleberrying, dancing. She was helpful to her parents, indoors and in the field.

Cora fell in love with Frank Price. His parents had homesteaded on the north side of the Gros Ventre, in the Zenith area. Frank and Cora were married on Christmas day in 1901. What a Christmas celebration that was! They settled on the ranch Frank had homesteaded near Kelly. They romantically named it "The Ideal Ranch." Four children were born to them there: Robert, Douglas, Sarah and Frances. Their "ideal" years ended in a separation in the

❧ *John Martin Nelson acquired the nickname "Slough Grass" because his ranch embraced a slough known for its fine hay.* (JHM&HC)

twenties. Frank left the valley and settled in California. In 1934, Cora married John Barber whose homestead is now a part of the Jackson Hole Golf Course. Unfortunately, this congenial match was shortened by John's illness and death in 1935. Cora sold the ranch and bought a home in Jackson.

Except for short periods of living in Idaho and Oregon, Cora spent her life in the valley. She was a wonderful addition to it; a joyful companion, enjoying all of the activities life had to offer, both work and play.

She was an enthusiastic member of the Old Timers' Association. In her later years she was surrounded by children and grandchildren in her home. She loved the family gatherings and always engineered them at her house until age slowed the eagerness. She attended the

Old Timer's Dance in the winter of 1964 and had a wonderful time visiting and reminiscing with her friends. She died at Sacred Heart Hospital in Idaho Falls, June 11, 1965. She was eighty-one years, one month and one day of age. She is buried in the Aspen Cemetery, overlooking the valley where she spent so many happy years.

Of the children of Martin and Berthe Nelson, Milliam, Cora and Mose spent most of their lives in Jackson; James settled in California and Pearl married Wade Wilson, of Milford, Iowa. The elder Nelsons moved to California in their later years. Martin died in Jackson in 1930; Berthe died in California at the age of ninety. She is buried at San Gabriel at the side of her husband who had passed away twenty-one years before.

*T*HE *W*ILSONS OF *J*ACKSON'S *H*OLE

This history, written by Joyce Imeson Lucas, was presented by Judith Rosbrook Andersen at Researchers' Rendezvous sponsored by the Teton County Library, August 15, 1990.

SYLVESTER WILSON'S FAMILY HAS BEEN traced back to his grandfather, James Wilson, who was born in 1776 in North Carolina. Sylvester's father, Elijah, married Martha Kelly in 1830. They lived for a time in Jackson County, Missouri, then moved to Nauvoo, Illinois, where Sylvester was born on January 30, 1840. Sylvester had thirteen brothers and sisters.

The family was living in Iowa when they decided to cross the plains by ox wagons and settled in Grantsville, Utah, at the southern end of the Great Salt Lake by 1852. An ad appeared in the *Deseret News* on April 17, 1852. "Herding—This subscriber wishes to give notice that he is prepared to keep cattle on Stansbury Island. Terms 1 cent per day to be paid in wheat, flour or young cattle. Elijah Wilson."

Elijah died in 1861 and his family moved to Wellsville, Utah. Sylvester was then twenty-one. Soon after Elijah's death his son Nick (Elijah Nicolas) left, and later wrote in his book *Among the Shoshones,* "After the death of my father my brother and I could not get along very well together. He was a very hard worker, and I had never done much work, and it went pretty hard with me." The brother referred to was Sylvester.

Young Sylvester Wilson's leadership ability was recognized by Latter Day Saint church leaders. He was a man of strong convictions and had the fortitude and ambition to carry those convictions through. Because of these characteristics the church leaders sent him to new settlements to organize branches of the LDS church.

When Sylvester was twenty-one, he and sixteen-year-old Mary Wood were married. After five years and three children they moved to Oxford, Idaho, a fast-growing area. Soon all available land with water was taken and that, plus grasshopper and cricket infestations, caused many settlers to leave. Sylvester and family went to Elsinore, Utah, and leased a place temporarily. They then left for the Moab region by way of the old Spanish Trail, so called because it was the route used by Spanish traders between Santa Fe, New Mexico, and Spanish settlements around San Bernardino and Monterey, California, thus bypassing the Grand Canyon. The traders swapped horses for Indian women and children and took them to the Spanish settlements as slaves.

Since the Green River was dangerously high Sylvester and family settled on Cottonwood Creek, the first settlers there. A few others soon came. Sylvester ran a store and he and his brothers built a large one-roomed house that served as a tuition school, church and community hall. Some seven or so other families settled in that area, and the town was named Wilsonville in honor of the civic minded Wilsons. Sylvester was thirty-eight when he settled in Wilsonville with his wife and eight living children. While there three more children were born. Sylvester contracted to carry the mail between Salina, Utah, and Ouray, Colorado, a newly established route of 250 wild and rugged miles. It took six weeks by horseback to make the trip. Sylvester established a post office in Wilsonville and was its postmaster until 1882 when the railroad reached Price, Utah, making the horseback route unnecessary.

Some of Sylvester's children were grown and had married during the time they lived in Wilsonville. Land with water had become practically unavailable and that, plus drought conditions, prompted Sylvester's family, with two of their married children, to leave by wagon for St. Anthony, Idaho, seeking new homes. Sylvester was forty-nine. They left Wilsonville May 31, 1889, and arrived at St. Anthony, a 400 mile trip, on July 23, 1889. They averaged less than ten miles per day as they brought all their worldly goods and livestock with them. The families who made the trek were Sylvester and his wife, Mary, and younger children; their married daughter,

Mary Alice, and husband, Selar Cheney, and family; and their son, Ervin, and his wife, Mary Jane, who was expecting their first child in September.

They planned to settle around St. Anthony, which at that time had only one building. The men went to the timber for house logs, a trip which took two days for each load. They had one house up to the square and had gone for more logs. While they were getting supper in camp a man rode in and asked if he could spend the night with them. He turned out to be Sylvester's brother, Nick, whom they hadn't seen for many years and who was just returning to his home and family in Sugar City, Idaho. He had been in Jackson's Hole helping Will Crawford, a bachelor, put up hay. He assured the nephews there was plenty of hay in Jackson's Hole they could harvest to winter their stock. All plans changed and the two families prepared for a move to Jackson's Hole. Only a few days later Sylvester and sons, John, George and Charlie, daughter, Rebecca, and Nick's daughter, Kate, (the girls to cook for the men,) started for Jackson's Hole with their pack outfits and the running gears of a wagon. Sons Ervin, Elias, and Selar Cheney were left in St. Anthony with the families to tend the livestock until they were ready to come to the valley. When they reached Jackson's Hole, Sylvester and sons borrowed a mower and rake from Will Crawford and put up hay for themselves as well as helping Crawford finish his haying.

In the fall Sylvester returned to Idaho for his family. Nick decided to move his family as well. So they led the little band over Teton Pass into Jackson's Hole, first bringing the cattle to graze on Fish Creek, later and on a second trip bringing the families. They were the first to bring wagons over the pass. By this time Ervin's and Mary Jane's son had been born. He was a month old when they left St. Anthony on October 27, 1889, and six weeks old when they finally arrived on November 11. It took three weeks to come the ninety miles. To lighten their loads they built a crib on the west side of Teton Pass and stored their winter's supply of flour, grain and so forth, until they could return for it. Since there was no wagon trail, they had to cut trees and build roads as they came. In some places the pass was so steep they had to put a six-horse team on each wagon to pull it, then return for another wagon. They didn't get very far in one day. Imagine camping out on Teton Pass for two weeks in November with a six-week old baby in those days.

Since they arrived in the valley too late to build cabins, some of the bachelors already living in the area graciously and generously provided living quarters for them in their homes. John Carnes had just built a new home so offered his older one to the Sylvester Wilson family. Selar Cheney and family lived with John Holland. John Cherry took in the Ervin Wilson family. The Nick Wilson family lived that winter with Will Crawford, then returned to Idaho for a few years before moving back again. All of the bachelors living in the valley at that time, some thirty or forty, did their best to make the families welcome.

Their first Christmas was spent at the Will Crawford place with everyone contributing something—elk steak, roasted wild geese and ducks, vegetables, plum puddings, mince pies and doughnuts cooked in bear grease. After the bounteous feast they danced to an orchestra of violins played by Sylvester Wilson, Nick Wilson, Selar Cheney, John Carnes and John Holland, with Brig Adams on the banjo and Andy Madson on the guitar. Since ladies were far in the minority, men danced with men and everyone participated. They danced all night, breakfasted in the morning, then went home traveling in daylight. The first winter was spent tending their stock and having parties. By the time spring came, they had a first-class orchestra.

The first Easter Services in Jackson's Hole were held at John Holland's place. According to Melvina Wilson Robertson's history *The First Settlers of Jackson's Hole,* "They sang hymns and Sylvester Wilson delivered the appropriate sermon which touched the hearts of the bachelors deeply. Among other things he thanked God for guiding his little group to this valley which was abounding in wild game, berries, fish, fowl, good soil, good grass for grazing and for the kind friends who had given them such a hearty welcome. He prayed they would all prosper and remain the best of friends."

The Sylvester Wilson families homesteaded in the area they named South Park in the spring of 1890 and built their homes. They selected South Park because there the snow cover melted the earliest of anyplace in the valley.

On March 17, 1891, Effie Jane Wilson, the first white child born in Jackson's Hole, was born to Ervin and Mary Jane Wilson. June 20 of the same year, Joseph Howard Cheney, was born to Selar and Mary Alice Cheney, the first white boy in the valley.

These sturdy pioneer stock suffered all the hardships and privations of early times. They had no doctor. Sylvester's wife, Mary Wood, was what they called in those days, a practical nurse. In spite of having her own large family to care for (she and Sylvester had twelve children) she took care of sick neighbors and acted as midwife when children were born.

In 1891 a diphtheria epidemic broke out and two of Sylvester's children died. He chose a site up on a high bench in South Park for their burial because it would be dry. This became the South Park Cemetery, the first cemetery in Jackson's Hole.

The first church services were held in Sylvester's home. In 1893 the first LDS Church Branch was organized with officials from the LDS Church officiating. The meeting was held in Sylvester Wilson's house, as were most of the Branch sessions. Neighbors who were not LDS members also participated, being made welcome.

The first school in Jackson's Hole was also held in Sylvester's home in 1894 with some twelve to fifteen pupils attending. In 1895, there were twenty-five pupils, and it was decided a schoolhouse was needed, so the settlers got logs out and started building one. Building was interrupted soon after it was started because of the Indian scare of 1895, so the schoolhouse was not completed until 1896. It was built on land donated by Ervin and Mary Jane Wilson. In 1895 Sylvester applied to Uinta County for a school district and in that year School District No. 37 was organized with C. Carmichael, Ervin Wilson and Mrs. N.M. Ely as the first school board in Jackson's Hole.

During the summer of 1895 the settlers feared an Indian uprising so settlers from all over the valley forted up at the ranch home of Ervin and Mary Jane for three weeks or so, during which time Sylvester Wilson died at the age of fifty-six, and a baby, Ruth Pettigrew, was born. The Indian uprising didn't materialize. One was feared because the settlers wanted the Indians to observe the game laws of that period. Some Indians had come hunting on Battle

Mountain and there was a skirmish. Then many other Indians came to help them, hence the fear of an uprising.

Sylvester Wilson brought the first riding plow into Jackson's Hole.

In the book *Progressive Men of Wyoming* Sylvester is described [as a man] "who during [his] life [was] a prominent ranchman, a brave Indian fighter, a hardy pioneer and a progressive public spirited man...." He "had lived a strenuous life amid the scenes of savage cruelty and treachery, had met the Indians on their chosen ground and baffled them with their own tactics, had aided in redeeming the wilderness to fertility and systematic productiveness, and as a bishop of the Mormon Church and prominent in its councils, had spread the light and comfort of his religious faith among the people whom his presence helped and cheered.... And she [his wife, Mary Wood] has been at his side, with ever present aid, in all of his arduous labors and soul-harrowing experiences, so that her knowledge of human nature and of affairs was both comprehensive and practical...."

The early Wilson families planted deep and lasting roots in Jackson's Hole. Many descendants live in the valley yet, some retired, many still going strong. From the seven children of Sylvester and Mary who ranched here only two remain in the ranching business, the two ranchers who can boast the longest period of continuous family ranching in the valley.

$\mathcal{D}$ICK $\mathcal{T}$URPIN: $\mathcal{E}$ARLY $\mathcal{T}$RAPPER

ICK TURPIN HAS BEEN DEAD SINCE 1914, but his name is used in the everyday conversation of Jackson Hole. He spent some thirty-four years in the valley before he died, being one of the very first to settle here.

Turpin Creek, just northeast of Kelly, and Turpin Meadows, at the north end of Jackson Hole, bear his name—although there is some question about whether it really was his name.

Turpin came to the valley in 1880 to trap. He built trapping cabins on almost every good stream in the Hole at one time or another. He found the trapping here to his liking and never left. Eventually he took up a claim.

His homestead was just north of the present town of Jackson along Flat Creek. The wild hay grew lush in the moist meadow, and a man could cut enough with a scythe to take care of his horses for the long, deep-snow winters. Only Ben Holliday and John Carnes, with his Indian wife, shared the area with Dick the first two or three winters.

By 1890, the place was filling up with people. At one Thanksgiving feast where everyone "carried in" his share of the fixin's, some sixty-five residents—mostly bachelors—got together to celebrate the holiday for a week. By 1900, most of the open land had been taken up.

Early settlers to the country found Dick very obliging and helpful. He never married and he never talked of his past to anyone. However, he did tell Jimmy Simpson one time that he had been born in Union, Ohio, and that his real name was Richard Smalley. Another bit of information was that he had worked log rafts on the Mississippi River.

After years of trapping, Dick sort of retired from the rugged life to establish a saloon in Jackson. It was here he almost killed a man in a fit of anger. He would have succeeded if Si Ferrin had not seized his arm as he was in the act of hitting the man over the head with a pistol.

Turpin was extremely honest in all his dealings with the other residents of the Hole and is reported to have had a very likable disposition. However, he did have a violent temper, and it was surmised by the other locals that he might be avoiding the law by living in this valley. He did hide out from the law for awhile, but that was because of another incident here. He seemed to like to use his pistol for a billy club.

A man named John West, a native of Logan, Utah, had taken up some land near the Turpin ranch. One day as Turpin was returning from a trapping trip in the mountains, he found West cutting hay on Turpin land. In a wave of red anger he walked up behind the mowing machine and hit West over the head with a gun. West fell off the seat and the team ran away.

Turpin thought he had killed West, so he took to the hills. West recovered from the blow but didn't stay around Jackson very long after that. It is told that he made a fortune in the gold fields of Montana.

Turpin came down out of the hills and lived in the valley until his death in 1914, at the age of seventy years. He had gone to Denver for medical attention and died soon after reaching that city.

His home in Wyoming was bequeathed to the State. It is now a part of the National Elk Refuge.

ROBERT & GRACE MILLER:
PIONEERS WITH VISION

THE OLD SAYING THAT BEHIND EVERY good and able man stands a good woman is ably illustrated in the lives of Robert E. and Grace Green Miller. For all of their active lives in Jackson's Hole they exemplified another cliché—pillars of the community.

Robert was born at Argyle, Wisconsin. At the age of nineteen he set out to seek his fortune. He worked at Sidney, Nebraska, for the Union Pacific Railroad for a year, then moved on to Denver where he worked in a bank. He took a trip to Montana and on the way passed through Jackson's Hole. He was so impressed with the country he determined to come back to settle. The next year he did so. That was in 1885.

For a year or two he trapped, joining the trapping fraternity of bachelors already spending winters in the valley. While looking around the valley he chose a homestead site which seemed ideal. It already had a cabin on it, and a big spring nearby. It was said that the cabin had been built by the outlaw calling himself Teton Jackson. He was not in residence at the time and would probably not have wanted the exposure of legally filing for a homestead claim. It is not known if Miller paid for a relinquishment or if he ever saw the outlaw. He filed on the site and performed the necessary work to prove up on the claim which lies just to the east of the present town of Jackson and is incorporated into the Elk Refuge.

Robert fenced and built ditches, improved the cabin and, in the winters, trapped. He was the first to bring in a mowing machine. He took it apart and carried it over the pass by pack horse. When he had money ahead, he bought cattle. By 1893 he had his life and home advanced to where he could return to the east to claim his

34

bride. He married Grace Green, of Ottawa, Illinois, on October 26, 1893, at her home. They rode over the pass to the homestead only to discover that, in Robert's absence, someone had stolen the boards from the cabin floor to build a flume for prospecting. Grace had to start her homestead experience with a dirt floor, as many other homestead wives did.

Grace and Robert had a baby boy, who died shortly after birth. Their only child, he was buried at her family home at Ottawa.

Homesteaders continued to arrive and take up claims in the valley. Some of them left after hardship forced them to move to friendlier climes, selling or abandoning their claims. Some, like the Deloneys, Simpsons, and Pete Nelsons, established much needed services. A sense of community gradually developed, especially at the confluence of Flat Creek and Cache Creek, the natural hub of the valley—just west and a little south of the Millers. Post offices were established at ranch homes throughout the valley.

For a short time, while the Fred Whites were moving from their location on Flat Creek to the banks of the Snake, the Marysvale Post Office was located at the Millers. They never held the commission of postmaster—that passed from Fred White to Maggie Simpson in 1894. Maggie, the Millers' neighbor to the south, then changed the post office's name from Marysvale to Jackson.

Around this time Grace Miller filed on an eighty-acre desert claim lying to the west of the Miller homestead. This was the first desert claim to be taken up in the valley.

In 1895 the Millers started a two-story log house. (It has been accepted in the registry for historical homes.) It was completed in 1897. Besides the help at haying time, Mrs. Miller had carpenters to feed. Having no sisters, daughters or mother to help, she hired young girls if she could find any who could be spared by their mothers. When the Allen family arrived in the valley in 1896 with two unmarried young daughters, Mrs. Miller rode over to their camp to try to hire one, or both, to help her. (Riding to the Allen camp at the base of Teton Pass involved a distance of some ten miles west via Antelope Pass and fording Snake River.) Cassie Allen went to help the Millers, while her sister Avilla went to the Cunninghams to help out.

Help never lasted long as the girls were wooed away by the many bachelors about. Cassie met Harry Smith, who was carpentering for Millers and soon wedding bells deprived Grace of her help. Avilla met Albert Nelson with the same result. Rena Peterson started her life in the valley by coming over the pass from Teton Basin to help Grace. Frank Peterson, good neighbor though he was, soon had talked her into his arms and cabin. Help was hard to keep, Grace discovered.

Maggie Simpson had purchased from the government a forty-acre isolated tract near the mouth of Cache Creek. The price was ninety dollars. She received the patent in 1900. The following year she sold ten acres of this land to Grace Miller for the same amount. Grace had it platted and proceeded to sell lots. This was the first town plat. Grace's grandfather, John Green, had platted a good part of the town where Grace was born, so she probably had an awareness of such procedures—and saw the obvious need.

Grace planned a park "for the children" into the townsite. It is Miller Park. We do not know the name of the wise person who thought to have the town buy the lots comprising our "square."

Friends and relatives from the "outside" came to visit the Millers to share their western experience. Photographs show some of the ladies riding sidesaddles. These may have been the first sidesaddles to show up in Jackson. The pioneer women found it safer and more comfortable to ride astride. Although the divided riding skirt had not yet come into fashion, they depended upon the voluminous skirts to conceal their "limbs."

At the turn of the century, the newly formed Forest Service, prodded by the nation's growing awareness of the need to regulate its resources, began issuing permits for cattle grazing on the open range. In 1905, the Millers and one other valley rancher were the only ones to have as many as 400 head on the range, making them the biggest "spreads" in the country.

Robert Miller was appointed Forest Supervisor over Teton National Forest in 1908. He built a small log cabin at the ranch to serve as his office. He held the position until 1918 when the duties were turned over to Arthur McCain. The little office building, the first office for the Teton National Forest Preserve, has been moved to the present location of the Teton National Forest Service for preservation.

Miller organized the Jackson State Bank in 1914. Joyce Lucas, in her privately published *Sylvester Wilson Family History*, writes: "With Robert E. Miller as the first president, Harry Wagner the first cashier. Members of the Board of Directors were Miller, Hyrum W. Deloney, Frank S. Wood, John H. Wilson, T. W. Lloyd, O. F. Stewart, C. L. Brady, P. C. Hansen and Harry Wagner." Ten thousand dollars was raised by local subscription for the base fund. They soon had $15,000 for working capital. The bank charged twelve per cent interest, a return hard to produce on a cattle investment. Miller was called Old Twelve Percent by many disgruntled residents of the valley who were snowed under by debts and disasters.

However, if Miller could see that a man was a good operator and had a chance to come out from under his indebtedness, he was helpful with advice and extensions. Learning of forced sales because of drought on the Green River, he encouraged many Jackson's Hole ranchers to borrow money and stock more cattle while they could get them so close by and cheap. Miller continued as president of the bank until his death in 1934.

Miller was Forest Supervisor and his close friend and neighbor, Dan Nowlin, was State Game Warden when the growing concern for the starving elk was spreading nationally. When government agencies were finally ready to try to do something about the problem, Miller was ready to retire from the active labor of his ranch.

Having no children to carry on with the ranch, he sold most of his acres to the government in 1914, retaining a few acres near town for a home. Title was given January 4, 1915.

Grace Miller, always active in church and social affairs, and with no brood of her own to supervise, bent her considerable energies and organizational know-how toward improvements to the community growing up around her original town plat. Jackson hadn't had a governing body for too many years, and the coffers were always empty. The town just grew, like Topsy.

It's likely the ladies nagged their husbands, and the mayor, and the councilmen. These worthy gentlemen probably challenged the ladies to run for office themselves.

The upshot was the election of a whole slate of female officers in 1920. The men voting joyfully for their wives. "Let them see how they could handle it."

Although the election got only a short column in the *Jackson Courier*, naming the new slate of officers, the national press learned of it and blew it up. Here was a whole slate of female town officers, maybe the first time in the whole country! Photographers arrived, the ladies were interviewed, their names became known nationwide.

Mrs. Robert Miller (Grace) was the mayor; Mrs. Roy VanVleck (Genevieve), Mrs. Henry Crabtree (Rose), Mrs. William Deloney (Mae), Mrs. Dan Haight (Faustina), the councilmen. Mrs. Charles Huff (Edna) was health officer; Mrs. Richard Winger (Marta), clerk; Mrs. Otto Lunbeck (Viola), treasurer; and young and beautiful Pearl Williams was town marshal. *[A reprint of a newspaper interview with Pearl appears on page 284.]*

The ladies' government did make many improvements. First they made an assessment in order to have some money in the till. They passed an ordinance prohibiting pigs and milk cows to be loose in city limits. They granted Edward C. Benson a franchise to furnish electric power to the town. (It was a few years before he got the job done.) They acquired land from the Forest Service on which to put the Aspen Cemetery—also they had a road built to it. Many other matters were discussed and adjusted.

The ladies did such a good job that the men were perfectly willing to let them run again—with no opposition. But after two years of handling the affairs of the town, they declined to run again and turned the reins back to masculine hands.

When young Billy Mercill came to the valley around 1914, the Millers accepted him like a long lost son. Miller helped Billy get established in the grocery store at the southeast corner of the square and gave him the use of a cabin in the big yard of their house in town. Billy soon added a drygoods line to the grocery store.

Mercill's Store *and* Deloney's Store. The town was growing! With the Clubhouse housing the drugstore at one end, VanVlecks Mercantile in the middle, and Mercill's Store at the south end, the east side of the square was full of business.

The town's growth reflected the homestead development

throughout the valley. Almost all the good land with access to water had been taken up by men looking for land capable of supporting their families. More prosperous settlers, those with financial backing or established fortunes behind them, took up land with recreational or aesthetic potential if arable land was unavailable. A young tourist industry began to build.

The Snake River Land Company became interested in buying land in Jackson's Hole around 1928. It was normal for the buying officers to approach the bank to learn of ranches for sale. Robert Miller became a purchasing agent for the SRLC. People in a bind financially or wanting to sell for any reason soon turned over their land.

It is possible that Miller did not know at first that the Rockefeller interests were behind the Snake River Land Company. When the news leaked that the SRLC was a front, and that the ultimate use of the land would be an extension of Grand Teton National Park which had been recently established, valley residents split their allegiance on the issue. Some felt the planned withdrawal of public land was worthwhile and necessary. Others felt the government regulations that would inevitably follow would lead to intolerable conditions and restrictions.

Miller resigned as purchasing agent. Dick Winger, another native, took his place. Residents never knew if Miller was aware of the ultimate plans of the Rockefeller interests or not, and speculation about his involvement continued. He must have decided that the SRLC plan was not for the ultimate good of the valley.

While working in his yard and garden one day in 1934, Robert suffered a fatal heart attack. Billy Mercill helped Grace through the trying time, accompanying her back to her home with Robert's body. He was buried beside their infant son. Grace returned to her home in Jackson, where she continued her life and activities much as she had before until she, also, suffered a heart attack the next year. Dr. Huff counseled her to seek a lower altitude and milder climate, so she left her home in Jackson in the charge of Billy Mercill and his wife Edith and returned to her childhood home. Dr. Huff, nurse Grace McDonald, and Billy Mercill accompanied her. She died in Ottawa, in 1948, and rests beside her husband and son. She willed Billy and Edith Mercill the large home in Jackson.

STEPHEN LEEK:

THE MAN WHO SAVED THE ELK

STEPHEN LEEK WAS AMONG THE group of bachelor-trappers who first braved the Jackson's Hole winters, stayed year 'round, and so, became the valley's first white residents. The winter of 1886 saw men gather at the cabin of Steve Leek to celebrate Christmas. Organizing the party took some doing, but word was spread by snowshoe telegraph from rim to rim, from Togwotee Pass to Snake River Canyon. Steve's cabin was on Flat Creek (called the Little Gros Ventre at that time) near the upper end of South Park. Each fellow brought contributions for the Christmas feed. Steve's offering was a trumpeter swan, stuffed and dressed, for the main dish. If anyone had brought alcoholic beverages to the valley, they had been drunk as the winter days grew shorter and colder. Coffee was the drink available for Christmas; typical bachelor fare completed the menu—beans, dried fruit and sourdough bread— and someone even made a sourdough cake.

Jokes and cards provided entertainment. Someone had a mouth organ. A tin pan band was created, and soon there was dancing. How to distinguish the partner representing the lady? It was decided the men should wear hats, while those representing ladies should go bare headed. A good-natured distribution of hats and sexes followed. One of the "gents" pointed out that some of the "ladies" were too bare on top, so it was further ruled that the "gents" should be the bald headed ones—and still wear hats. The dance was a roaring success.

The day after Christmas dawned clear and cold. The men were having so much fun with their togetherness—after so much aloneness—that they hated to break up and return to their far-flung cabins. So, what to do next for fun? It is possible that one of the stories about Leek originated that day....

Each trapper had his little stack of wild hay, put up in the autumn to feed his few horses through the winter. The stack had to have a high fence to keep the hungry elk from eating it. An elk could stand on its hind legs and reach the hay above a seven foot fence.

As usual a little herd of elk was hanging around Leek's stack that morning. They moved away as Steve and some of the fellows went out to pitch a little hay to the horses. As the horses moved up to eat the hay so did the elk.

"Those critters ought to be good for somethin' besides eatin' up our winter's hay," one of the men remarked.

"They're as big as a small horse," another commented. "I wonder if anyone has ever tried to ride one?"

"Why don't we try it right now?" Steve urged, and swung up to the top of the fence.

From there he dropped astraddle of a big cow elk that was dining on some scraps of hay lying on the ground alongside the fence. An explosion of elk and Leek erupted at the edge of the corral.

Horses, elk and men were dodging for safety as the cow elk performed gyrations never dreamed of by a horse. She tossed Steve into the air, and when he hit the ground, she jumped on the middle of him with all four feet. Men ran at her from all directions, waving and shouting.

She turned tail and ran off to join the herd.

"Jesus, Steve. You hurt bad?"

Steve struggled up, tried his arms and legs, looked himself up and down, then announced in his low drawl, "Seems like I'm all here, but the darned female stuck her leg in my hind pocket and ripped my pants from hip to hem. Anybody got a needle and thread?"

The closest store was a hundred miles away in St. Anthony. Of course, Steve, like all the trappers, had needles and thread.

After the winter of trapping in the northern part of the valley, Steve claimed his homestead rights in South Park, about three miles south of the place where the town of Jackson would grow.

The attendant work of a homesteader filled his life: grubbing and burning sage; laying out and digging irrigation ditches; planting the fields, then harvesting the hay. (Hay was the only crop with a ready market locally. Markets for any other goods were far away and seasons were short. Any surplus of hay was fed to cattle, and the cattle were then cowboyed on the hoof out of the valley to market.)

Steve started a little herd of cattle which he increased at every opportunity. As his income producing projects were being pushed along, he also was building. First a cabin, then outbuildings and a barn. While getting timber for buildings, fencing, hay cribs and winter wood, Steve also found time to acquire a sawmill and set up a water-powered mill in 1893. John Wilson helped him haul it in and set it up. It was the first in the valley; later it was used to saw the logs for the first schoolhouse to be built in the valley.

Steve was a tall, thin, good-looking man with the frontiersman's ability to master all the crafts necessary to living in the wilds. He was horseman, cattleman, farmer, builder, timberman, trapper, hunter. The last two pursuits were his favorites, and through the years, his life was shaped around them.

The arrival of the Wilson families in 1889 and 1890 brought some young ladies of marriageable age into the valley. Social enjoyment rose to a high pitch. The valley bachelors were soon making fewer trips out of the valley. Log rollings, picnics, dances and Sunday Meetings were introduced to the valley.

Steve soon singled out Etta Wilson, daughter of "Uncle Nick" Wilson, to be his partner for life. They were married in 1896. To this union was born two sons, Lester and Holly, who grew to manhood on their parents' ranch, following in their father's footsteps as ranchers, big-game guides and fishing resort owners.

(Lester married Helen Simpson, daughter of Jimmy Simpson; Holly married Oral Lloyd, daughter of Butch Lloyd. Steve and Etta eventually had four grandchildren: Lester and Helen were parents of Jack; Holly and Oral were parents of Lillian, Nancy and Stephen. Their lives were intertwined with the growth and businesses of Jackson.)

While his sons were young, Steve had branched out from ranching to become a big game and fishing guide. He established a fishing and hunting camp on the west side of Jackson Lake. Later he acquired a lease on the property which he held until Grand Teton Park was created. (The Park negotiated a trade of the original campsite for one on the east side of the lake which is still known as

"Leek's Camp," although the Leek family no longer owns it.)

When some of Leek's hunters brought cameras to his camps, Steve became very interested in photography. He acquired cameras of the latest make and taught himself the fundamentals, not only of photography, but also film processing, producing his own prints and slides. He learned the art of projecting slides on a screen and gave "picture shows" to the residents of the valley.

These were put on in the upstairs of the Clubhouse, with his son Lester running the projector, while Steve gave a running commentary about the place and people, the animals, or the reason for the shot. With his sons, Lester and Holly, he proceeded from showing slides to running the first movie business in town—still up in the old Clubhouse.

The movies came packaged in several canisters, one reel per canister. He would show two or three reels of news and comics, then seven reels of the feature presentation.

Between each reel the lights would be turned up, giving the viewers a chance to turn to their neighbors and visit while the reels were rewound. This was a good time for any current announcements, usually given in Mr. Leek's slow drawl. Some eastern critics say all western men drawl. Maybe so. Steve's was surely the lowest and slowest heard on this range.

All the while, Leek was acquiring the know-how and connections that allowed him to make the greatest contribution to Jackson's Hole that anyone has made. True, it took a lot of work from many people to bring this about, but Stephen Leek was the spark.

Steve saw interesting subjects for his pictures in every part of his life. But his interest in wildlife, particularly the plight of the elk, led him to take pictures of the elk in summer, fall and winter. It was impossible to ignore their starving condition around the haystacks in winter, impossible to feed his own cattle without a herd of elk on the same feed ground eating up the precious hay.

(Each homesteader had to develop a fine knowledge of how much hay to keep for winter feed for his stock. Too much hay meant waste and loss of value or profit. Too little hay meant hungry or starving livestock, or buying more hay, if it was still available, from a neighbor.)

The valley residents were also very concerned. Not only did a great deal of their income depend upon hunting parties in the fall, but the poor starving creatures touched the sympathies of all. How could the valley folks get someone to address the problem?

Steve had pictures, scores of them. He also had a backlog of hunters' names he could contact. He started a lecture tour.

The tours not only served the purpose of signing up hunters for the next season, but also stressed the plight of the starving elk. He feared that without some form of feeding program, the magnificent elk herd of Wyoming might become as scarce as the buffalo were at that time.

In 1907, S.N. Leek was elected Uinta County Representative. He helped to draft further legislation for the protection of Wyoming game animals. Word spread and Steve was invited to speak and show his pictures to legislators and conservation clubs—including the Izaak Waltons. His tours, plus letters written by many of the influential people of the state, impelled the Legislature to appropriate $5,000 to buy hay for the elk of Jackson's Hole in the winter of 1909.

With the coming of moving pictures, Steve sent to France and obtained the best motion picture camera and equipment money could buy. With his moving picture shows and his still picture presentations, he was invited to join the Orpheum Lecture Circuit. He was billed as the "Father of the Elk."

He did not carry on this work for profit, but rather to bring attention to the problem of winter feed for the elk.

The winter of 1911 proved especially bad for elk. The March 2 *Evanston Times* reported:

> Sheriff Ward and Mark Manley, of Mountain View, who were delegated by Governor Carey to go into the Jackson Hole country and inquire into the condition of the elk, which were reported starving and dying off rapidly, returned to Evanston last Friday after having carefully gone over the situation. Conditions were not so bad as reported, although they found much suffering amongst the antlered tribe.
>
> Mr. Manley reports the snow in Jackson as between three and four feet deep and much deeper in the surrounding mountains. The sheriff and his assistant crossed forty-one

snowslides within a distance of four miles on Teton Pass. The storms were so serious about a month ago that the mail was delayed for a number of days and then only the letter mail got through by someone bringing it over the Pass on snowshoes. Merchant Charles Deloney, a former resident of Evanston, had a load of freight buried under one slide and it is estimated that the supplies are now under twenty feet of snow, where they will probably remain until June.

"As a heavy snowfall came much earlier this year than usual," remarked Mr. Manley yesterday to a *Times* reporter, "the elk drifted down to the lower valleys, where the snow is not so deep and conditions are more favorable. These elk, from all reports, are in fair condition. Unless more heavy storms come the loss should be comparatively small. Approximately 5000 head remain in the valley around Jackson and this is where the heaviest loss is. Possibly fifty percent of the calves have died owing to the crusted condition of the snow, and more will die even if fed hay. The only feed they have been able to secure for some time has been willows, and the small amount of hay they could steal from the rancher's stacks."

Continuing, Mr. Manley said that the elk have become a great nuisance to the ranchers, destroying haystacks and fences in their mad efforts to reach food. The ranchers, in order to save hay for their stock, are obliged to stay on their feed grounds and herd the elk away. They are, in many instances, compelled to sleep in their haystacks and keep waking up all night to keep the elk from devouring their hay.

Hay was very scarce in the valley on the arrival of Ward and Manley. Up to the time of their departure only, 110 tons had been secured to help in the feeding program. It is possible, however, that fifty or sixty more tons may be secured from the ranchers. In the event of an early spring even this amount may save many elk from starvation, as about one pound daily is sufficient feed for an elk. It was expected that a number of ranchers would buy hay in Victor and drive their stock over there to feed, thus releasing their hay in Jackson Hole to be purchased for the elk. None of the ranchers seemed willing to move their herds as the roads over the pass were so bad and the hay in Victor had raised in price, selling as high as $10.00 per ton, the sellers to do the feeding at this price. Mr. W. H. Sebaum was left in charge of trying to get more hay for the elk feeding program.

Sheriff Ward and Mr. Manley say that the ranchers of Jackson Hole are progressive and hospitable and concerned about saving the elk herd. They did much to make the mission of the Governor's committee pleasant under trying conditions, and they have so stated in their report.

In 1911, the U.S. Congress appropriated $20,000 toward hay purchases. During the succeeding two years, Congress bought property along Flat Creek northeast of Jackson totaling 1,760 acres, and added 1,040 acres of undeeded public land. This was the nucleus of the National Elk Refuge. (This first purchase included the Robert E. Miller homestead.) From that time to the present, additional government purchases, plus donations from the Izaak Walton League and the John D. Rockefeller, Jr., Corporation, have enlarged the refuge to its present size. The Wyoming Game and Fish Commission and the National Elk Refuge share the cost of the elk feeding program.

Having provided the necessary impetus to force public awareness toward better game management, Steve turned his attention back towards his work in the valley. He and his sons became more involved in the fishing camp and big game business.

The movies continued under their operation, and for a good many years, Lester, Helen and Holly, along with Ray Reed at the drums, supplied the orchestra which furnished all the music for the dances held in the Clubhouse, the Legion Building, or wherever there was a get-together. Steve leased out the ranch, retiring to one of the matching, two-story log homes he and his sons had built in Jackson. He spent his later years organizing his collections of pictures and historic memorabilia—trying to record his memories of the valley he had done so much to bring from a primitive state to an important, progressive area. He died before finishing this task.

𝓜ARY 𝓦HITE: 𝓥ALLEY'S 𝓕IRST 𝓟OSTMASTER

ARYSVALE WAS THE FIRST post office in the valley, and was named for Mrs. Fred (Mary) White, the first post-mistress. It was located at the north part of the Flat Creek Flats, just east of the Botcher place (Botcher Hill). Started in 1892, there weren't too many patrons at the time.

In letters written fifty-nine years later to Cora Barber, Mary White Tuttle, then in her late eighties, reminisced about her arrival in the valley and the White's efforts to get the post office assignment. Cora Barber, née Cora Nelson, was the daughter of John Martin (Slough Grass) Nelson. Cora gave me copies of two letters written by Mary. Part of the second letter reads:

> ...Your letter, which came this week, was surely most interesting. How it did take my mind back across the years to the time I first met you in Jackson's Hole. I can remember as if it had been yesterday when I rode the pinto pony up to the old Holland ranch and the wide grin with which your mother came to meet me. We were the first two white women to come to that valley. You were the first little girl and your brother Milliam was about two years old. We had our first visit that day, and I can picture you yet. The three of you came walking all the way across the flat and waded Flat Creek to visit me, my first and only lady callers for about four years, and you all three rode the gentle half-blind horse as I went home with you. Seems impossible that it was sixty years ago, and still it was.
>
> Don't you remember how we saw or spoke to a neighbor only once or twice a year and we never got word or mail

from the outside from snowfall to spring thaw unless some hardy individual took it into his head to ski across the mountain and bring everybody's mail, and as soon as we heard about it how we all made ski tracks to that man's cabin, pronto.

Didn't we think we had the whole world in our grip when we got a little Post Office of our own. And the job of keeping it fell to me and I did it for the first three or four years while we lived in the cabin at the head of the swamp.

What a time we had getting that Post Office! The petition that we sent to Uncle Sam had so few signatures, and yet we had every possible name we could get in the valley—and a few from out Victor way. The route was so difficult that they made us carry our own mail sack on schedule for a year—to prove that it could be done, I suppose—but every signer took his turn at making the trip, and after the year was up Uncle Sam provided us with a regular mail carrier.

Then we really did feel important. We could order things from the mail order houses and get them without waiting six months. I remember the first order I sent was for a pair of slippers and Montgomery Ward sent me a pair of wooden shoes that would weigh about ten pounds, and the poor mail man had to carry that awful parcel on his back and on skis over that terrible hill.

Next morning when he had to carry them back again, what he said about wooden shoes and my bright mind probably melted some snow. A few years later when I made that ski trip myself, I didn't blame him any. I thought his speech hadn't been strong enough.

That ski trip is one thing I never will forget. Going up the hill, especially that last pitch, took some very skillful side stepping straight up. It took us all forenoon and we stopped for lunch in the mail carrier's little snow cabin, or I should say "igloo," at the top of the pass. The snow was so deep over it that there was just a hole in the snow down which we had to slide yards and yards till we got to the entrance, and then when we made a fire in the corner chimney to boil our coffee, the melted snow began to drip down on us. It was easier going down the other side!

After we had left the swamp ranch and went to live on the Snake river bank, it was Bob Miller who took over the post office, then the Simpsons, and by that time it had become "Jackson," the beginning of what you now have. Just think, a church, a museum and a telephone office! Sounds like any big metropolis....

Marysvale was a central location for the time; settlers were "taking up" the land along Flat Creek, South Park, the Spring Gulch and along the Gros Ventre. In January of 1893, the Whites changed the name of the post office to "Gros Ventre." That name was used until they gave the post office over to Maggie Simpson, the next postmaster of record. (The Whites must have relinquished the operation for a time to the Robert Millers before the change of postmaster was official.) If the Whites ever filed on their land, they did not go ahead and prove up on the claim. Charlie Peterson, Sr., remembers playing around the White place as a child. He says there were no foundation remains; that his father said the post office was kept in a covered wagon sitting on the ground. The Whites no doubt lived in a homestead shack, easily torn down or moved, for the few years they were there.

The fact that a post office was there at the White ranch did not encourage a settlement at the northern end of Botcher Hill. The spot is now open field, at the north end of the Flat Creek flats, in the Fish and Wildlife refuge.

Mary doesn't say in her letters to Cora what happened to Fred White, nor to her second husband Mr. Tuttle. The fact that she signed her given name "Mae" rather than Mary indicates another change since her Jackson's Hole days.

Her correspondence with Cora includes a gay and articulate account of the problems and pleasures of pioneering such an isolated place. She said:

> ...I notice that among those that you have mentioned as having passed on are the names of all those old timers whose

names were on that post office petition. It makes me feel as
if I had lived to be the last inhabitant of the earth! Are you
and I the only ones left who knew the valley...?

> "Ere the blight of man was on it,
> And the endless acres lay
> Just as God Almighty left them
> On the restful seventh day."

Do you remember the Fourth of July celebration we
held that year on the Jenny's Lake? There weren't more than
a dozen of us, but old man Atherton, from up on Little
Gros Ventre, remarked that the population was getting "too
darn numerous" and he moved his cabin back miles further
into the hills.

And then the tall tales Mr. Cherry told us about his
being the first man ever to fish in that lake? He always made
a raft, he said, to fish from, because the fish he caught were
so big that they pulled him on his raft all around the lake all
day, just like riding on a steamboat. He came from Texas,
Mr. Cherry did, where everything is big!

We never did catch any fish that size, but do you
remember the day we spent fishing along Snake River
because some fish-line manufacturer down east had offered
a substantial prize for the person who caught the most fish
in one day on that particular brand of fishline, and Mr.
White caught two gunny sacks full of trout? We had taken
Mr. Pettigrew, who was a court commissioner, along to cer-
tify to the amount of the catch, but the fishline manufacturer wouldn't believe it anyway, so we got no prize, and most
of the fish were wasted, though everybody ate all they could.
If I could have one sackful of them here now it would be
prize enough.

There was so much game wasted those days. When I
have to buy meat at the market at a dollar a pound now, it
makes me shudder to think of the times we have shot down
a fat elk and taken only the hams and the loins and left the
rest to the coyotes. Game was so plentiful and so easy to get
those days.

Remember the time we took the running gears off the farm wagon from the old White ranch and went for fence poles along the Gros Ventre River and I sat on those two forked rods and the wagon reach and held the rifle in case we should run onto some kind of game, and when we made the turn at the head of Spring Gulch, about two hundred antelope came rushing over the ridge and tangled up with our team and upset me from my precarious perch, and we didn't get the frightened horses stopped till the antelope were a mile away. Do they come back in the spring now as they used to do?

And do the elk wander in herds down into the swamp at the first fall of snow? Remember the bunch of a thousand or more that came and stayed all winter around our cabin at the head of the swamp? What a nuisance they were! They ate everything about the place, even to the soap from off the wash bench at the kitchen door. And they made a determined effort to eat the little stack of hay that had been reserved for the family cow. Every morning we drove them away and built the fence a couple of rounds higher, but never succeeded in keeping them out.

Then, remember the ruckus the game wardens kicked up when the Indians came and shot an elk or two? Old Capt. Smith got shot—and I always believed that the idiot did it himself—and they killed a couple of Indians, and the last Indian fight that Uncle Sam ever had to settle was on. Remember how we gathered at the Erv Wilson place expecting to be scalped any dark night and the men stood guard over the camp at night, and we ladies had quite a social time until Mr. Crawford shot at the calf one midnight, mistaking it for an Indian marauder, and scared all the fun out of us. Can you remember where you were when the lights were doused that night, and wasn't it one mad scramble?

I tell all this to my son, who has his office in Washington's Pentagon Building, how I began the upward climb toward a coveted place in the sun in a little one room trappers cabin with a dirt floor, and shot bear and deer and elk from the door, and was scared by Indians and traveled on skis when I went to call on my neighbors. He only half believes me and he calls me "Mrs. Kit Carson," but I remind him that we lived a safer life then than he does now among the crowd. Our skis were less dangerous than his modern automobile and we didn't need so many repair stations along the way, in order to get where we were going; and that I still prefer the mountains and the lakes and the wide out of doors to the city streets. Still, I believe that for each of us there is a predestined path, that there are no short cuts but we must walk in it every step of the way. Else why my pilgrimage through Jackson's Hole?

Write me again very soon, won't you? With love to you and luck with the kiddies, as always, your friend,

Mae [White Tuttle]

Mary's letter states that they moved from the Flat Creek location to the bank of the Snake River. I find a homestead entry there in the name of Frank White. Nothing for Fred White. How I wish I knew more of Mary (Mae) White Tuttle's history. There was a saloonkeeper here named Tuttle. Could they have met again elsewhere? And what happened to Fred?

THE SIMPSONS GAVE JACKSON ITS NAME

THE FIRST POST OFFICE IN JACKSON's Hole stayed at the ranch of Fred and Mary White at the upper end of the Flat Creek meadows for two years and two months and was called Marysvale. Then, in 1894, Maggie (Mrs. John) Simpson became postmaster, and the office was moved to their homestead near the mouth of Cache Creek canyon. The valley was well known as "Jackson's Hole" so Mrs. Simpson thought the post office should be called Jackson, and so named it.

The Simpsons came into Jackson's Hole from the Lander area, where they had been working at the Amoretti ranch near Dubois. They came up the Wind River, over Union Pass and down the Gros Ventre, a trail used by Indians, John Colter, the trapper brigades, the army, President Arthur's expedition, many hunting parties and now, families seeking homesites. They came with wagons, teams, extra horses, household and building equipment, and four of their six children. Alva, Claude, and James were almost grown young men; the youngest, Ida, a girl of eleven. John made the trek in 1892 and Maggie in 1893. By 1894 they had established themselves in a two-story log house beside the clear, tumbling waters of Cache Creek, where it flattens out after emerging from the canyon. (The now-giant spruce trees on Hall Avenue mark the homesite.) From all over the valley folks beat a track to the Simpson ranch to get their mail.

The early day postal job was not well paid. The compensation was based on the stamp cancellation; it was not a job a man could waste his time with. Since the lady of the house could seldom leave it in those days, the office usually fell to her. Maggie Simpson not only carried on her housewifely duties but kept community affairs stirring as well. A community meeting place was sorely needed. John and Maggie gave a five-acre tract at the corner of their homestead for the purpose. The fellows of the valley formed a "Jackson Hole Gun Club." Membership was twenty-five dollars and labor toward the building. Claude Simpson was given a membership in return for the land. The "Clubhouse" still stands at the northeast corner of the town square; the first public building, the nucleus of the town.

Others besides homesteaders were coming to Jackson's Hole. Some needed a small plot for business or home. As homesteads were proved up and patents to the land obtained, some people were able to buy a few acres. Maggie learned of a forty-acre tract which could be filed on (probably an isolated tract). She filed, proved up, and received a patent for this land in 1900. A year later she sold ten acres of the forty to Mrs. Grace Miller for ninety dollars, just what she had paid for the whole piece. The forty-acre plot can be roughly described as bounded by Deloney Street in the south, Flat Creek on the north and west, and somewhat east of Cache Creek to the east.

Mrs. Miller had her ten acres platted and sold lots. The first town plat was bounded by Deloney Street, Cache Avenue, and Flat Creek to the north and west. Mrs. Miller had the forethought to donate a block of this land to the children of Jackson, and it became Miller Park.

Lots quickly sold and soon Charles Deloney had built a store at Glenwood and Deloney. The Jackson Hotel, the Wort Livery Stable and a saloon clustered around the corner of what is now Deloney Street and Cache Avenue. The town grew.

The Simpson family members, as well as their land, were instrumental in the growth of the town. Son Will followed his family to the valley in 1896, bringing his bride, also named Margaret. They established residency on the forty-acre plot Maggie had acquired. Their house sat at what is now the location of the Anvil Motel. In 1897 Will and Margaret's son Milward was born there. When Charles Deloney came to the valley in 1901 or 1902, he and Will Simpson became partners in the store Deloney started in this building. It was the first store in Jackson's Hole.

Son James built a home in what was called "the swamp." James

❧ Maggie Simpson, shown here with husband John, is credited for giving Jackson its name when she renamed the Marysvale post office. (JHM&HC)

also started a drugstore in the lower floor of the Clubhouse. Son Claude homesteaded a tract of land near the parents' claim. This was bordered on the south by the ridge on which the cemetery rests; in fact, the cemetery may contain some of his land. Son Alva left the valley to pursue a forestry career in Colorado. Daughter Ida married Bill Redmond in 1897. The Redmonds also played an important part in the development of the town; Bill was one of those who subdivided the lots belonging to the Jackson Hole Gun and Commercial Club.

John Simpson died in 1921 and was buried in the Aspen Cemetery overlooking the home he had built during the latter years of his life. Maggie had developed a heart condition and needed a less rugged life. She sold the ranch to John Hall and moved to San Diego where her daughter, Pearl Keister, a widow of former Wyoming Senator Steve Keister, lived. At the death of Maggie in 1922, the family returned her to Jackson's Hole, to rest beside her husband on the ridge overlooking the ranch (now a part of Jackson) which they had claimed as their part of Jackson's Hole.

❧

Maggie Simpson wrote these notes about her life [Empty brackets indicate phrases which cannot be deciphered]:

Married at Bergon's Ranch, Bear Creek, Colorado, December 25, 1865 [John was 28; Maggie, 19]. Moved that spring to Joe Rists Ranch on Bear Creek, ten miles from Denver. John had the hay contract at Fort Morgan, Colorado. I moved down to Fremont Orchard with him. Had eight men to cook for and someone off the road every night as it was a road ranch. Stood it six weeks and went home to father's on Bear Creek sick. Took typhoid August 10th. Was sick until Christmas. Moved to Fort Morgan, Colorado. John had the wood contract and a gang to cook for there.

It had a store and road ranch. The spring of 1867, we went with the troops from Fort Morgan to Fort Reynolds, eighteen miles below Pueblo, Colorado. John had the timber contract and the beef contract. We were a month on the road. It took ten ox teams [   ] for transportation. Went in the ambulance with Mrs. Gillette, Annie and Katie and [   ]. Captain Gillette was in command. We saw Indians every day at a distance but there was one company of soldiers of the Seventh Cavalry and a lot of citizens so they didn't attack us. We built a house a mile from Fort Reynolds on the Arkansas River. William Lee was born there January 26, 1868. Cal Boone lived just across the river from us—a grandson of Daniel Boone—also a brother of Dan Boone.

Mrs. Dan Boone was with me when Will was born. Had Dr. Toombs of Pueblo. When Will was four months old, John sold out to Hugh Melrose. We moved to Pueblo—stayed there a month or so, then went to father's on Bear Creek. I lived there and John went back to Fort Logan. Saw lots of Indian trouble there. The spring of 1869, we moved to the Big Thompson. We ran a stage station there. The coaches ran from Cheyenne to Denver. Was there from July 1, until October. Took in $1,800—$1.00 a meal. That summer my sister, Isabell Alcesta died of typhoid—eighteen years old on July 31. Willie, as we called him, took very sick and it settled in his right leg. It was partly paralized. He didn't walk for a year, just crawled and drug his leg after him. He outgrew it some but has always been lame. He was overheated and teething. He walked when he was nine months and didn't have a tooth.

In October, we moved to Denver and John ran a dray. Joseph Clinton was born in Denver—East Denver July 14, 1870. Mrs. Armstrong, an old friend, took care of me—all the care I had. John went into the Elephant Corral that fall. We moved the next spring to North Denver. Had an acre lot over there. Pearl was born there, June 29, 1872. James Sullivan Simpson was born there in 1874. In 1877, John went to the Black Hills. We moved twice [   ] in North Denver.

Father came and moved us to the Big Thompson in 1878. Brother Will took us to the Black Hills, Deadwood with a five mule team. Father kept Willie. We lived in a house of Mort Boughtens. John bought a lot up City Creek with a cabin I cooked in and that fall a big tent. He built a house of two rooms. Ida Byrd was born there March 28, 1879. She was the sweetest baby but not any sweeter than Pearl was. We were there in the big fire. Clint took cold, it was in October—had typhoid. Then Jimmy had typhoid. Next fall, I wanted to go back to Colorado. My brother, Joe, was killed with a bucking horse and in 1876, the Indians killed my brother, Andrew, up at Fort Fetterman, Wyoming.

The fall of 1880 Clint died of Diptheria on the 8th of November. Ida was twenty months old. She had membranous croup. Took it the night after Clint was buried. For twelve days, she never made a noise. After it broke up, it smelled like diptheria. I went on the coach to Sidney, Nebraska in December, then to Loveland, Colorado to fathers. We bought some cows and took them to the mountains at Fremont and Will [   ] George Rists in the fall. I moved to Loveland to get the children in school. John came home the next spring. He lived at Deadwood two years after I left. That spring, father let us take his timber claim and we built a two room house. We had cows and John ran a milk wagon into Loveland. The winter before Claude was born, I milked nine cows and the tears would freeze on my cheeks. We got a swell girl who could milk in the spring. Claude DeWitte was born there August 13, 1883 and Alva Adams was born the February 9, 1887.

Father died while we lived on the ranch four miles north of

Loveland. He died July 23, 1888. We moved to Denver that fall. John went in the stable business but didn't do any good. The next spring, in June 1889, we went to Wind River, Wyoming on the E. A. Ranch owned by the Amarettas [*sic*]. I cooked and washed for the cowboys for two years. In 1892, we moved to Lander. Will was prosecuting attorney. Jim worked in a drug store. July 12, 1893, Pearl and Stephen Keister were married and in September, we moved to Jackson Hole. Will and Maggie Burnett were married October 18 [1893]. John had gone to Jackson Hole the year before. We moved twice in Lander—down to the Urich house where Pearl was married.

In 1894 [1895], we had Indian trouble in Jackson. The troops came in and people went into camps and left their homes. We had the P. O. I was appointed P. M. that year. Served nearly six years. Will and Maggie came in that fall and we had to [   ] ranch [   ] Will [   ].

We traded cattle for Will's ranch. Thirty-one head of my cattle went into it. We built a house. The first shingled roof in Jackson and the first chimney built of rock. There was no brick. There was no hotel and we had to keep people and the boys were in the tourist business and I had to cook for them.

James S. Simpson and Edith Younger were married March 12, 1899 at Lockwood's ranch [the stage stop at foot of Teton Pass, east side]. Ida Byrd Simpson and William Preston Redmond were married December 1, 1897 at our home in Jackson.

MAGGIE MCBRIDE'S DIARY

WE ARE STARTING OUT TO FIND US A new home. We are going to Jackson Hole, Wyoming. It is the year 1896 and my husband Roy McBride and I have been living at Rockland, Idaho....

Thus begins that part of the diary of Maggie McBride which covers her trip by wagon from Rockland, Idaho, to Jackson's Hole with her husband Roy and a group of fellow travelers seeking new homes in the beautiful valley of Jackson's Hole.

The group consisted of the James Ira May family, the Charles J. Allen Family (Charles Allen and Jim May were cousins), the newly-married McBrides and the newly-married James Budges. Mary Ann Budge (Nan) was a daughter of Charles Allen.

In 1895, Allen had been sent to help with the Indian troubles in Jackson's Hole. He decided to move his family there. His glowing descriptions of plentiful hunting and fishing and available land encouraged others to follow suit.

....It seems hard to leave our folks behind, but we intend to go back every year, if possible.

Sister Jo stayed with me the last week to help me get ready. We had a farewell family dinner, June 15. All our folks were there except brother John, and sister Minerva. We were sorry they could not be there.

Thursday: Roy and I went up to Aunt Lydias. Jo stayed home and ironed and took up a carpet for me.

Friday: Roy, Jo and I went up Spring Creek to bid Cade and her family goodbye. Mamma came down with us, stayed all night.

Saturday: Jo, Nettie, Elva Tyler, Roy and I went to bid Alta and family goodbye. Mamma went as far as the store with me, had a nice time. Came home Sunday. Stopped to Clare's to bid her goodbye. Bid John and dear mamma goodbye. Packed everything in the wagon.

Sunday: Kate and family were up awhile. Jo stayed all night with Nettie.

Monday, June 22, 1896: We got up this morning and ate breakfast at Mrs. McBride's, and bid her goodbye. The rest came down to the house, then we bid them goodbye. My husband and I left our home in Rockland this morning about 8:00 o'clock. Jo rode as far as the school house with Roy. I rode Waif and led Cap.

We overtook Charley Allen, his wife and family, and Jim Budge and wife on their way to Jackson Hole. We arrived at the Falls at noon, did some trading. Mr. Bennett gave us some ginger snaps and salmon. Mr. Cook gave me a hat. We camped at Allen's Wells, the mosquitoes are very bad.

June 23: The mosquitoes just about ate us up. I didn't sleep a wink. Left camp about sunrise. I rode Waif, with Roy's saddle and my bloomer riding suit. I did not ride very far, got tired. I killed one rabbit with my shot gun. At noon we were at Mershem. Roy and I went to Hoverson to camp, got an Indian wagon and went to Pocatello to see the Dr. Called on Sparks's and Della. Got supper at the restaurant then came back to camp.

June 24: The mosquitoes are not bad. It is noon, and we are on a sand ridge between Ross Fork and Blackfoot. Have the wagons near together and quilts put over for a shade. I had a bad chill this morning, my head aches now. The men have got the horses, so I will stop writing. We are camped south of Blackfoot.

June 25: Drove into Blackfoot this morning. Roy had a horse shod. I went to see Mrs. Woodin and Maggie Raymond. She was very glad to see me, wanted us to stay to dinner, but as the rest of the crowd were ahead of us we could not stay. We overtook the crowd camped on a canal. So here we stopped, a very desolate place. Still have a bad cold. Roy and the rest are asleep. The roosters are crowing. We drove this side of Basalt, saw Clem Drue, she is as pretty as ever. Her brother will come out to camp to see us.

June 26: We are all ready to start. Here we are camped south of Idaho Falls. We passed through Shelley, Roy got some tomatoes and a bottle of soda water. We heard Jimmy May and family were camped outside of town waiting for us. Charley stopped to look for them. Roy and I went up town to mail some letters to our mothers. Got our teeth filled, and did some trading. I created quite a sensation. I wore my outing suit, went to see Mrs. Jim Gordon. I think she is a lovely lady, came back to camp. Went out and tried to find a rabbit, but could not. Henry May drove his cattle to our camp. The rest of the family will overtake us tomorrow.

Henry May is just a very young man and I think I will always remember him sitting on the wagon tongue playing the harmonica. I think he gets homesick at times.

June 27: Roy and I are out north of Idaho Falls waiting for the rest to come. They are in town trading. We came through and got what things we left there, got some bananas. At noon we were eight miles from Idaho Falls. We went one road and the rest went the other. I guess we will meet again. I have never seen so many rabbits before, there are trails all over. I killed two and missed two. We are camped in a lane near a man by the name of Hudman. Roy got hay from him. He is acquainted with Johnny Reed and lots of other men down home.

June 28: Roy and I are having noon meal on the banks of south fork of Snake River, north of Menan. The mosquitoes are about to eat us up. We crossed the river this morning on a bridge. It is Sunday today. When we came through Menan, they were going to church. They are all Mormons. They have a very nice church. I think this is a pretty country, but Oh! the mosquitoes. We will get ready and pull out. Here we are camped just off the Pools Island. Still mosquitoes. The other outfit caught us.

June 29: Monday, we are now in Rexburg, having a horse shod. Last night the mosquitoes were very bad. We went to bed, but could not sleep, got up and went to the other camp, they had just got in. Went back and moved our bed, they were not so bad. We pulled out before the rest. We are still in town. The rest of the crowd are here. Charley is having his wagon fixed, the rest are trading.

This is a very lively country. People are going all the time. Some very nice rigs, camped on Moody Creek. Villia [Avilla Allen] and I went hunting. I killed a woodchuck. I helped drive the horses this forenoon.

June 30: Made a big drive, did not stop for noon. I helped drive the stock. Roy got me a pair of spurs, and I made Waif go. We are camped on a pretty stream called Canyon Creek. A family lives here, they keep boarders. Most of folks have gone fishing. They have come back, caught some fish. The men were shooting at a mark with winchesters. Mrs. Allen and I tried our luck, we did as well as the men.

July 1: (Wednesday) Made another long drive. I rode in the wagon. We drove in a mile of snow, are now surrounded by snow. We are camped on Teton River. The Teton Peaks are grand. Everyone has been fishing. Mr. and Mrs. May caught seven, Roy caught three.

July 2: We are still camped on Teton River. Will stay till tomorrow. Roy caught a fish for breakfast. The men have gone fishing on Badger Creek. I washed this forenoon. Mrs. Allen is washing now. This is a very long valley. It is called Teton Basin. Good deal of traveling, both ways, but most of them are going to Jackson Hole. Charley, Jim May and Val [Allen] went fishing, fished till dark, caught 25 nice ones.

July 3: We are all packed ready to go. The men are catching the horses. The mosquitoes are awful. So thick I can neither read nor write. They leave at dark, but come at sunrise. We have to have breakfast before sunrise. It is noon and we are at Driggs P.O., still fighting mosquitoes. The people here want us to stay for the dance tomorrow night. Charley is having his wagon fixed. The men went to look at a ranch to take, but they did not like it. We did not stop for the dance. They had a pulling match, most of them were drunk. We left there about six o'clock, drove till dusk. Got stuck in the mud, we were still there when Val came and said there was a deer back a ways. Roy left the team stuck in the mud and went flying after the deer. We had camped when he caught us, he did not get the deer.

July 4: We were awakened by the firing of guns and firecrackers. We are late in starting this morning. We passed through Victor.

They were celebrating the Fourth. We are now camped on a creek, it is a lovely stream just at the foot of the great mountains we are to climb. Roy and I took our guns, went hunting on mountain, but did not see anything to shoot at. Saw some lovely groves. That is the way we spent our Fourth. Mrs. Allen is not well. We are in Wyoming now.

July 5: Camped on Swift Creek. The girls and I rode horseback, had a nice time, but the teams did not. The mountain road was too steep, had to double twice. Camped about 2:30 o'clock. Roy and Jim went hunting. Nan, Villia, Cassie [Allen] and I went strolling on the mountain, We rolled rock down. I took a roll down myself, but didn't get hurt. Had a good laugh. Nan slipped off a foot bridge. We all made crowns for us, then went to camp, and had a combing bee.

July 6, Monday: Two weeks ago today we left home. Come about two miles, then doubled on three wagons, brought them to the top of the mountain, but had to put three teams on before we reached the top. The men went back after the other wagons, while we fixed dinner. We had tea made from snow water. We are on the summit now—I can see Jackson Hole. We got the wagons up all right.

Roy and I were always the last wagon on the trip. The three other wagons had chicken boxes on behind and the chickens were laying eggs. Lots of the eggs rolled out and of course we picked many of them up. They come in handy as we near Jackson Hole. Sometimes we camp in one camp for two or three days to shoe horses and rest them up. I use some of the eggs to make custard pies and cake baked in our dutch oven.

We are now camped near the foot of the mountain, in Jackson Hole. It is a nice valley, lots of timber. Lost the shot gun, Roy went back after it. I drove to camp, Cassie rode with me. Roy found the gun the other side of the mountain, on the road. We are all tired out. Most of the folks walked up the mountain and down most of the way. I rode Waif.

July 7: The girls and I carved our names on some trees this morning. Found one home but passed it. Nooned on a creek near a cabin and found lots of strawberries. Camped for the night on a nice stream.

July 8: Part of the crowd went to a lake fishing, four miles from camp. We went horseback. There was no road, we went through timber and rocks, when we got near the lake we tied our horses and walked. Roy struck out up the lake through fallen timber, underbrush and boulders. I followed him, when I got where there was good fishing I was tired out. Roy caught nine, I caught five, then Roy made a fire on a rock, and fried some fish. Ate our dinner; then struck out for camp, but Roy had to fish some more, so I came home with Jim and Nan, we went flying. Camped at the same camp ground. Mosquitoes worse than ever. Mr. and Mrs. Spencer called at our camp. The first Jackson people we saw.

We camped there two days.

July 9: We drove to the Ferry. Took a long time to get our outfit across. The loose horses swam the river. We tried to jew Mr. Menor down on the ferry bill, but nothing doing, even tried to pay him in flour and cured pork, but after we got across and paid him in cash then he wanted some bacon, but we didn't let it go, kept it for our winter supply. Camped on the north bank of Ditch Creek.

July 10. Drove on down to Grovont River and camped in the Cottonwoods. (Later it became the Sebastian ranch.)

July 24: Jim Lannigan and Jim Simpson called on us, of course they were interested in the girls.

We went gooseberrying, took Charley and Jimmie to Nowlins. We got lots of gooseberries, got in the wagon to go up the creek, drove through a dip, Nan and I were in the back seat, we went out on our heads, berries and all. On our way home Mrs. Nowlin overtook us, she wanted Villia, to help her cook for the hay men. Then Mr. and Mrs. Miller came and wanted one of the girls. Mrs. Allen said Cassie could go.

July 25: Roy and Jim went up on Grosventre river for mining tools. I laid around all day. Nan and I were the only ones in camp, the rest went berrying, and took the girls to their work.

July 26: Roy and Jim came home today.

July 27: A crowd of us went fishing on the Grosventre river. Roy and I went horseback. We found Woodins outfit camped there. Roy caught 14 fish, gave Mr. W. two.

July 28: A stormy day. Roy and Charley went up to Nowlins to hay.

July 29: I washed today, am very tired now, my head aches.

July 30: I slept with Mrs. Allen. It rained this morning.

July 31: Villia and I went to the post office. Got a letter from Mrs. McBride.

That fall the men helped [other homesteaders] with haying [taking part of their wages in hay for their own livestock—a common practice of the time]. That winter Roy and I lived with Jim Lannigan. Charley Allen and family, also Jim and Nan Budge, lived in the old Johnny Carnes home. [The Budge's first child, Allen, was born there the next spring.] Jim May and family lived in one of the Slough Grass Nelson cabins.

The first time we saw the Robert Millers was on the Flat Creek flat. They were in a buckboard and had the Nowlin boys with them. They were looking for help to cook for the haymen.

❧

Roy and Maggie later homesteaded on Flat Creek; Jim and Nan Budge chose to file north of the Gros Ventre, near Blacktail Butte, as did James May. Charles and Maria Allen filed a claim on the banks of the Snake River, in the Oxbow Bend, about a mile west of the outlet of Jackson Lake.

JACKSON HOLE GUN CLUB

BY 1897, JACKSON'S HOLE WAS becoming quite populous. In the nine short years since the Wilsons had come to the valley and found half a dozen bachelors plus Johnny Carnes and his Indian wife, a steady stream of settlers had come and taken up homesteads. A smaller outbound stream of disillusioned folks had been forced by circumstances to sell out, leaving behind little evidence of their sojourn in the valley other than their homestead improvements and here and there a place name or landmark named after them.

True, there was as yet no store, and the only school was down at South Park, but there was a post office. In fact, by July there were two post offices, as Maggie Cunningham had a post office at Elk and the Marysvale Post Office had been moved to the Simpson ranch and renamed "Jackson." [*See other chapters in this book.*]

There was quite a nest of ranches in the little circle of buttes and foothills surrounding the Flat Creek flats near the mouth of Cache Creek. With not even a schoolhouse for a public meeting place, the lack of a public building was apparent. The men talked about this need and decided they could do something about it. To get together and build a building was a simple matter, and with everyone helping, not too expensive or time consuming, but it had to have some sort of legal existence. They decided to form a club.

It is too bad that we do not have the minutes of the meetings. From the scraps of legal documents that have been preserved we have to piece out the story of the Clubhouse and the Jackson Hole Gun Club.

On June 15, 1897, a deed was given by John Porter Simpson and wife Maggie Simpson to the Jackson Hole Gun Club for a triangular-shaped piece of land containing five and four-tenths acres, more or less. It was signed by W. L. (Bill) Simpson as president of the club and Frank L. Peterson, secretary.

This document may never have been filed in the courthouse. If it was, it must not have been transcribed from Uinta, to Lincoln, to Teton in the various moves when the county split, because it is not in the Teton books at present.

By gleaning some names from deeds, we are able to report the names of some of the members who sparked this venture. By far the best source of names of club members comes from a little "Programme" which the club had printed for the "Initial Grand Ball" given by the Jackson Gun Club on July 5, 1897. This small memento was in the souvenirs of the late Roy VanVleck, who hadn't arrived here at that time. It is thanks to him for acquiring and saving it, and to Jeanie Stewart for lending it, that we can name the committee members who helped with the Grand Ball. The program lists the committees as:

Arrangement: James Simpson, J. H. Davis, James Lannigan, W. F. Spencer. Reception: S. L. Adams, George Matson, Ed. Hunter, P. H. Karns, W. L. Simpson, D. C. Nowlin, Ham Wort, M. Detwieler, F. L. Peterson, John Hicks, R. E. Miller, John Cherry, S. N. Leek. Floor: Frank Wood, James Simpson, J. H. Davis, H. Stelz, John Shives, W. F. Spencer, James Lannigan. Door: W. P. Redmond, Albert Nelson, Martin Nelson and W. Manning.

It is interesting that the date of the Grand Ball was July 5, 1897, just three weeks after the deed was given. Did the club throw up a building in twenty days? Or did they have the Grand Ball in someone's house? We may never know now, but of one thing we may be certain—they "Had A Ball."

Several Jacksonites can remember going to school in the newly built Clubhouse in the winter of 1899. At that time it was built of log and was in the form of a cross, a long central room with anterooms on each side. One anteroom contained a cook stove and tables for food preparation. The other was used as coat room, store room and a place to bed down the kids when they fell asleep.

For two or three years the building was used as meeting house for the gun club, schoolhouse for the kids and dance hall for all parties. (There were built-in restrictions against alcoholic beverages in the deed.)

The Clubhouse, Jackson's oldest commercial building still standing and being used today, had been serving as a general meeting house for the little community and as a temporary schoolhouse for two years before the first town plat of 1901 was surveyed on land belonging to Grace Miller.

This original townsite stretched from what is now Broadway to North Street, and from Cache Avenue, to Flat Creek on the north. Lots could be bought for ten or fifteen dollars apiece. Almer Nelson remarked in an interview, "When my father bought the Jackson Hotel, he bought a lot next to it for fifteen dollars. You could have probably bought the whole town for a hundred dollars."

In 1905, the Gun Club expanded its membership and aims for, on January 14, 1905, at a special meeting, they voted a change of bylaws. This new bylaws document was found in Steve Leek's files and a copy was given to the Jackson Hole Historical Society by Ed Lloyd.

It seems the object of the club was changing with the times. The pertinent changes follow:

"The name of said club shall be the Jackson Hole Gun and Commercial Club.

"The object of the club shall be the betterment of social and commercial conditions in Jackson Hole.

"The members shall solicit the patronage of all good citizens to become members of the club, that our club be more effectual for any and all good causes.

"That the wife of all members be made honorary members and have a voice in all decisions and vote in all meetings of the club."

The new bylaws were then signed into effect by all members present at the meeting: S. N. Leek, Robert Miller, Claude Simpson, Frank S. Wood, S. E. Osborn, P. H. Karns, Roy McBride, George M. Matson and Frank L. Peterson.

The site was ideal for a business location, so it may be that at the same meeting they voted to remodel the building. The work should be completed by July 1, 1905.

One more interesting legal transaction took place in 1905. The 1897 deed may never have been filed in the courthouse in

Evanston. There is a 1905 deed which is of record in the Teton County Clerk's office.

Whereas the first tract of land given in 1897 was triangular in shape, following the section line on two sides and contained 5.4 acres, this second deed described a rectangular piece of ground 4.66 acres, with a thirty-foot easement from section lines for street purposes. The club's lot covered what is now the city square, the Clubhouse block just east of it, the Jackson Drug/B&W block, to the north of the square and the Bank block to the east of that. The Clubhouse was the only building in it at that time.

The remodeling job must have been completed in the specified time because the lower floor of the building became a mercantile store during the autumn of 1906 when a couple of enterprising young fellows came through Jackson Hole on their way to Butte, Montana, with a load of potatoes.

The potatoes were all they had to show for a couple of business ventures in the mining towns of Colorado and Encampment, Wyoming. When the mines went to pot, business had also.

Roy and Frank VanVleck liked the looks of Jackson Hole, and the settlers needed the potatoes. The young fellows traded their stock of potatoes for enough money and trade goods to set up a small stock of mercantile goods. They freighted in kerosene, tools, drygoods, traps, farm implements and just about everything a growing community could want.

They slept in the back of the store and boarded at the Jackson Hotel with the Pete Nelsons, who owned it at that time. Frank started a barber shop in the north end of the store and an amusing family story has been handed down concerning his tonsorial efforts.

A dude came in to get a haircut and shave but found a native just ahead of him. The native was "Shakey" Shinkle, a resident of Kelly who suffered from a very bad case of palsy. All the natives knew how impossible it was for Shakey to hold still, but the dude didn't.

Frank escorted Shakey to a chair, strapped him down with a big wide harness strap around his shoulder and behind the chair, then proceeded to stir up a cup of lather. He soaped Shakey and turned to strop his razor, playing "Clippity, getcher hair cut" on the stovepipe. When he took hold of Shakey's nose and made a long swipe

🌾 *This photograph was taken from the current town square before the plotting of lots. The gun club, housing the Jackson Mercantile on the ground floor, is in the background.* (JHM&HC)

down his cheek, Shakey squirmed and shivered. The dude picked up his hat, murmured, "Now I've seen everything," and lit out.

Initially the club's name implied a membership interested in shooting activities with community gatherings as a secondary objective. A swing to interest in building up the business of the town is evident in a change of the bylaws of the club dated 1905 when the name was changed from Jackson Hole Gun Club to Jackson Hole Commercial Club.

In 1908, a deed was made from the Gun Club to the Commercial Club transferring the entire property. In the addenda to the deed, there is a statement that the members of the Gun Club were paid $25 each. Did those who wished to withdraw take their original membership fee and quit? There is no mention of the added value the membership should have earned with the construction of the building.

Those with membership in force at the time of the deed transfer were: John Cherry, Claude Simpson, Jack Shives, William Manning, John Bircher, Charles Wilson, T. W. Lloyd, James Budge, Henry Botcher, Charles J. Allen, Stephen N. Leek, William P. Redmond, James S. Simpson, J. P. Cunningham, U. G. Foster, Charles Spencer, Roy Anderson, Albert Nelson, Peter Karns, and Frank Peterson.

So the Gun Club no longer existed.

No membership records of the Commercial Club have come to light, but at least some of the Gun Club members belonged to the new club. The next business of record concerning the Jackson Hole Commercial Club is the sale of the entire tract, presumably including the Clubhouse, on January 23, 1912.

The price was three thousand dollars, and the buyer was Frank Wood. He must have been buying for others because the next day he transferred the property to T. W. Lloyd and Pierce Cunningham for the same amount. The deed was signed by William Manning, president, and Peter Karns, secretary, of the Jackson Hole Commercial Club.

As soon as spring took the snow from the valley, Pierce Cunningham and T. W. Lloyd had the tract surveyed and subdivided (maybe the town's first real estate promoters). Otho Williams surveyed it May 14, 1912. The survey was acknowledged June 14, 1913, and the plat was not filed until June 29, 1914. They really did need a courthouse nearer than Evanston.

Partners T. W. Lloyd and Pierce Cunningham sold some of the lots as a partnership, but some were sold by each as individuals. T. W. Lloyd transferred most of his lots to his wife Suzie Lloyd, while Cunningham sold most of his interests to William Redmond. They made one sale as partners, this being lot one of block one which they sold to the Woodmen of the World. A lodge building was erected on this lot either by the Woodmen or by the Odd Fellows who bought it next. This building stood on the southwest corner of the present city park. In 1916, Redmond and Suzie Lloyd sold the other seven lots of block one to the city for $350 to each seller. The city minutes show that they purchased the seven lots for $750. (There is no record of where the extra fifty dollars went.)

In approximately 1934, the city council, under Mayor Dr. Huff, bought a lot on the north side of the square and built a similar building for the Odd Fellows and traded them out of the building on the southwest corner, thus completing the square. The square was then cleaned up landscaped and fenced by community effort, and eventually grew into the lovely little park of today.

Lot three and one half of lot four of block four of the Clubhouse Addition (the one and one-half lots the Clubhouse occupies)

❧ The Odd Fellows building sat within the town square on the southwest corner until 1932 when it was moved. (JHM&HC)

were transferred to the Jackson Drug Company. There is no deed of record in the Teton County courthouse of this transaction. The next deed of record is a transfer from James Simpson for a one-half undivided interest in the Jackson Drug Company to Bruce Porter in 1919. The Porter Estate still owns the building.

Over the years the Clubhouse has fulfilled its objective as a center for community life, commercially as well as socially. After Roy and Frank VanVleck moved into their own building next door to the Clubhouse, the Jackson Drug Company started a drugstore in the downstairs. Robinson and Miss Moon were the first druggists to conduct the business.

In 1914 Bruce Porter, an enterprising young druggist, came to work for Jimmy Simpson. Bruce soon went off to the First World War, but upon his return, he purchased the drugstore from Jimmy in 1919. From 1923 until 1935, the post office was in the Clubhouse. Postmaster W. E. Lloyd (Butch) also had a meat market in the lower floor of the building. When the drugstore and post office moved to the north side of the square, the Clubhouse continued to house important businesses.

The upstairs continued to be a community dance hall and gathering place. Plays were given and community weekly "sings" were held there. The first movies shown there were Steve Leek's game and scenic pictures narrated by Mr. Leek in his low-pitched drawl.

Sometime around 1923 or 1924, Hollywood came to Jackson! With Hollywood magic, a train seemingly pulled to a stop across the street from the Clubhouse, and Mary Miles Minter stepped down. Tom Mix was on the scene, likewise his horse Tony.

Time dims the sequence of the story, but Tom tossed the villain down the Clubhouse steps. In one scene, there was a shoot-out on the square. It was a made-to-order western set. Tony was guarded day and night, and, to the astonishment of us youngsters, cleaned up more often than any kid in town. He was the main attraction of the whole Hollywood crew for small Jacksonites. The film: *The Cowboy and the Lady.*

While the Clubhouse was at its heyday as town center in the early 1920s, no place in town had any indoor plumbing. The plumbing needs were filled by water being hauled from Cache Creek by the barrel, and by an outhouse out in the alley. A tragicomic incident happened one day in the time of year when the mail was being hauled in by sleigh.

A man named Scott had the mail contract at the time. Both Scott and his helper came in on the mail sleigh on the evening of this event. Since the road was tough and the weather cold, as usual, they had taken many nips from the bottle of moonshine they had along for such trying times. Before unloading the mail (a heavy job, since the merchants all ordered their stocks of groceries sent in by parcel post) they decided they should repair to the Clubhouse outhouse and have another nip from the bottle. Since this was during prohibition days, one didn't just tip up a bottle in public. They invited a couple of friends, who were standing around on the Clubhouse steps, to join them.

Now the Clubhouse outhouse was fairly commodious, being designed to serve a public place. It stood on the edge of the little bench behind the Clubhouse with the door opening outward, facing west. The back of the hole was built up with rockwork and boards ten feet or more to the level of the bench, the front was dug straight down to the bottom of the hole. The floor was a platform extending over the sides of the hole. With the weight of the four big fellows the boards gave way at ground level and the whole edifice settled down into the hole.

Scott and his companions tried the door, which could not open out against the ground, then tried to break some boards, somewhere, anywhere! The surrounding ground and rockwork held everything firm and solid. They were trapped.

At first they just shouted guardedly, hoping to attract the attention of Butch Lloyd, the postmaster, or Bruce Porter, the druggist. When they got no response they set up a shouting that could be heard all over town. Butch and Bruce had heard them in the first place and had run out to assess the trouble. It was so funny (and such a big problem) that at first they couldn't do anything but try to plan, through their laughing.

Scott had been out in the frigid winter air all day, nipping frequently. He soon got on a crying jag.

"Get me out of here!" He would moan. "I fight the blizzards! I fight the snows! I fight the slides!—Now I've got to die in a god-damned outhouse!" This didn't speed up the rescue because the rescuers were convulsed again and again and had to go into the drugstore to wipe their eyes and try to plan.

Soon everyone around the square was in on the rescue efforts. Scott's repeated cries of distress went up, loud and long, heard all up and down the alley, swooping and soaring, subsiding into plaintive threats and curses, only to start up again with renewed fervor. "Chees-suss kee-rist. Can't some-body do something? ... I fight the snow! ...I fight the blizzards! ...I fight the slides.... Now I've got to die in a god-damned *outhouse!*"

In spite of the hilarity outside of the outhouse, and unbeknownst to Scott, work was progressing. Somebody produced a block and tackle and someone found some long, stout poles to make a tripod. With most of the men in town hauling on the ropes, the outhouse was winched up out of the hole. The four outhouse occupants were not exactly received with open arms. They slunk off in different directions to try to clean up.

Butch and the bystanders had to unload the mail sled. Butch and his wife, Leanore, got home pretty late that night, having distributed mail after midnight.

A small sequel to the story: sometime in the predawn hours of the next morning, Irene Hodges' cow wandered along the alley behind the Clubhouse and fell in the toilet hole. Next morning the block and tackle, along with the tripod, had to be put to use again, and some brave soul had to fasten the rope around the cow. Although the Hodges ran the cow back and forth in the deepest part of the creek and then gave her a good washing, Irene said she just couldn't stand to use the milk. I guess she wasn't exaggerating, because they sold the cow.

*N*AN *B*UDGE: *M*ERRY *P*IONEER

"THE MERRY PIONEER" IS A FITTING title for Aunt Nan Budge. She raised a big family, made a home in frontier conditions, helped with the outside work—all this she considered fun. Even her entrance into the valley was in the nature of a summer-long picnic.

Mary Ann (Nan) Allen was born in Calls Fort, Utah, April 25, 1877. She was married to James Budge on April 25, 1896, at Rockland, Idaho. By June 21 of that year, they had set off with a group of friends and relatives headed for Jackson's Hole. The train was composed of four covered wagons, fifteen people, about fifty head of cattle and horses and eight hens and a rooster. The chickens belonged to the Budges. [*See "Maggie McBride's Diary," page 59*]

Members of the wagon train were Mr. and Mrs. Charles J. Allen (Nan's parents), with five of their children, Mrs. and Mrs. J. I. May with their children, Mr. and Mrs. Roy McBride, and James and Nan Budge.

Travel was slow but they enjoyed the scenery and had no traffic accidents. They arrived at the foot of Teton Pass on July 5. Another four days saw them over on Ditch Creek where the men looked around for homesteads. Traveling seemed to agree with the hens for they kept the party in eggs all summer. Some hunting and fishing went on, then the men started haying for Slough Grass Nelson. They had to work in hip boots, but they got some hay for wages and used it that winter.

Mr. Budge homesteaded his place the fall of 1897. The house was a log cabin with sod-covered poles for a roof. When it rained Nan had to put the babies under the table to keep them dry. It rained two or three hours longer in the house than it did outside.

Outside, the antelope played around over the top of the root cellar, and elk stayed on Blacktail Butte. The stretch of homesteads, including the Budges', along the east side of Blacktail Butte soon became known as Mormon Row.

The Gros Ventre was full of fish and Aunt Nan introduced horseback fishing. She owned perhaps the world's only fisherhorse. His name was Quitip (Kee-tip)—a long legged sorrel. He seemed to know when the fish she caught was small. He would stand indifferent, even bored, while Aunt Nan reeled in the catch. But let the fish be a large one, and Quitip would head for the best landing bank, whichever side of the river it was on. He went just the proper distance and speed, with no direction or urging from Aunt Nan—good thing, because she would be busy reeling in her catch.

He seemed to know the pools where the fish were and to enjoy standing in the water up to the saddle skirts until they caught one. The big ones never got away from Aunt Nan and Quitip!

Nan loved to ride over to Huckleberry Ridge to berry, taking whatever children were not big enough to help in the fields. With a baby or two before and behind the saddle, they would ride over, ford the Snake, pick all day, and return. Sometimes a few women and many children would take food and bedding and camp at the berry patch a few days.

About 1898 the government granted a post office to the locality. It was called Grovont (with that change in spelling) and Aunt Nan was the first postmaster. The post office remained at the Budge ranch on Mormon Row about twenty years. It then traveled around the various ranches, eventually returning to the Budge ranch. Aunt Nan was postmaster at the time they sold their ranch in 1941.

James Budge was a County Commissioner of Lincoln County from 1915-1921; he was also assistant assessor of Lincoln County for one term. When Teton County was organized, he was made assessor, serving from 1925 to 1928. He then served as Teton County Commissioner from 1931 to 1934. He was among the first members of the Jackson Hole Cattle and Horse Association.

The Budges built up a fine ranch and herd of cattle from the four cows, nine chickens and twenty dollars in cash they brought into the country. When their family was grown, they sold the ranch, then bought and retired to a small place in Wilson. The ranch on Mormon Row went to Lester May—grandson of the J. I. May with whom they pioneered to the country. When the Grovont Post Office was abandoned in 1950, Mrs. Lester May, the last Postmaster, wrote to Mrs. Budge, the first, and this letter Aunt Nan treasured as the last letter to be canceled by "her" post office, closed after fifty-two years of service.

Another memento of her post office days is a badge returned to her after being lost for thirty-two years. The Budges and Bill Menor had been vacationing in 1915. They took in the World Fair where the badge was lost.

It was returned by a Mrs. Wear in January 1947. She explained that her son had just found it.

Mr. Budge passed away October 13, 1943, after a short illness, and after his death Aunt Nan continued to reside in her home on the bank of Fish Creek. She had a pet saddle horse to care for and also made pets of any birds, animals or even fish that came her way. She had a school of huge old trout which got a ration of hamburger from her and which she was known to defend from greedy fishermen with her life, honor and the help of the law!

Mr. and Mrs. Budge had the spirit and courage necessary to pioneer a new country, the ambition to work and plan, and the patience to watch the seeds of their efforts grow to maturity. Aunt Nan died September 28, 1961. The valley will miss her.

*E*D *H*ARRINGTON:

*A*LIAS *T*RAFTON, *H*IGHWAYMAN

BEFORE THE EARLIEST WHITE MEN stayed the year around in Jackson's Hole, the valley was trapped in the winters by various white trappers. Among them was an old fellow named Goodwin whose favorite trapping areas were the heads of Sheep, Flat and Nowlin Creeks. Henry Gunther told of finding one of Goodwin's distinctive box-type bear traps with sliding doors on Miller Butte, and some more of the same up in the foothills.

Goodwin trapped the area east of the town of Jackson long and skillfully enough to get some landmarks named for him. Lovely little Goodwin Lake is named for him, and the prominent triangular-shaped peak now called Jackson Peak at first bore his name until the Forest Service changed it.

Goodwin's home base was in Idaho, somewhere near the confluence of the North and South forks of the Snake River. He would arrive in Jackson in the fall with his traps and pack train of supplies, then send the horses back home to Idaho with someone traveling that way. He had no hay for wintering them. At the end of the spring trapping he would walk out to Idaho, leaving his furs cached. There he would gather up his pack outfit and come back to pack out his furs.

Goodwin was pretty well known in the sparsely-settled basins on both sides of the Tetons, but he disappeared one spring and no one ever learned what happened to him. History is concerned with facts; speculation is concerned with rationalizing or explaining a situation's mysterious and unknown dynamics. If it is never proved, it remains gossip. The rest of the story of Goodwin's fate is just that.

For years on his travels back and forth through Teton Basin, Goodwin always stopped at his friend Hank Goe's—this was before

Hank Goe and his sons moved into Jackson. Goodwin had made his usual stop at the Goe's one spring when he was on his way into Jackson's Hole with his pack outfit to gather up his winter's catch. When the Teton Basin folks didn't see him come back out they weren't concerned, since he could easily have ridden further on toward home before stopping.

No one missed him or sent out a general inquiry or alarm.

In those days everyone tended to his own business, trappers most of all. He wasn't missed for a long time, and there is no record of a search being made. When it did become apparent that Goodwin was just gone, not to return, then the speculation and the gossip started among his friends and acquaintances.

Ed Harrington was a suspect. He was a resident of Teton Basin, strong-willed and trouble-prone. Harrington had already served time for horse stealing and stick-up deals. He was no trapper, but someone remembered that he had sold a catch of furs that spring.

Ed was apt to have various kinds and colors of horses in his string, but someone else remembered his having a particular pinto which was colored just like a pinto old Goodwin had owned. Still no organized search was made. It had been so long since he disappeared. What kind of evidence was a pinto horse in someone's string which was probably traded off by now? Or a catch of furs, which Ed could claim he had caught. How could anybody prove he hadn't?

Harrington was never questioned, and Goodwin was never found. If foul play was the cause of his disappearance, he probably rests in peace somewhere in the vicinity of the lovely little lake which bears his name.

❧

In the early days Jackson Hole was given credit for harboring many bad men. It would be fine if we could shrug Ed Harrington off as an Idaho bad man. Sometime later, however, he came to Jackson to work on the Jackson Lake dam while it was under construction, and so he lived in Jackson for a brief time. Ed found a way to get into trouble at that time too.

During the time the dam was under construction, about 1913–14, Yellowstone Park was supervised by the U.S. Army. Dudes arriving in Jackson and wishing to go through the park had to hire a boat trip from Moran on the old steam-powered side wheeler named the "Titanic," a scow run by Captain McDermott. This craft ferried them to the north end of Jackson Lake where they were met by a "white-top rig"—this was a three-seated two-horse buggy capable of carrying nine people—which in turn delivered them to Thumb.

From Thumb they were ferried across Yellowstone Lake to Lake Lodge. From there on, the Yellowstone Park Company handled the transportation. Their coaches were big eleven-passenger coaches drawn by a four-horse team (double span).

Buster Estes was a Jackson lad who drove the white-top rig leg of the trip for the Sheffield Lodge.

Ed Harrington was living under the name of Trafton while working at the dam. He made it a point to visit with Buster in the evenings, and finally broached the idea that it would be mighty easy to hold up the Yellowstone Park coaches and get a lot of money and jewelry from the rich dudes.

Buster just thought the guy was joking and agreed it would be a good deal. Trafton then outlined a plan he had been thinking out. He would build a boat and take it to the north end of Jackson Lake. There he would overturn it and it would look like he had drowned. Then he intended to make his way to a spot where he could hold up the stages. Then he'd disappear into the forest afoot.

Trafton built the boat. One night he told Buster he was ready for them to execute his plan. Buster still didn't think he was serious. He told Trafton he was pretty busy, and Trafton should go ahead without him. When the boat and Trafton were gone from Moran next morning, Buster began to wonder whether Trafton really intended to carry out his harebrained idea.

A day or two later Buster went to Mammoth for a load of dudes to bring to Sheffield Lodge. On the way he passed nineteen park coaches with Charles (White Mountain) Smith driving the lead coach. They were stopped at Kepler Cascades. Buster proceeded on to Thumb. Later that day he saw the same string of coaches come tearing in to Thumb.

When the passengers tumbled out in great distress they told of being held up by a lone bandit at Shoshone Point. The following day the Sheffields reported Trafton's boat found capsized, and that they feared the man was drowned. At last Buster knew that Trafton's plan was not a joke.

Buster either looked guilty, or the soldiers had found out Trafton had been seen with him, for on his next trip, Buster was stopped by Sergeant Jim Webb and told he was under arrest for being an accomplice of Trafton.

Buster laughed and said he would have to take his load of dudes to Thumb first. After some argument, Sergeant Webb allowed him to do this. A couple of soldiers went along to see that Buster came back.

So conducted by the soldiers, Buster arrived at Fort Yellowstone (Mammoth). He told Major Brett what he knew of Trafton's plans. They asked him if he could identify Trafton, and he was shown a scared little Irishman who had been in the wrong vicinity without horse, pack or proof of identity. Buster did recognize this anxious fellow; he was not Trafton but a man who had been in Moran recently looking for work. Trafton had successfully eluded capture.

He built a cabin hideout on the west side of Jackson Lake—hidden so successfully that it wasn't found until 1931 by Slim Lawrence.

Just as he had planned, Trafton made his getaway with the loot. He was later heard of in Denver. His downfall came because he was spending money like mad on wine, women and gaiety before returning to his wife in Idaho.

She had somehow gotten word of his high jinks with the Denver women, and later when he returned to Sandpoint, Idaho, she notified authorities where Ed Harrington (alias Trafton) could be found. He was tracked down in Idaho, tried in Cheyenne, and sentenced to five years in Leavenworth, for the Yellowstone caper.

As Trafton's life came to light during the trial, Jacksonites learned he had already served two sentences for horse stealing and had robbed his own mother of a large sum of money. This evidence renewed speculation that he was involved with Goodwin's disappearance.

After discharge from Leavenworth he led a straight life—so far as Jacksonites knew.

Too Big a Dream

AT THIS LATE DATE IT IS HARD TO ASSESS the character of the man; especially since he did not not seem to join in the community spirit of visiting and sharing which made other families of the sparsely settled upper valley of Jackson's Hole very knowledgeable about each other. The things we know about John Dudley Sargent consist of some facts and much gossip; which, I suppose, is about all we can use when spinning a character sketch of any human being.

Sargent was born into a prosperous and important Maine family with connections in Sullivan, Calais and Machias. His grandfather Ignatious and his great uncle John D. were active both in business and politics in these towns. Records of a merchandising and building corporation and other documents provide some basic information about John Sargent: Birth date, 1861, father; Henry C. Sargent; mother, Alice Hemmenway.

It is rumored that he was a scapegrace at Yale college. This is also said of his partner, Robert Hamilton, who joined him in the Jackson's Hole adventure. The families may have advanced money for the project these young men undertook, or the men may have received allowances. Whatever, they received an income — making them remittance men — something the other homesteaders didn't have, and therefore setting them apart, and making them a little suspect. But I'm getting ahead of the sequence.

Sargent first entered Jackson's Hole in 1886 and was so impressed with the beauty of the place that he determined to return some day. In 1888, he returned with a partner, Robert Ray Hamilton. Hamilton is said to be a descendant of the Robert Hamilton, financier, who managed the financing of the Civil War. Even though the young men apparently enjoyed that first summer, they did not spend the winter, but returned East.

We do not have the date of Sargent's marriage to his first wife, Adelaide Crane, but it must have been before that winter, because their first child, Hemmenway, was born in Machias in 1885, and the second child, Mary, was born in 1887.

Eighteen eighty-nine was the summer which saw Sargent's ten-room house going up on the north end of Jackson Lake and much clearing and fencing being done. Although Hamilton's name does not appear on any filing claims nor deeds, he was acting as a full partner in the work and expense. Quoting from a letter written to Slim Lawrence by John Dodge, who was a friend of the partners, "Hamilton got log men from Ashton who rip-sawed the logs on three sides and laid them with pegged corners." Hamilton had his own cabin built on the place. They named the ranch Merye Mere.

Their plan, which was a good one (just a little too early for the amount of travel), was to create a roadhouse to accommodate Yellowstone Park travelers, or fishing or hunting parties which would stay several weeks. They freighted in expensive furnishings and dishes by mule pack over the Conant Pass trail—even bringing a baby-grand piano slung between two mules on an improvised travois. The legs were removed (that grand was not as wide as the modern variety), still, a very worthy feat. The piano is still in Jackson's Hole, residing now at the home of Bessie Barney, of Wilson, Wyoming.

By 1890 the home-business venture was ready, and that spring Adelaide rode into the valley with the partners, carrying her baby, Martha, born in 1889 in Machias, in her arms.

There is no record of their activities of that summer of 1890, but it could only be one of hard work and hard play. Groceries, railroad, and mail were seventy horse-back miles to Ashton. The nearest community was ten miles south where a few scattered settlers were just getting started. The few other children were fifty miles away in the southern end of the valley.

Just getting in the wood, cutting and carrying it, getting meat or fish for the larder, tending livestock and improving the place must have kept the men busy. Caring for the babies, the meals, and the house was a full day for a woman. The beautiful surroundings with the abundance of fish, wildlife, and birds could make for happy living. They must have gone "outside" for the second winter, at least for part of it, because the fourth child, Katherine, was born in Salt Lake City in 1892.

The summer of 1891 brought a tragedy and the first signs of something of a neighborly suspicion of Sargent. The partners had gone on a hunt for antelope, supposedly to the pot-holes area. They hunted in the pot-holes area west of Snake River, south of Signal Mountain, and they became separated. When Hamilton didn't show up Sargent sought help. In none of the accounts have I seen that Sargent sought help to find Hamilton, but such must have been the case. A search party was organized, and since they would be fanned out riding both sides of the Snake River, it was agreed that anyone finding him would make a fire and smoke signal on the butte north of the river. This is how Signal Mountain got its name.

Hamilton's body was found. The fire was built. Some say his horse was found with the antelope still tied onto the saddle. Many years later, Mary Sargent Sears sent her version of the incident to the *Jackson Hole Guide*, August 28, 1958:

August 28, 1958
Calistoga, California

Dear Editor of Guide,

I see where some people are writing a column about past history of Jackson for the Guide. Would you kindly print a few lines for me?

I am John Dudley Sargent's eldest daughter of a family of four girls and one boy. Father went into Jackson the first time in 1886, later with a partner, Robert Ray Hamilton, in 1888. They took up a homestead at the north end of Jackson Lake, a beautiful view of the Lake. It took four years to build the ten room house.

The second year they were in residence [1889: Mary was two] Robert Hamilton was drowned in the Snake River while crossing with a deer in the saddle. They found his body later with the saddle, which had turned, his foot was still in the stirrup, and washed ashore.

So many people tell things which are untrue, but I know, for I heard it many times.

He was buried down in front of our house but later his folks came from the East and took his body back there to bury. The grave hole was not filled and us children played around it many times. There was no mystery about Hamilton's disappearance, as some say.

I read Mr. Barbee's column and enjoyed it except that part which isn't true. Hoping you will kindly print this in your paper, I am, sincerely yours;

Mary Sargent Sears

The implication which Mary referred to was that Hamilton had been led to, or sent to, an unsafe crossing by Sargent, which had cost him his life. Old timers from the upper end of the valley disclaim hearing any of this kind of gossip until many years after the event.

Of the next few years we have no memoirs. Apparently Sargent was engaged in pioneering work, eased with some music and literature, it would seem, since he had imported the piano and also had a Victrola with many classical records. We do have documents of homesteading residence showing that the Sargents were in Salt Lake City during the winter of 1892 and in Idaho for the winters of 1894 and 1895. The fifth child, Adelaide, was born at the ranch in 1895, with local midwife Grandma Sam Osborn at hand. This must have been a summertime confinement. These moves with all of these small children, could not have been an easy life. Maybe it is just as well that their roadhouse was not busy.

John Sargent kept a journal. It reveals his sensitivity to the beautiful surroundings in which they lived and shows quite a bit of family pride, fun, and feelings. One entry, "A Single Full Summer Day," was written some years after the event, according to the date at the bottom. Another, an account of a trip over the mountains, accompanied by his four-year-old daughter Martha, is also written sometime after the event. It is an interesting and very plausible account of a trying trip crossing the mountains in a heavy snowstorm while alone with a small child and five pack horses. The journal includes an account of a winter—or late spring—trip over Conant Pass on skis. It is suspenseful reading, with a storm blotting out just the right crossing of the pass to make possible an easy descent of the Berry Creek canyon. On this trip he started from the railroad at St. Anthony, coming over the pass to Jackson Lake. A friend he named only with a capital L was with him. Sargent arrived home safely to find his fat cat taking care of things.

From this period in the 1890s there are pictures of the ranch and of the children, beautiful, well-dressed little girls and a boy, a large and comfortable (for that time and isolated place) log house with several other buildings.

In the spring of 1897, tragedy struck the family again. Time has blurred the details. The story, as it was repeated in the valley, is: Soldiers from Yellowstone Park's southern gate, on the way to Moran, stopped by the Sargent home and knocked on the door, expecting to visit a bit and offer to take or bring back any mail or needs of the family, a common practice. Sargent, acting very strangely, would not let them in. They may have heard a cry or have seen something to make them suspicious. At any rate, they told settlers at the community of Moran that someone needed to look into the Sargent home. A group of the Moran folk went to the Sargent home and found Mrs. Sargent helpless in bed. John was not there.

The ground was still snow-covered there, so Mrs. Sargent was pulled to Moran on a toboggan. From there she was to be taken to Jackson in a buggy or wagon. It must have been a very rough ride, so early in the spring. Four or five miles from Jackson, on the Curtis or Nowlin ranch, the drivers stopped, for Adelaide appeared so low they were afraid to go on. Adelaide died at the Curtis ranch. She was buried there on the place, as there was no designated cemetery at the time. Many years later her remains were moved to the Jackson cemetery after her daughter Mary had grown to adulthood and arranged the removal.

There are different versions of the injury which killed Mrs. Sargent. One source stated: "Mrs. Sargent died May 15, 1897, from injuries thought to be inflicted by her husband." Another cause, passed around as fact, was that she had slipped on the icy porch when doing housework, had broken her hip or pelvic bones, and had been allowed to remain without medical aid or any knowledgeable help until the condition became critical. A third version was that a miscarriage, or an attempted abortion, had become infected.

Sargent's disappearance added to the speculation.

Factual statement: Sargent left Jackson's Hole in the spring of 1897 and did not return until 1899.

One wonders what was happening to the five children the oldest only nine or ten, at the time of Mrs. Sargent's removal from the house. Did Sargent come back for them? Were they taken to Moran and boarded with neighbors until relatives could send for them? Did Sargent have *anything* to do with getting them placed or settled? Or did he just light out over the Conant trail and leave the situation to solve itself?

In some of the material about him, it is stated that he stood an investigation at Cheyenne but was released for insufficient evidence.

One other legend passed along through the years: When Mrs. Sargent lay dying someone asked her if she wished to make a statement. She answered that if she lived there was plenty she could tell, but if she was going to die it could go with her.

Sargent must have spent the period from the spring of 1897, when he left the valley, until October of 1899, when he returned, at the family home in Maine. All of the children were with relatives there at that time. Mention is made in family correspondence that grandparent Henry Clay Sargent raised Hemmenway, Martha and Adelaide. Mary may have stayed in Maine for a few years, but she did not like the east and came back to Wyoming to join her father. Katherine, also, was at Merye Mere while very small.

Yellowstone Park soldiers on their way to Moran (which had a post office, and hence a name by then) overtook Sargent pulling a toboggan on which was his seven- or eight-year-old daughter Katherine. When he realized the soldiers were approaching from the rear, he dropped the toboggan rope and webbed off into the timber; soon he was out of sight. The soldiers could not overtake him, so they pulled the toboggan on in to Moran, stopping at the Allen ranch, which was the post office, hotel and store also.

According to Grandma Allen, the little girl was sore and crying and walked stiffly. Grandma Allen soon had her bathed and put to bed.

A neighboring ranch wife near Moran relates in a letter to Slim Lawrence that a posse of men went up to the Sargent place, with thoughts of lynching, but that Sargent had made it out to the railroad and could not be found. So maybe there was some reaction after all. Again we have no word of what happened to the child. Was Mary at the ranch?

I came across another reference to Sargent's high-strung nature in a journal of a trip through Yellowstone, with a side-trip to Jackson Lake, taken by the Thwaites in 1903.

> It was the twelfth of July when we reached the shores of Jackson Lake. Mosquitoes were much more abundant there than at the higher altitudes, and at one swamp they lit on my father's back so thickly that you could not see the color of his shirt. We camped on a small bay not far from Sargent's ranch, and soon were visited by John Dudley Sargent, the hermit of Jackson's Hole. He was a great talker, very nervous, and obviously an Easterner. He stayed for supper and offered to rent us his boat for less than the quarter of a dollar for quarter of an hour, which was advertised on his signs.

Sargent, after his wife's death, was not too popular in the settlement, so was probably very lonesome.

There are pictures taken by friends and neighbors showing Katherine riding a pony being led by her father. The horse was apparently just being trained to carry a person because the rope and halter, and the way Katherine holds the reins, and the pony's ears all indicate caution and mistrust. She appears to be twelve or thirteen in the picture, taken in 1908. By then, Sargent had remarried.

Mrs. Germann relates in a letter an interesting sidelight on the time of the marriage of Sargent to his second wife, Edith, somewhere between 1906 and 1908. The letter says, "I remember very well when they came out into Idaho to be married. They came to a dance in Victor and they began to waltz. Everyone left the floor and stood back to watch them as they whirled and whirled crazily around, and it really was a sight to see." If they "came out" to get married they must have been in Jackson at the ranch. Was she a dude sent to the ranch for a visit or for health reasons? Or had he met her back east and brought her to the west to be his bride?

Some neighbors said that she had mental problems and Sargent agreed, in return for a fee, to marry her and take care of her. Today, however, as another old-timer says, "she would just be considered a 'nature child'"—nothing more than eccentric.

Edith and John must have had some happy times. She was also musical and wrote poetry. She encouraged him to write. There are pictures in the album showing Edith playing the violin to the accompaniment of the Victrola, all out in the yard. Another shows them off for a toboggan trip with a group of friends from the dam, which was by then a major influence in the upper valley.

Edith liked to sunbathe and was observed engaged in this unusual activity by several of the residents of the community as they rode back and forth on the road past the ranch. Herb Whiteman saw her stretched nude on a blanket in the yard. Being a shy young man he rode on by, hoping she wouldn't know he saw her. She had. She just waved in an unconcerned manner. Another traveler told of seeing her up in a tree, playing her violin, naked.

Whether this was true or not, they did have a large pine tree from which John had trimmed the lower limbs and left stubs of branches to make a ladder to an aerie about twelve or fifteen feet above the ground. It was a favorite perch for Edith. Years later when the Lawrences lived at Merye Mere, Slim and Verba found a small derringer pistol in a crotch of a limb which had fallen. Mary identified it as Edith's.

Edith's stay at the ranch was from sometime in 1906-07 to 1913. Sargent evidently took Edith to San Diego. A note in his journal states: "...Shock...San Diego, December. 6890 feet to sea in five days. 10 P.M. Saturday..." Then the journal turns to reminiscences. It would be nice to know what broke up what appears from this distance in time to be a good arrangement. The couple seems to have retained a loving respect for each other. One of the last things in Sargent's journal was a reference to a letter from his wife, received on May Day, 1913. He notes, "God Bless my wife." The letter that Sargent had received had been written by Edith in Long Beach on April 19, 1913, and it is very encouraging:

❧ *John Sargent sitting in front of his fireplace in the same location as he was found after he shot himself.* (JHM&HC)

Be not impatient of delay, but wait, as one who understands. Action contracts, while thought dilates. Think, think, and develop your brain cells to their highest pitch, and be strong.

My cure for worrying… If you don't fret about a thing you'll see your way out. Worrying causes a stop in the brain, shutting out other thoughts. Like corking up a poison. The bad microbes grow fat, without right thinking to kill them… Not action but mental work is the best cure for nervousness. Action and talk excite the nerves, right thoughts bring perfect calm. What you are doing is more important than what you are feeling… Your thoughts have brought you where you are, through the law of your being, no element of chance in that.

She was later committed to a sanitarium.

During this time, Sargent seemed to begin to have financial worries. Perhaps his income from his family in Maine was exhausted or cut-off. He had known many years of loneliness and dreaded to go back to living alone.

Not long after Edith's departure, Sargent placed a Bach record on the Victrola, arranged his rifle with a string from trigger to toe, sat in his chair by the fireplace, listened to the strains of *Nur, wer die Schusucht* (Ye Who Have Yearned Alone) and pulled the trigger.

As much as two weeks may have passed before he was discovered by a group of riders from Moran, out for a pleasure ride. The group included Mr. Mahoney and his daughter, Emily Thompson, Lennie Van Winkle and a man named Brown. They hurried back to Moran and alerted Valdez Allen, who was the Justice of the Peace for the community. He gathered a group of men and went up to see what could be done.

The flies were so bad and the body so decomposed that it was hard to do anything in the house. After assessing the cause of death, a piece of canvas was found, and the body, wrapped in that, was taken to a hole which some of the party had dug in the ranch-house clearing. A prayer to rest his soul was quickly said by this small party, and the grave was filled as quickly as possible, too. The odor was sickening and all-pervasive. Herb Whiteman, Ted Miller, Newman and Valdez Allen comprised the burial party.

So ended the dream of John Dudley Sargent. Maybe the dream was too big for the man. At least he had twenty-three years of living in one of the beauty spots of the world. And he appreciated that beauty! Some of the years were pleasant, some tragic.

Maybe he wasn't a big enough man for the mountains.

The Sargent children got nothing from their home. It stood idle until 1919, when it was acquired by Harry Wagner for six hundred dollars. Apparently there were back taxes and clearing costs. When the ranch was sold to W. Louis Johnson in 1926, Edith Sargent, or her estate, wrote asking for a settlement, but she was informed that the ranch had legally passed from the Sargent estate several years before.

⁕

A SINGLE FULL SUMMER DAY
[excerpt from the journal of J. D. Sargent]

The Sargent children were the first and only settlers on Jackson Lake, which is not, as commonly supposed, in Jackson's Hole, and not far south of the south boundary of the Yellowstone National Park.

Jackson Lake itself is fifteen miles long and four wide. The Teton Mountains form its west shores. The East shores are hills and ridges of Pine, Spruce, Aspin [sic] and Bitter Cottonwood along the beaches of the lake.

There are occasional open Parks on these East ridges and in one of these, at the N.E. end of the lake was the childrens Home, a long one story log cabin of ten rooms; big fire places, and windows and a south porch overlooking about all the lake and its fine islands. One of these islands, the "Big Island", as the children called it, is two miles long, a mile wide nearly and has many high ridges and prominent heads.

The N.W. end of this island, a quite high bluff, had on the beach under the bluff one June a big snow bank, plainly seen from the Cabin's porch although it was seven miles away.

The children's father told them he'd take them all down to the Big Island on 4th of July if the snow drift lasted till then, and they'd make ice cream with the snow. On July 3rd the snow drift could only be seen from the cabin porch with field glasses it was so melted away, but Mrs. Sargent made a big freezer full of ice cream custard, packed up a hamper of good things to eat, and plenty of salt to mix with the snow to freeze the ice cream, and at 7 a.m. the morning of the 4th the four children, their mother and father, boarded the little sail boat and set sail for the Big Island before a gentle north breeze.

In two hours or less they landed on the island under the bluff and found just enough of the snow bank left to freeze the ice cream. Before the last of the ice cream was eaten up the snow had entirely melted away on the beach.

The day was very warm, grass green, the aspins and cotton woods along the shores of the island all leaved out and Cow Elk with their month old calves in hiding from the midday sun all through the pine trees of the mid-island.

After unanimously voting to Christian [christen] the headland of the island where they found the snow, Ice Cream Point, they all boarded the sale of the boat and sailed out for home before the afternoon breeze, which is always from the Southwest on Jackson Lake. The sun went down as they passed between Catharine and Martha's Islands and with the sun the wind, so the children's father rowed the remaining three miles home in the beautiful afterglow, to the sweet music of old songs on a lake of azure darkening to black as the night shadows fell and stars came out and were reflected in the now jet black water, while the Evening star hung like a lamp from Heavens Portal in an afterglow of fading, but slowly fading gold, over the crest of the Cascade Peak on the west shore of the lake directly opposite the childrens home.

JOHN D. SARGENT

UPPER JACKSON LAKE, AUGUST 26, 1903

HERB WHITEMAN BEAR-LY ESCAPES

HERB WHITEMAN WAS SEVENTEEN when he came into the Jackson Hole country in the summer of 1896 with Edgar M. Heigho and a woman named Cora. Cora and Edgar may have been married. If they were not, her maiden name has escaped the memory of the oldest old-timers.

These three intrepid young people had been working in a big department store in Detroit. Hating the city atmosphere and rush, they decided to pool their resources and go West. They'd heard of the beautiful Jackson Hole country and planned to start a dude ranch.

They chose a site and homesteaded on the shore of Jackson Lake, just north of the Sargent place. They built a house, a cabin or two and some outbuildings. They expected to get paying guests from the traffic through the south gate of the Yellowstone. Cora established the Antler Post Office, March 3, 1899, but it was discontinued mid-December of the same year.

Travel was light, and their small capital was soon gone. The partners had to disperse to seek employment. The plan and the site for the dude ranch were both excellent. It was sad that it was just a little early for a dude ranch and that their finances were so limited.

Heigho, in whose name the place was filed, left the country to seek a job. The homestead claim lapsed. Not much is known about his life, but evidently he married another woman after leaving Jackson's Hole. Many years later a daughter came to Slim Lawrence asking if he could show her the site on the lake where the ill-fated dude ranch was located. Slim showed her the foundations and the remaining building and toilet.

Cora took a job cooking on a dude ranch. She even cooked on the Eaton Trail Rides through Yellowstone Park, which would indicate much ability and love for the outdoor life. She married a rancher, Frank Sebastian, whose home was along the Gros Ventre River a few miles west of Kelly. Frank died with severe stomach cramps, probably from a ruptured appendix. Since Cora married the hired man, Max Edick, soon afterward, there was some malicious gossip about how stomach cramps could be "induced." Since there was no doctor in attendance, and no coroner in this remote part of then-Uinta County, there was no investigation.

The Edicks lived at the Sebastian place until it was washed away in the Kelly Flood of 1927. Mrs. Edick had driven their little car to higher ground while Max and the hired man, Clint Stevens, brought a hayrack loaded with possessions. The flood caught the rack, tipping it over. Max caught onto a cottonwood tree which was the only tree to remain standing in a radius of half a mile. Clint was drowned.

With their buildings and some of the livestock lost, the Edicks sold to the Snake River Land Company, the company buying land for the Rockefeller interests for the purpose of making a national park. The Edicks moved to Parker, Idaho, where they lived out the rest of their lives.

But this story isn't about Heigho or Cora Sebastian Edick anyway. It is about Herb Whiteman.

When the dude ranch dream had to be abandoned, Herb took jobs as they were available. He guided and freighted for Ben Sheffield. Before Ben established his lodge at Moran, he operated hunting parties based in Livingston, Montana. Herb freighted from there. When he was old enough, Herb homesteaded a claim in the willow meadow at the edge of Moran. He was a part of the big excitement on the various dam constructions. You could say that his neat two-room log cabin was "in" Moran and that he was one of the first citizens and founding fathers of that community.

As Herb worked, he purchased a few cattle. In summer he held jobs while caring for his fields and hay. In winter he fed his livestock and trapped. His slight size and fair, boyish complexion belied his strength. He covered his six day-long trap lines on his self-made skis with speed and efficiency.

Maybe Herb was so efficient that he never needed a wife, for he never married. His cabin, the walls lined with books and magazines, was always clean and well stocked with groceries. He was also a good cook. Until old-age maladies claimed his life, he was never ill. Loved and respected by his friends and neighbors, Herb ran a smooth operation.

Marten, mink, bobcat, lynx, coyote and bear were Herb's game on his trap line. When the Wyoming Game and Fish Department made the trapping of bear illegal, Herb was not quite ready to take this trophy off his list. He continued to set his bear traps, discreetly. One early spring day he found a bear in one of his traps and was skinning out the hide when he spotted someone coming. With no time to do more than pocket his knife and strap on his skis, he lit out, trying to keep out of sight of the man behind him. As Herb suspected, it was a game warden.

The warden took time for only the most cursory glance around because, having seen a man depart, he was sure he could catch him or at least get close enough to recognize him. But he never came close enough for a good look. Herb had an advantage in this country he knew so well. He cut a big circle and then, to confuse his pursuer, he joined up with some of his old ski tracks. Sure that his trail couldn't be accurately followed, Herb skied back to check on the bear. After all, if it wasn't a warden, some other yahoo might be stealing his bear skin.

The bear was very much as he had left it. The stranger's tracks followed his own. Herb took out his knife and resumed the skinning job. He hoped that he had lost the guy on the old ski trail, but Herb kept a sharp look out as he worked. It was well he did. The pesky hide was still not off when Herb spied a figure crossing an open space on the back trail. Again Herb took off, using his old trail for a while.

When the warden arrived at the bear he could see that the poacher had been back at the job. Knowing he couldn't have much start, the warden put on a burst of speed and followed the well-worn tracks. Herb used every ploy he knew, climbing uphill where he could keep out of sight, hoping to wear out the legs of a less hardened skier. He made a circle which he felt sure would discourage his tracker and wound up back at the bear to see what had happened there.

Nothing was changed at the site of the trap, so once more Herb started the skinning job. He hoped to be able to take the hide if he had to run again. Not so. Again, before he could finish the skinning job, he caught sight of a figure on his back trail. Herb was disgusted. The hide was a forty to fifty dollar investment, but not worth going to jail for. He picked up his trap and headed back to the traveled sleigh road. It was getting dark by the time he hit the road; it would be hard for a tracker to tell which way he traveled from there. Herb made it back to his snug cabin in time for a late supper and a good night's sleep in his warm bed.

Back at the bear carcass, the warden had decided to get smart this time around and wait there until the trapper came back. The warden knew the trapper was a persistent cuss and that he meant to have that bear hide, that was plain to see. The warden backed up the trail to a hidey spot and settled down where he could keep the carcass under observation. He got as comfortable as he could and waited.

He waited and waited. As soon as it got dark, the cold increased. He got colder and colder. He wanted to be hidden so he couldn't start a fire to warm up; he couldn't even get up and stomp around. He was still convinced the poacher would come back to finish skinning out his bear. Hours rolled by.

Presently the moon rose and bathed the snow with a silvery whiteness. If a poacher wanted to skin a bear he would have as much light as day could offer. No one came to claim the hide. When the night was far advanced, the warden became so chilled he was sure he would lose some toes. Finally he struggled from his cramped position and made his way on the back trail to his home.

Word got around, as it always does, of the warden's lonely, frigid, unrewarded vigil. Other unscrupulous natives might have laughed at such a plight, but Herb was such a gentle man, he would have hated it, had he known he caused anyone such misery.

Herb is one of the handful of pioneers resting in the little cemetery on the bench overlooking the meadow where once stood the settlement of Moran. When he arrived in Jackson Hole he remarked, "This is where I'm going to stay. I don't want to ever go back."

I don't think he ever did, even to visit.

THE ELK HORN HOTEL

WHEN MARIA AND CHARLES ALLEN came to Jackson in 1896 they looked around and settled upon one of the most beautiful spots in the valley to homestead.

Beside the Oxbow Bend of the Snake River, a short distance below the outlet of Jackson Lake, they built their home. It was soon a center of community life. Maria was the first postmistress of Moran, getting the appointment in 1902. There were no businesses at Moran, so the Allens soon found themselves running a roadhouse, serving meals and renting rooms to travelers. The business became known as the Elk Horn Hotel.

"Pap" Deloney stocked some shelves in their home with general merchandise from his store in Jackson. In an adjacent building, Charles Allen set up a supply of liquor. The home was even used as a hospital at times, with Grandma Allen, as Maria was known, serving as a good practical nurse and midwife.

Her own daughters, having married soon in this woman-hungry land, went to "Mother's" at birthing time. It is recorded that two of her daughters were there at one time, awaiting new arrivals; Otto Nelson and Marion Allen were born in adjoining rooms at almost the same moment. Anna Nelson and Clinton Kelly were born nearly simultaneously at the Allen home at another time.

With so much living, there was also some loss. The Allens lost two young sons to accidents, and some of the little new arrivals could not make it. A beautiful spot on the bench overlooking the ranch, the lake, and the mountains was chosen and set aside for a family burying ground.

Before the 1920s, the Allens sold their Moran ranch, but retained title to the three-acre burial ground, which held many of their family and a few close neighbors. Charles and Maria lived in Kelly in the 1920s, then went to Idaho for a few years. When they retired from active farming they returned to Jackson and built a home on the three acres near the little cemetery.

A busy life is hard to relinquish. Since their cabin was beside the highway, the Allens put in a gas pump for the tourist trade. This led to a few supplies for sale, and soon Grandma Allen had a little lunch counter and was serving light lunches. Next, they built a few cabins.

All this activity soon proved too much for the Allens, so they leased the cabins and spent their remaining retirement years actually retired. They were laid to rest beside their children in the Allen cemetery.

The leasee added more cabins, a tall pump house and other civilized appurtenances on the small plot, almost surrounding the cemetery. When the lease ran out, Grand Teton National Park purchased the site from the Allen heir. The pressing need for housing for Park personnel kept the cabins in use until 1972.

Now the cabins have been moved away, the pump house is torn down, the concrete slabs broken up and hauled away. The little ridge top cemetery overlooks the homestead in much the same natural state that Maria and Charles Allen found it.

THE DELONEY REMINISCENCES

AFTER THE CREATION OF YELLOWSTONE National Park in 1872 met with such popular approval, conservationists urged that some protection should be given to the forests of the nation. In 1891 President Benjamin Harrison, by executive order, created the Yellowstone Forest Reserve.

It covered Yellowstone and extended beyond the park boundaries on all sides. On the south, the Reserve boundary was forty-four degrees north latitude, which put its southern boundary on a line even with Owl Creek to the west and Mount Reid to the east and crossing the northern end of Jackson Lake.

In 1897, again by executive order, Teton Forest Reserve was created from "that area south of the south boundary of the Yellowstone," extending south and east and west of the Yellowstone Park southern line to include most of the timbered area north of the Gros Ventre River. Where the two areas overlapped each other, jurisdiction was assigned to the Teton Forest Reserve. Thus, the appointment sent June 9, 1899, to Charles W. Deloney [sometimes spelled DeLoney] delegating him the first superintendent of the Teton Forest Reserve, included "that portion of the Yellowstone Forest Reserve lying south of the Yellowstone Park boundaries."

In keeping with customary practice in making such governmental appointments, officials representing the involved area had proposed a candidate for the president to consider. Teton Forest Reserve was in sparsely populated Uinta County with the county seat in Evanston. Deloney received his appointment through the recommendation of U. S. Senator Clarence D. Clark, his neighbor and political co-worker in Evanston. It was President McKinley's first executive appointment upon taking office.

The 1899 appointment referred to Deloney as Forest Supervisor Deloney. Early U.S. Department of Agriculture records appear to indicate he had a prior appointment as forest superintendent, although a copy of the appointment has not been discovered. He did apply for a furlough from the department in 1898.

According to his daughter Frances, upon receiving his first Forest Supervisory appointment, Deloney packed a few necessities, left his family in Evanston, and with one helper set out to fulfill his duties. After a breakdown in his health late in the summer, he applied for, and received, a furlough. In 1899, he was reappointed, and at that time he moved his wife and the young children still living with them to the small settlement of Jackson, some two hundred miles to the north of Evanston.

Visiting with Frances Deloney Clark about her childhood in early-day Jackson Hole, her family, and the Deloney history was like one's first trip into the valley. In both cases, one received more impressions than one could possibly have anticipated. Frances had a wonderful eye for detail and a tenacious memory.

Frances said that for Charles and Clara, Jackson Hole was just another spot to pioneer. Both of them had crossed the plains, separately, before the transcontinental railroad had been completed.

Charles' ancestors, both Deloneys and Charbonneaus, were of pure French descent. The family was originally all Catholic. Some of them were among the first to break faith with the Roman Catholic Church and form the Waldenses, a Reformationist group founded by Peter Waldo. The group left France in the 1300s and migrated to the mountains of Italy, where they were allowed to worship free of the prevailing Catholic restrictions. This, Frances pointed out, was the cause of the erroneous idea that the Deloneys were of Italian descent.

Charles (in his later years called Pap) Deloney, the son of Richard and Sallie Deloney, was born in Mt. Clemens, Michigan, August 24, 1842, (some of the remaining records set the year as 1842, some as 1843). Very little is actually known of his childhood and early life. The only authentic story of Pap's early life is a letter written to his daughter Frances by his friend and comrade in arms Charles Gosler:

It was early in 1852, when your grandparents, Richard and Sallie Deloney with their two sons and three daughters arrived here from River Rouge. When your father and I were school age we attended a little log school house where we received a limited education. At the age of fourteen we went to work in the lumbering camps and sawmills, where we worked from daylight to dark for a very small wage. When the civil war broke out we enlisted in Company B 29th Mich. Volunteer Infantry. We were sixteen years old.

In forty days we were thrown into battle against a formidable enemy. We took part in the following battles; Decatur, Ala. Oct. 26, 27, 28; Overall Creek, Tenn. Dec. 7; Winsted Church, Tenn. Dec. 13; Shelbyville Pike, Tenn. 15, 16, and 17, and later Nolonsville, Missionary Ridge and Chickamagua.

At Stoneriver, in a bloody fight, your father was wounded and taken prisoner and thrown in the Andersonville prison. He escaped and rejoined his regiment and was honorably discharged and mustered out in Detroit Sept. 20, 1865.

In 1867 your father went west. As a soldier, I assure you, there never was a better one; as a friend and comrade no one ever knew a truer.

The spring of 1867 marked the beginning of Charles Deloney's business adventure on the headwaters of the Green River. And, according to Frances, "That was a long time before there was a Sublette County!"

It was also before Wyoming was a territory. With the Civil War over, former soldiers were seeking new opportunities in the west. The much talked about and widely reported transcontinental railroad was on the move and many veterans found work on railway crews or with contractors supplying Union Pacific.

Underfunded and slow to start in 1862, the transcontinental railroad made little headway. New impetus provided by a second Pacific railway act in 1864 allowed the Union Pacific to speed up its pace, and by July 1867, the rails had reached North Platte, Nebraska. As the tracks progressed westward, harassment from the Indians increased. Congress provided army assistance, some of these men fresh from Civil War battles, to keep order.

In early July 1867, Grenville M. Dodge, a Civil War general now with Union Pacific, went ahead to locate a route division point at Cheyenne and to plat the townsite. General C.C. Augur, accompanying Dodge, located Fort D.A. Russell nearby. By November 18, 1867, some three thousand citizens welcomed the first work train to Cheyenne.

Cheyenne's citizens—and all the territorial neighbors they could bring to their viewpoint—petitioned Congress to establish Wyoming Territory from parts of the Dakota, Utah, and Idaho Territories. Congress had been thinking of such a territory since 1865. On July 25, 1868, Wyoming Territory was established by an organic act of Congress.

Four counties had been established from Dakota Territory by the time of territorial organization: Laramie and Carter (later Sweetwater) Counties in 1867, Carbon and Albany Counties in 1868. Finally, a strip of land from Wyoming's southern boundary north to the Montana border was annexed from Utah and Idaho Territories and named Uinta County. Wyoming, untouched by the war, was a beckoning place of new beginnings.

An economic motive may have prompted Charles' decision to go west in the spring of 1867, but Frances liked to think it was the hope of finding a better and freer way of life. It was to be expected, after all the training in the forests of Michigan, that Charles was interested in getting out ties for the Union Pacific Railroad. He bid for and received a contract to supply ties to Green River City in the spring of 1868.

His first operation in 1867 was to construct a boom across the river at Green River City to catch the ties he expected to float down with high water the next spring. He hired a crew of thirty husky men and equipped them with heavy clothing, timbering tools and food, then started the long trek to the headwaters of the Green. It was a hard trip of one hundred and thirty miles into new territory. The men made their own road as they advanced.

He hired freighters to deliver the supplies to the proposed timbering site. Charles and the tie hacks walked. It took sound judgment to provision the crew for all eventualities for an eight-month stay in isolation. Even the civilized center of Green River City had little in the way of medications, preventatives, and restoratives, and all supplies were very expensive.

After the long, hazardous trip, the camp was established on the west bank of the Green River at the mouth of Rock Creek. The freighters remained with the crew for some time, helping to build the commissary, office, cook shack and bunkhouses. They even skidded some timber before returning to Green River City with the promise to return to camp with more provisions as soon as spring arrived.

As winter set in, the tie hacks cut timber near the headquarters and built a skid down the steep mountainside. Trees on the upper slopes were cut, worked out of the timber, and pointed down the skid where they shot down to the area where the ties were shaped. As they were made, the ties were piled along the stream banks waiting for the high waters of June to float them to the railroad.

Frances remembered her father saying that the living quarters were fairly comfortable, yet wanting in every vestige of civilized furnishings. The culture of the camp was thin, with men loudly and profanely voicing their wants and gripes, requiring from Charles a great deal of diplomacy to handle the crew. As the winter wore on the men became increasingly restless and irritable, but work continued at a good pace.

Soon the stream banks were piled high, and stacks of ties had to be located further back from the stream, awaiting the return of the freighters. It was their job to haul them to the stream when it came time to send the ties downstream.

Spring crept in slowly, the snow receded in the timber, staples and supplies of all kinds were getting dangerously low. The food seemed to melt away with the snow. Still no freighters appeared.

The men could ignore mosquitoes, work with frostbitten fingers and toes, live with the greater threat of blizzards and Indians, but when the meals were scrimped, they blamed the boss. The hungry tie hacks mutinied, refused to work, and made threats if food was not provided, and soon.

Charles was sure the freighters were near, so he set out afoot to hurry the provisions along. In spite of his abounding vitality, a few days of walking without food or shelter sapped his strength. A "squawman" found Charles lying unconscious in the sagebrush near the old Lombard (or Oregon) ferry. Actually, it was the man's dog that found him and led his master to where Charles lay.

Charles was taken to the cabin at the ferry and nursed back to strength. Having learned that the freighters had passed that way, he returned to the camp as soon as he was strong enough. He had missed the freight train because they had been on the west side of the river, trying for a better road. No one at the camp had thought to send a searcher for him.

With the supplies on hand, order and confidence were restored, and the work in the forest was completed.

The drive of logs to Green River City took about a month. The men worked the ties along and kept them free of log jams with their pevees (pivas or pivots). Indians curiously followed along the way, never attacking, but causing a constant worry. The men were armed only with their pevees, as the work they were doing would keep firearms constantly wet.

Cautiously the tie hacks slept on sandbars in the river and tried to stay in groups for mutual protection. It seemed the Indians were only curious.

The logs arrived in Green River in July 1869, with no trouble from the Indians. Charles spent another winter at logging before moving on to other enterprises.

From Green River City he went to Bear Town (in Uinta, associated with Bear River) where he helped to clear out the gamblers and outlaw element in the Famous Bear Town affray. He moved from Bear Town to Wasatch (another of the end-of-track towns on the U.P. Railroad that did not survive) to Evanston. All were small starts of towns of about the same size at that time.

In Evanston in 1870 he opened a barber shop. Later that year he fell in love with the tiny (four-foot nine-inch, shoe size two-and-a-half) blonde and beautiful Clara Burton, daughter of the bakery owner. They were married by Elder Brown of the L.D.S. Church, November 24, 1871. A family man, Charles remained in Evanston until 1899, when he was appointed first Forest Supervisor of the newly created Teton National Reserve.

Pap (fifty-seven years old at the time) found Jackson Hole fresh and unspoiled when he arrived. "When we moved into the valley," Frances recalled, "I was six years old, and I very well remember the trip." They traveled by train from Evanston to Pocatello and on to St. Anthony. "We were met in St. Anthony by a friend of my father's. He had a white-top spring wagon and a spirited team. From St. Anthony we took the long dry road south to Victor across the rolling hills of Idaho. Jim was just a baby on my mother's lap. Viola, the sister just older than I, was about ten years old and got to ride beside the driver. I sat with my mother and remember with some resentment that I was tied to the seat, as I was not so quiet or dependable, and never stayed put."

The ride from Victor over Teton Pass was much more interesting for the children, and even, at times, frightening. The first wild bear they had ever seen, as well as deer and elk, were sighted on that trip over the hill.

In Frances' memory, that early-day road went "straight up one side of the mountain and down the other." Portions of the road bed were corduroyed with poles over boggy places. "On the top we stopped while the wheels were roughlocked and a log was chained to the rear for braking purposes."

The swollen flood waters of June made it necessary to cross the Snake in a boat. Lee Clover rowed them across. It was a hazardous experience, but their only tragedy was a lost valise. "The worst part about the lost valise was that it contained my doll," Frances joked. "My father and Si Ferrin met us at the river, and we traveled on to Jackson in another wagon."

Their new home was a log building which had been built for the Deloneys by John Emery. It was located where the Anvil Motel sits at present (215 N. Cache). The largest room was stocked with merchandise and turned into a store, with living quarters in the rest of the rooms.

The store seemed "quite pretentious" to young Frances, and right away she discovered that "my father had stacks of candy and gum on the shelves. There were two counters and a big pot-bellied stove around which were nail kegs and horseshoe kegs and boxes used as stools."

Spittoons surrounded the stove because it was here the fellows congregated in the evenings. "Father and Mother slept under one of the counters on a roll-out camp bed of sorts. Viola and I slept on hay mattresses stuffed with slough grass in the all-purpose kitchen-living-bedroom, and Jim had a little hay mattress in a packing box. They were good beds and had a delicious odor."

In the store was a big old safe. "I don't know how it ever found its way into Jackson, or where it is now. It must be indestructible. But there it was, and for many years it was the town's safety depository. Everyone banked there. It seemed to me there were stacks of money. In those days there was one payday a year for the ranchers (and many others), and that safe was the clearinghouse."

Food came into the valley in huge quantities, as very little except meat was raised locally. Frances remembered four- and six-horse freight outfits driven by Si Ferrin and Dave Timmins, two of her father's freighters, arriving every day or so.

"Sugar and flour came in hundred-pound sacks; crackers, coconut, macaroni and such dry things came in twenty-pound boxes. Dried fruits came in bulk boxes also. Beans of all kinds and colors came in hundred-pound bags. And sow-belly to flavor them came in huge slabs.

"Jelly and jam and pickles came in kegs, and syrup came in little cans shaped like a log cabin. Kerosene for the lamps came in huge drums and had to be loaded wisely to keep any damage from spillage away from the groceries.

"The only lights we had were the smelly kerosene kind which had to be filled every day, the wicks trimmed and the globes washed. How we hated that job! Long plugs of Horseshoe and Climax chewing tobacco hung near the counter which held the Duke's Mixture and Bull Durham and the pipes and snoose which were the most salable items. Arbuckle and Lions Brothers Coffee Beans came in hundred-pound sacks, to be ground in a big iron grinder when purchased.

"Gun powder came in bulk, and Naphtha and Castile Soap came in long bars which were cut off at the desired length when purchased. There were bottles of ammonia, camphor, turpentine, liniment, and lots of mustard. The mustard was used in mustard plasters, as well as for seasoning. No family wanted to be without mustard plasters when the pneumonia season rolled around!

"Among our first visitors—at home, not the store—were Mr. and Mrs. John Anderson, with Oliver and Mark and Myrtle. Mrs. Anderson ran the post office at the Antelope Gap (now called the Y). Later they moved the post office and hotel into Jackson and the families became good and lasting friends." Frances was quiet for a few minutes, remembering days long gone, people lost in time.

"Let me name some of those early residents, some of whom left the valley, but many whose names still appear at present: the J. D. and O. P. Ferrins, S. N. Leek, Ralph Spencer, the Bill Crawfords, the Jack Fees, Jack Shive, the Charlie Hedricks, the Ed Blairs, the Mort Elys, the Frank Petersons, Bill Manning, the Pap Simpsons, Albert T. Nelson, Walt Spicer, Dick Turpin, the Charles Allens, the Pierce Cunninghams, Johnnie Counts (the man who paid his store bill with gold nuggets), Old Puzzle Face (a fugitive from justice), Beaver Tooth Neal (poacher extraordinaire), the Bob Millers, all the Wilson brothers and their families, the Wards, the Cheneys, Mose Giltner, Dick and Ed Myers, Jake Johnson, Cal Carrington and Old John Cherry (who told me that when he came to Jackson Hole the three Tetons were small holes in the ground)." A pause—a smile. "And I believed it!"

The Deloneys soon fitted in the life of the little community like the pocket in a shirt. Over the years, Charles and Clara became known as Pap and Grandma Deloney to these people; the store was the center of business and news exchange. Grandma became nurse and doctor almost at once. She kept a bundle consisting of sterile sheets, bandaging and basic medicines at hand in a cupboard ready to take to any emergency.

Grandma Deloney had known tough experiences ever since she came to the U.S. She had come with her family as Mormon converts, starting from England, July 13, 1867, in the vessel *The City of Washington*. They were on the seas for eleven days, and an epidemic of typhoid broke out. Many passengers died and were buried at sea. Upon arrival in New York they were held in quarantine until it was too late to travel across the plains, so they were forced to remain in New York all winter.

"During this time, my mother lived in the home of a doctor, and he, realizing that she was going into a life where little medical help could be had, gave her a good course of instruction in medical practice—the importance of sterilizing and cleanliness, the drugs and herbs for various illnesses, how to sterilize and sew up wounds, and general nursing and midwife care of the sick. It would be impossible to estimate how many people this training later cured, or even saved.

"In 1868, the family crossed the plains with ox teams. Grandfather Burton was the captain of the train and had been asked by the church authorities to include some converts who had just been released from the hospital. He kindly included them, but he little knew what a heartbreaking experience they would create. The illness, and having to lay over the extra time in New York, made money for the needed wagons and supplies short.

"Many had to walk the full distance from Benton, Wyoming, the end of the railroad, to Salt Lake City, the destination." Benton, located on the North Platte about ten miles east of Rawlins Springs, was first a stage station on the Overland Trail, then a temporary end-of-line railroad town which blossomed and died away within the year.

"Clara was one of the walkers. She walked every step of the way 'except crossing the rivers.' The converts who had joined the party after their stay in the hospital were too weak to stand the rugged trip, and one after another they weakened. They were carried along in the wagons, but almost every morning there was a burial, sometimes the grave had to be dug big enough for several bodies. They buried thirty-six people of the train in the twenty-five days it took to cross the plains."

This was the last organized Mormon wagon train to cross the plains, as the rails were laid to Ogden before the next summer. While Clara Burton walked westward across the plains of Wyoming Territory, Charles Deloney and his men were timbering in the mountains to the north of them, providing ties for the railroad's westward push. Within a year or two, Clara and Charles met and married, living in Evanston some nineteen years and raising most of their family before once again packing up and moving—this time going north into the Jackson Hole valley.

"I well remember how my mother—already nearly half a century old when she came to this valley, and so tiny beside her six-foot-three husband—how she helped the young ones into this life and the old ones out of it.

"She brought with her a medical bag with sharp scalpels, scissors, rolls of bandage and sterile pads which she had made and sterilized in the oven. She was a wonderful diagnostician—a feel of the head, a look down the throat, an ear to the chest, a feel of the pulse and a few questions, from this she made a diagnosis and went to work."

Frances, as observer, was convinced the psychological effect of Clara's self-assured approach to the illness had great curative powers for the patient. "She was pragmatic; I once heard her tell a young woman, 'If you think you might be pregnant, you are pregnant. Let's make it legal before it shows.' And they did as she told them!

"She had a kit of home remedies packed for her by Dr. Blackburn, of Evanston, from which she administered if someone came to her complaining. She believed in them heartily." Decisively Frances added, "And so do I—even yet.

"I well remember the belladonna for headache; nux vomica for the stomach, bryonia and phosphorous for bronchial and lung congestion. Ipecac was used for croup; camomile for cross, feverish, teething babies; scorched flour for sore bottoms. And always bed rest and lots of good pure drinking water....

"Grandma Deloney was a prayerful woman herself and always admonished her patients, 'Pray for help, and when it comes, thank your God.'

"In that day we carried water from Cache Creek in buckets and bathed in an old tin tub. Mother, Viola and I had long hair down to our waists which was a chore to wash....

"My father wore white shirts, always. I never in my life saw him in a colored shirt. He wore black half-sleeves, and in cold weather a dark sweater, but always the white shirts. I think of the hard wash boards of the day with horror and wonder how my mother managed to keep all of us fit for the constant public inspection we had every day of our lives.

"In the summertime we kids lived in the creeks, in the winter in the snowbanks. We were a healthy lot....

"In the fall of 1899, we Deloneys moved back to Evanston as there was no school in Jackson. When we returned in the spring of 1900, we crossed the river on Menor's ferry. From then on the family stayed in Jackson as a school was started by subscription. Miss Gallagher, later to become Mrs. Fisk, taught the first school in the town. It was held in the Clubhouse, which was under construction, and only one room was finished off so the school could be started. Sawdust covered the dirt floor, and the kids came to Pap's store so that each could carry back an apple or cracker box for his seat. A big wood heater was installed, one long table provided desk and writing space for all, and school proceeded.

"I don't remember how many years school was held in the Clubhouse, but I do know that very soon a floor was laid and then country dances were held regularly. Bunks were built around the walls where the small fry could be bedded. Everybody attended and brought quantities of food. A wing was added to one side for kitchen facilities, with cook stove and tables.

"Coffee was made in a big wash boiler, the coffee grounds tied up in a cloth sack and tossed in until it had boiled awhile, then removed. The eating started about six o'clock in the evening with sandwiches, cakes, and pies in quantity—and hot dishes like roasts and scalloped potatoes too. The dishes were cleared away and the dance began with the caller crying, 'Everybody waltz!' or 'Circle two step!' and everybody did! Even the kids. 'Four more couples for a quadrille!' and four more couples would materialize.

"Some of the dancers who 'cut quite a figure' on the dance floor were Enoch Ferrin with Nellie Wilson (soon married), Charlie Hedrick and Rilla Hill (soon married), Frank and Retta Woods. Steve Leek and Charlie Wort and Ben Goe.... Everybody danced, even Grandma and Pap, at times. Some of the early-day musicians that I remember were Uncle Nick Wilson, Selar Cheney, Dick Myers and Jake Jackson, real good fiddlers and good fellows."

At midnight everybody ate again. The kids were shuffled into makeshift beds and the dance resumed until dawn. Exhausted but happy people collected kids and dishes and stowed them in the sleigh, or wagon as the season might be, and drove off to start the day's work at home.

❧ *S.L. Spicer, Rube Tuttle, William Minor, Sr., T. Lloyd, W.L. Spicer, Frank La Shaw, Jack Gray, and Alva Simpson at the bar in the Rube Tuttle Saloon. Postcards made of this photograph incorrectly name the men in reverse order.* (JHM&HC)

"The dancing makes me think of the band that was started by Dr. Melton. He came to the valley in 1904 to teach school and he was a remarkable addition to the community. He started a band, and everyone he could entice into it played. There were twenty-two people in that band. Quite a lot for the size of the town then. Phoebe Beagle and I were the youngest and both played cornets.

"We sang, also. Community sings out-of-doors, gathered around the sagebrush smudgepots. The mosquitoes were terrific!

"I remember Uncle Joe Adle…. Such a gentleman always. He lived in the swamp north of town—riding into town in the evening to join the group singing. 'Tenting Tonight On The Old Campground,' 'Juanita,' and all the old songs…. Uncle Joe had a beautiful tenor voice. And he knew them all. All the Deloneys sang, Pap, Grandma, and us kids. With the dancing and the singing and the band, I remember it as a happy musical time.

"In the spring of 1902, our brother Hyrum joined the family store. He had been in Ogden where he took a bookkeeping course. From then on he was a great help to my father. Also in that year, the Andersons moved the post office and hotel into town from

Antelope Gap and enlarged it. Mr. Tuttle built a new building for his saloon, and I believe Dr. Bloom, a dentist, built an office on the corner of Broadway and Cache.

"The town had just been laid out in 1901 and many of people were getting lots, there was a real building boom. Two fellows, Mullen and Parker, started a brick and lime kiln, and all the buildings going up were made of brick. My father bought lots on the corner of Second Street and Milward, and soon he had started a new home, and a new store building right across from it. Later the Jackson Hole Museum was housed in that store building. A new log school building was built on the west side of town. The Latter Day Saints built a brick church on Second Street and the Episcopal Mission built a church on Milward Street. The town was growing.

"Let me interject a recollection about old Pap Nichols, whose homestead was at the warm springs about six miles north of town. He was a delightful character who was as hard-boiled as they come. Pap Nichols and Pap Deloney were veterans of the Civil War who had fought on opposite sides. The Civil War was refought every time they met and had time to chat. I loved to sit around and listen in. Once Pap Nichols said to me, 'You are a smart little girl. Now don't let your Pap influence you with those damn Yankee stories of the Civil War, and don't let Grandma influence you too much about Joseph Smith. People get overcome and bogged down in their own weighted religion and politics.' These were his own words…. He told me this many times.

"After we were moved to the new store location, Pap purchased the only livery stable in town, a large corral in the block south and east of the store, called the elephant corral, for some reason. Then he bought the brick and lime kiln and was really in business."

[There is a possible precedent for the term 'elephant corral' in Maggie Simpson's brief memoir. She records that her husband John, while working in the Denver area in 1870, "went into the Elephant Corral that Fall."]

"Old Dr. Palmer moved to town about this time. Like Pap, he was a Civil War veteran. He built the house which later became the Reed Hotel, then the Crabtree Hotel.

"There was no mortician in those days. People helped each other to lay out their dead, and coffins were made by the best carpenter available. The coffins were padded and trimmed by the women, very often right in the Deloney livingroom.

"The first funerals I remember were those of Mrs. Si Ferrin and Rex Ely. Both were buried in the South Park Cemetery. I don't know if there was a cemetery in Jackson then.

"Before the Mormon Church was built in Jackson, the Sunday School and Meetings were held in the Deloney home, and always ended with a big community feed. On occasion couples were married there. We had a little portable organ which Dr. Melton had brought to the country. It served for meetings, funerals, weddings, and sings, and traveled about wherever needed."

While Frances remembered the store, the home life, the people, and the parties, her younger brother Jim recalled the outdoor things.

"Pap did a lot of his own freighting," Jim told me. "I can remember how he could unload the drums of kerosene by himself, and the big barrels of vinegar and all kinds of liquid stuff that comes in a bottle now. Pap was a big man, six foot three and strong in proportion.... I helped to haul freight, too, when I got big enough.

"I must have been no more than thirteen when Elias Wilson got caught in the slide on the pass. It was spring and the road was breaking up. All the freighters on the hill that day were relaying the teams—hooking all the teams on one load to pull it to the top, then leaving that sleigh and going back for another.

"Elias had just put his team in line to hook up when the slide hit him. It swept several teams and teamsters down the mountain side. We followed the slide downhill and caught two of the horses. I came to where a piece of halter rope was sticking out of the snow. I grabbed that and pulled, and a horse's head came up. Down under the horse's neck was Elias. The horse was still alive and so was Elias. We dug with everything we could lay hands on and got him out alive.

"One other fellow was dug out alive. Another short fellow—I don't remember his name—but he was about five foot six. He got wrapped around a tree. It broke about every bone in his body and stretched him out until he was about seven feet long.... We had to haul him in dead. Several of the horses were killed, and they lost about twelve loads of machinery."

[Jim Deloney's memory of this particular incident varies from Jim Imeson's account. Jim Imeson was also present at the site. *See chapter: Snow Slide Buried Elias Wilson.*]

Jim Deloney remembered a close call for his father: "Pap just about lost his life freighting, but this was in the summer. A front wheel hit a quaking aspen stump and crumpled up. That threw Pap off in front of the wagon and one of the other wheels ran over his chest and shoulder. The hill was steep there, so Pap rolled down quite a ways.... The team pulled the wagon along.

"When a search finally got started they looked for three days before they found him. He had rolled down near a spring trickle. He could reach out and get a little water in his cupped hand. He tried eating some fresh-water snails. He was conscious, but he couldn't raise up. They found him because a coyote was yapping nearby. He had found Pap and was just sitting around waiting for him to die." Pap was brought to Jackson to Grandma Deloney's excellent home care.

"Dr. Reese was the doctor here then. He didn't know much about setting bones, but he looked at Pap and said he would get along all right.... Pap didn't get along all right. He had to be hauled to St. Anthony in a wagon, and from there he was shipped to Ogden on the train. They used x-ray and patched him up, but he was down there two or three months.

"When he got home, he had to be very quiet for another long time. The x-ray showed a bullet lodged below the shoulder blade and grown around with cartilage. It was one of the Civil War wounds. The doctors said it was too late to disturb it after this long time."

Pap recovered his health and put in many more years at the store, but he didn't do much more freighting. He had bought the Estes place in South Park as a place to keep his teams and raise some hay. Viola and her husband Otto Lunbeck ran it for awhile, and then Pap rented it out.

Speaking of Dr. Reese reminded Jim of a story. When Doctor Reese got married to Phoebe Beagle a few years later, the town boys put on one of their famous shivarees. According to Jim:

"Phoebe and Doc shouldn't have got married here, that's sure. They should have ridden over the hill to Driggs like everybody else did that didn't want to face the music. The boys took Doc Reese right away from the wedding ceremony and took him down to the saloon and poured whiskey down him. Then somebody had a better idea, and they took him out of town to a cabin and locked him up for three days. Poor Phoebe was about wild 'cause she didn't know where he was, or if he was still alive. Finally somebody took pity on him and went and let him out."

"Facing the music," Jim's term for sticking around and getting caught in the customary wedding-day shivaree, took either a lot of nerve, a temporarily misplaced faith in one's friends, or just plain lack of planning. Unfortunately, even the most careful of organizers could not manipulate or control the weather. Sometimes, as in the case of Bert and Frances Deloney Clark, totally wrecked plans do work out. And what a story for the family archives!

It was in the early fall of 1912 when Bert Clark crossed the mountains from Pinedale on his way to Oregon and stopped in Jackson Hole for a visit. Pap Carter needed a few days' help finishing up haying, and Bert was glad to oblige.

The girls in Jackson, one of whom was Frances Deloney, impressed Bert so much that he decided to stay and took a job as mail carrier over Teton Pass. He and Frances often rode horseback together and danced together in a courtship that led straight to marriage.

Winter set in, and January of that year was one to be remembered. On the night of January 16, a raging blizzard swept Jackson's Hole, but inside the home of Pap and Grandma Deloney, bright fires blazed. Happiness and anticipation were rampant. Pap was not too well, but little Grandma was, as always, "up and at it." The old home was dressed and ready for a wedding! Old-fashioned house plants, starched and stiff, decorated Grandma's living room, and everyone was dressed in finery befitting the nuptials of a favorite daughter.

The night of January 16 had been specifically chosen as the wedding night because the big party of the year, an annual affair which old and young all attended, was to take place that night at the S. N. Leek ranch south of Jackson. The Leek party, it was believed, would provide an avenue of escape from the friendly, but sometimes undignified, shivaree!

Bad roads made the arrival of the wedding license very late, so it was not until 12:15 A.M. that the wedding was performed. Then the wedding party retired to the Leek ranch to enjoy the festivities.

Attending the Leek party, watching every move of the newlyweds with dire predictions of what would soon happen to them, were Long Tom Imeson, Bob Johnson, Charley Spencer, Peck Miner, Roy and Frank VanVleck, Ed Myers, Myron and Clay Seaton, Walter Spicer, and others. They had, they said, big plans. And they meant it.

At four in the morning the newlyweds, tucked in the mail sled which was drawn by four spirited horses, left Jackson headed for the Hotel Utah.

When the sled reached Wilson, the mail carrier refused to take them over Teton Pass because it was his belief a big slide was ready to run. Dan Hudson, the State Game Warden, also a passenger on that stage, was allowed to take his chances and left with the driver. A big slide did run. The young driver and his horses were killed, buried in tons of icy snow. Dan Hudson, miraculously, was found alive.

Marooned in Wilson by the storm, Bert and Frances took refuge in the old Wilson Hotel. The proprietors, Mr. and Mrs. Nethercott, gave them an upstairs room which was warmed by a stove pipe from the stove in the room below. About ten in the evening a shot was fired up through the floor of the bridal chamber, and Bert was given ten minutes to get into his pants and join the boys. There was no argument. The rest of the night's events went unrecorded.

The next night the newlyweds gave a wedding dance at Wilson with Uncle Nick Wilson doing the fiddling. In just a few days, the Jackson boys fought snow and drifts and carried the happy couple back to Jackson where they were shivareed in style. Another wedding dance was given in Jackson, and Dick Myers and Jake Jackson fiddled for all till the wee hours of the morning.

After the storm passed and the roads were reopened, the honeymoon was spent as planned—at the Hotel Utah. When the Clarks reached Pinedale on their return journey, they were again shivareed, and they gave another wedding dance. The warm welcome

Ma Reed, owner of Reed Hotel (in background), didn't tolerate drunken cowboys. She served good meals and tart homespun philosophy. (JHM&HC)

awaiting them at home at the Rustic Lodge Ranch at Cora was cherished for years.

Gregarious, vivacious and a bundle of energy, Frances became a familiar figure throughout Wyoming in succeeding years. She served many years, first as Reading Clerk, then as Chief Clerk, in the State Legislature. Active in the Order of the Eastern Star, Frances proceeded through the chairs of the state's Grand Chapter and was Worthy Grand Matron of the body in 1958. At the time this article first appeared in the Jackson Hole Guide in 1972, she was serving on the Governor's Committee on the Status of Women.

Though they all shared the Deloney personality traits so evident in Frances, the other Deloney children led quieter lives. Hyrum married Jean Curtis, Viola married Otto Lunbeck, and Jim married Tony Crisp, the sister of Bob and Claude Crisp—two men, incidentally, who were well known for their sense of humor. But given a valley-wide community dependent on its own resources for entertainment, and citizens who displayed a well-developed bent for rowdy good fun, I suspect there may still be a tale or two to be told about the Deloney family's memorable occasions.

Offering a left-handed example of typical high jinks (but notably excluding his own family), Jim once mentioned, "Some of the boys would get a little wild when they came to town and got something to drink.... I remember one time when Ed Myers and Tom Imeson were riding around—shooting off their guns, and their mouths. They wanted to stay in town overnight, so they went to Ma Reed's Hotel and demanded a room. Ma said, 'I ain't got any rooms, I'm full.' 'That's nothing, I'm full too. Ha! Ha! Ha!' Tom roared. Ma just reached in the kitchen and got a big cleaver in her hand and chased him out the door and down the street far enough to get him out of her sight." Jim concluded, "Ma didn't hold any truck with drunken cowboys."

Pap and Grandma Deloney were at the center of events for twenty-five active and eventful years after coming to Jackson. They were just at the edge of the modern leap into the future when Pap died in 1925. He died of the hiccups, a rare and seemingly insignificant disorder to take a big and rugged man's life. Grandma did not outlive him by many years, but she was her active, helpful self until the stroke which took her life. The modern conveniences which made life easier came to Jackson Hole just after they passed on. Pap and Grandma Deloney gave of themselves with work, with planning, with care. It made their lives full.

⁂

Members of the Deloney family were understandably distressed when Robert E. Miller was identified as the first superintendent of Teton National Forest in the February 29, 1968, issue of the *Jackson Hole Guide*. Frances wrote Senator Clifford Hansen to enlist his help in correcting the record. After receiving a preliminary report from the Forest Service Office of the U.S. Department of Agriculture, the Senator wrote her on his UNITED STATES SENATE letterhead as follows:

> Thank you for your letter of March 4, concerning a news story which appeared in the "Jackson Hole Guide" on February 29, 1968.

My office got the information for the statement which was made in that news release concerning Robert Miller's service as a Supervisor of Teton National Forest from a report which was prepared on the Robert Miller house by Grand Teton National Park. The Park Service was under the impression that Robert Miller was the first Superintendent of the forest. Nevertheless, the May 12, 1967 letter from the U.S. Forest Service specifically outlines the correct history of Forest Supervisors around the turn of the century. And, as you so very correctly point out, the information supplied by the Forest Service is at direct variance with the information supplied by the Park Service.

Let me apologize to you personally for the erroneous information that was printed in the February 29 "Jackson Hole Guide." I am as anxious as you are to see that a proper history on this whole subject is made. Therefore, I am proposing to send the enclosed release to the "Jackson Hole Guide" and hope that they print it so that no one in the area remains under any misapprehensions concerning the early day supervisors of Teton National Forest.

I certainly hope that this has clarified the situation and that this has taken care of most of your concerns.

Sincerely,

Clifford P. Hansen
U.S.S.

❧

The enclosed press release sent to the *Jackson Hole Guide* reads:

To: Jackson Hole Guide

U.S. Senator Cliff Hansen has sought to clarify a historical point concerning the old Bobbie Miller House which is located on the National Elk Refuge near Jackson.

Hansen said, "It has been brought to my attention by Mrs. Frances D. Clark that the Forest Service takes a different view than that which had been previously reported in the "Jackson Hole Guide" concerning the history of early day Forest Superintendents on the Teton National Forest."

Hansen said that he has a letter from the Deputy Chief of U.S. Forest Service in Washington D. C. which reads as follows:

Mr. Charles (Pap) Deloney had a Forest Superintendent appointment in 1898, and was furloughed during the late fall. On June 9, 1899, he was appointed Supervisor of that portion of the Yellowstone National Park Timberland Reserve lying south of Yellowstone National Park. This information is somewhat cloudy as to just when he was appointed and for which area. A telegram definitely appointed him to take over that portion of the Teton lying south of Yellowstone National Park, but the telegram was addressed to Superintendent Charles Deloney, so he must have already had that appointment or title for some other area.

Mr. W. Armor Thompson was Supervisor until August 1902, with headquarters at Elk, Wyoming.

Mr. Robert E. Miller was appointed on August 20, 1902, and his appointment became effective on August 25, 1902. He resigned on June 30, 1918.

Hansen said that his office had received information earlier from the National Park Service which stated that Robert E. Miller was the first Supervisor of the Teton National Forest. Hansen said, however, that this additional information from the Forest Service now clearly indicates that while Robert E. Miller was not the first Supervisor of the Teton Forest, he in fact was Supervisor there from 1902 to 1918.

Hansen said that he wanted to make sure that the record was perfectly clear on this point since many local residents have expressed a keen interest in the matter.

※

The 1899 appointment and a part of the area involved is corroborated in the following letter to Deloney from A. D. Chamberlin, then superintendent of the Yellow Stone National Park Timber Land Reserve:

Cody, Wyoming
June 9, 1899

Chas. Deloney,
Forest Supervisor,
Jackson, Wyo.

Sir:

I am directed by Sup't Garbutt to turn over that portion of the Yellow Stone National Park Timber Land Reserve lieing [*sic*] south of the National Park to your supervision. As I have no rangers in that portion of the reserve there is nothing for you to do as far as I am concerned but to go up there and take it.

Yours

A. D. Chamberlin
Forest Sup't.

CROSSROADS AT THE DEW PLACE

THE DEW PACE LIES IN A BIG MEADOW where the Gros Ventre makes its second big bend and starts flowing west. Bacon Creek and Fish Creek join the river here, so the place is a natural crossroads for travel up the river.

Follow the river upstream ten miles, swing up Kinky Creek and you can cross an easy divide and come onto the Green River. Follow Fish Creek to its head near Union Pass and another easy divide leads to the headwaters of the Wind River.

This three-way crossroads was heavily used by the Indians, by the trappers, by the army—General Sheridan brought troops across in 1822—and then by the settlers.

A landmark that the army left when they crossed Union Pass is indicative of army attitude at the time.

Union Peak is a high point in the mountain chain commanding a view of much of this headwater area. General Sheridan wanted a view from this vantage so he took a detachment of cavalry and rode from the camp near the head of Fish Creek up the slopes of the peak.

The going got very tough near the top, steep slopes of crumbled boulders completely surrounded the peak. The horses were made to climb through this broken rock-slide cover, fit only for mountain sheep or goat. Several horses caught their hooves between rocks, some slipped and fell, the soldiers cursed, and it was obvious that the trip down was going to be worse.

When the general finished his observations and calculations, he ordered his officers to have the men lay stones. "We will have a six-foot wide roadway filled with stones, laid close enough that a horse hoof will not be caught between them."

General Sheridan was able to ride his horse down off the mountain, and if you should have any business on top of Union Peak today, you will find a good, laid-stone, easy grade road the last mile to the top.

ʑ⯑

The majority of the homesteads up the Gros Ventre River were taken up by bachelors, but a few were filed on by families. The Dews had a large family, but since they were all boys who would soon grow up to be bachelors, it did not help the balance of nature any.

Mrs. Dew was crippled and had to run her large, masculine-dominated household from a wheelchair. Theirs was a congenial if rough-talking family.

The elder Dews were proud of the boys. Mr. Dew was especially prone to brag about their cowboying abilities, to the point of irritating his listeners. So when the tale spread of son Dick shoeing his favorite horse, it was listened to with a little malicious glee.

It was on a Sunday afternoon that Dick allowed as how he might as well get some shoes on Brownie. He had let Brownie go as long as he could because the little bastard was so hard to shoe. Brothers and visitors aplenty were on hand to help, if help was needed.

At the corral, Dick roped his horse, haltered him, and laid out the shoeing tools. The horse allowed Dick to pick up a foot, but if Dick started to work on it the horse fought. Dick tied up one foot with thick soft rope, but still the horse struggled and fought until nothing could be accomplished.

"I guess we'll have to throw him and tie up his feet," Dick decided.

The cowboys made Brownie jump around on three legs until he lost his balance and fell. Immediately someone sat on his head while someone got a pole, and others tied all four feet together. Then they pushed the pole between his legs, half hitched his feet to the pole, tied the halter to it also, and with someone sitting on each end of the pole, the shoeing went ahead.

Pappy Dew hopped around like a banty rooster, giving advice but not much help. He shrilled, "Dick, you got a kink in that pony's windpipe. You best let him up a minute."

"He's all right, Old Man," Dick grunted around the horseshoe nails he was holding in his mouth. "Go mind your own business."

The horse's breathing was labored, but his feet were still for a change, so the shoeing went on apace.

Dick was intent on showing off how fast he could put a set of shoes on—if the horse would hold still. Comments floated about the corral concerning the horse's condition, led by Pappy Dew.

"Dick, I'm tellin' ya, that horse has kinked his pipes."

"Shut up, Old Man. I'll be through in a minute," was all the response Dick gave. Finally he drove and clinched the last nail, and the fellows unwound the ropes. When the halter was loosened from the pole, the horse's head fell to the ground with a very lifeless thud.

"See there, you damn fool kid, I told you his pipes was kinked."

Pappy Dew had the last word and Dick had a dead horse, dressed up with four new shoes.

$\mathcal{F}$IGHT $\mathcal{O}$VER THE $\mathcal{F}$IRST $\mathcal{C}$HURCH $\mathcal{L}$OGS

JOE NETHERCOTT WAS ONE OF THE EARLY homesteaders on the west side of the Snake River in Jackson's Hole. He had to homestead twice since his first claim (where Earl Hardeman now lives) reverted to the government because Joe failed to put in the residence required by law. This was not Joe's fault. He ran into a bit of trouble and was "restrained" from living on his claim. A bad deal, but the government was fussy about the residence requirement. When the claim reverted, someone else took it up. Joe had to begin all over, quite a bit later.

Around 1900 there were some relatives living on the west side of the river when Joe first came to the valley. Joe picked out a homestead along Fish Creek, staked it out and filed his claim.

Joe Nethercott was a tall, strapping young fellow with a determined disposition and a reputation for being afraid of absolutely nothing. His reputation seeped into the valley ahead of him. One story was that he had jumped his horse into the Wind River at the head of the canyon, obviously a deep and treacherous place, and both swam across. Of course this daring-do was spurred by the hot pursuit of a posse. It seems Joe had been up to no good somewhere. The sheriff leading the posse was not foolhardy enough to follow Joe's lead. Drawing up on the bank, he announced that anybody brave enough to jump a horse in at that spot deserved to go free.

As summer faded into fall, Joe got out a nice set of house logs and hauled them to his claim, piling them where he planned to build. Since winter was approaching and he wasn't prepared to 'winter in' he took off for California, and a job.

The book, *History of Teton Valley*, by B. W. Driggs, L. J. Clements, and H. S. Forbush, contains this pertinent item, "Jackson

Hole is included in the Teton Stake of Zion (Teton Basin). A ward was organized at Wilson, September 18, 1898." This was no doubt the first official church group in Jackson's Hole. The members must have been feeling the need of a church. While Joe was gone, they started building one.

As the building's donated materials and labor progressed, the congregation became very much aware of the fine set of house logs just lying there nearly on the site of their building. As the building went higher Joe's logs were included.

Perhaps the church builders' reasoning went like this, "Well, there is that set of logs Nethercott got out, just lying there, probably rotting. He probably starved out on the claim and might not even come back. If he does come back we can always replace the logs, when it's easier for us to get into the timber. No use letting a good set of logs lie there and rot; he ought to donate them to the church anyway."

Following this "divine" reasoning they soon had the logs cut to length, coped, laid, chinked and daubed. Nethercott's logs could not be distinguished from any of the other "donated" logs.

Joe worked as a deputy in the Oakland sheriff's office all winter. Come spring, he made tracks back to his homestead to resume his proving-up requirements. Along the way he fell in with Bill Van Winkle, whose brother also was homesteading along Fish Creek. Together they came into the valley. Arriving at the homestead, the first thing Joe noticed was the empty spot where his logs had been piled.

Non-Mormon neighbors were only too tickled to tell him where his logs had gone. They were supporting walls of the House of God. Of course Joe was mad. The more he thought of the work and sweat it had cost him to cut, trim, skid, haul and stack those logs, the madder he became. He might not be able to get his logs back, but by so-and-so the dirty so-and-so guys who pulled such a so-and-so stinkin' trick were not going to get them for free. Joe decided to go to a church meeting.

It is very likely that the church members who gathered at the big celebration to dedicate the new church were not aware that Joe was even back in the country. However, when they saw Joe Nethercott and Bill Van Winkle arrive in the churchyard, the door was hastily slammed and bolted. Seeing themselves shut out, Joe and Bill went to the side and kicked in a window. Pandemonium reigned.

Some of the women and children dove under the raised platform which held the lectern and the speaker's chair. Bill pulled a gun on the men and ordered them to line up against one wall. Meanwhile Joe laid down some rules. One at a time the men could come forth to the middle of the floor and fight him. While Bill held the others off at gun point Joe whipped fourteen "brothers" one at a time. (Probably the whole male portion of the membership.)

Had there been as many lawyers around the country then as there are now, Joe might have been persuaded to sue for payment for his logs, plus damages. If he had jumped the members verbally he might have had the logs replaced. Somehow I feel that Joe didn't mind donating them to the Lord...in his own way.

However, even in those days, and even though he started out by being the injured party, such flagrant disturbing of the peace did not go unpunished. Joe was arrested, tried, found guilty and sentenced to two years at hard labor. It is not known why Bill Van Winkle did not share in the sentence, but he served no prison time. Part of the hard labor Joe put in was on the construction of the underpass in Evanston. This may have been the start for his later career as a construction contractor here in Jackson.

Since he could not live on his homestead while paying for his crime in Evanston, Joe's residency requirement on the homestead went unfulfilled and the claim lapsed. Someone else filed on the claim before Joe returned.

When he did return several years later, he had married and brought his family with him. No "disturbance" interfered with his proving up on his second claim. Perhaps both sides had learned to live and let live. This second homestead, called the Riverbluff ranch, once known as the Jarvis place, is where the young Nethercotts grew up. It was the home from which Joe started the construction business which flourished through the twenties and thirties. Building was the heritage Joe left to his sons.

ALBERT T. NELSON:
WYOMING'S FIRST GAME WARDEN

IN THE RAILROAD YARDS AT ROCK SPRINGS one summer day in 1884, a group of two or three cars was shunted onto a spur track with a bit too much speed. It was obvious that the cars were going to overshoot the end of the track and pile up at the bottom of a gully. A young roustabout ran to overtake them, grabbed hold of the ladder on the side of one of the cars, climbed topside, and started to set the brake.

Other men had seen the plight of the cars and all were yelling at the young man. "Let it be!" "You'll be killed!" "You haven't got time!"

He was a strong young man. As he cinched down the brake wheel, the cars slowed, then squealed to a stop at the last possible moment. One of the railroad officials happened to be in the yards that morning and saw the incident. "Who is that young damn fool that just saved us a string of cars?" he wanted to know.

"He's Albert Nelson," he was told. "A young Swede roustabout we haven't had on too long. He doesn't speak much English, but he's a good worker. You don't have to tell him much. He takes into any job like he knows all about it."

"He'll be a dead Swede if he takes into jobs like that very often," the official commented. "Send him around to me. I want to talk to him."

In the course of the official's "talk" with Nelson, he discovered that the young man had just completed two years in an agricultural college in southern Sweden, while also working with horses on a large farm. So Nelson, not too many months in the U.S., was sent to work on the boss's ranch where he would be more in his element. Although Albert was at home with the horses, he was not familiar with cattle brands and the Western methods of working cattle. He

130

was put to work as a cowboy until the outfit suddenly lost their cook, then he was elected to fill the vacancy.

Albert had never been a cook, either. But he soon learned. One of his first batches of biscuits were hard as stones. He'd forgotten to add baking powder. When the cowboys tried to bite on the squatty little rocks, they just about broke their teeth. They kidded Albert in words he couldn't understand but guessed at. Naturally, as cowboys are prone to do, it wasn't long before they started "horsing" around, throwing the biscuits at each other like snowballs. The horseplay soon became serious business and Albert thought for sure he was going to be run out of cowcamp. A cowboy called Mexican Joe managed to ease the tension and from that time Nelson was accepted as one of the crew.

One thing the men really appreciated was the way he kept the larder stocked with fresh meat. There were no game laws in 1884. The ranchers scorned using their beef to feed their men and depended instead on the country for their meat supply. Albert was a good hunter and a crack shot. He kept the crew well supplied with frying meat—and remembered to put soda in the sourdoughs.

Albert Theophil Nilsson was born in Stoby, Sweden, October 30, 1861, to Pehr and Oliva Josephine Ohlson Nilsson. He was the eighth child in a family of twelve children. He outlived them all; the last surviving sister died in Sweden in 1945. He was the only one of his family to leave Sweden. His father was a merchant as well as a lawyer. While Albert was receiving his elementary education, he often helped out in the store. An older brother, Otto, was a major in the Swedish Army and encouraged Albert to undertake a military career. Albert did enlist for a three-year period, and while in the army his education in history, math, geography and physical education continued. He was particularly apt in the physical education program, was a member of the army swim team and also chosen with one other soldier to put on a fencing exhibition for the Crown Prince of Sweden.

Serving in the army through an enlistment period had no effect on the draft status of a young man in Sweden. Albert had been out of the army only a little more than a year when his draft number came up. He had decided that he did not want the army as a career, nor was he inclined to the indoor work of a merchant or professional man. The thing that caught his interest the most was the pioneer life described in a Swedish translation of *The Leatherstocking Tales* by James Fenimore Cooper. Upon receipt of the draft notice, Albert had to make a decision in a hurry. He quit his job and took a boat to Germany where he waited until he could get passage on a German freighter bound for America. Since his mother had passed away earlier in that year and his father had preceded his mother in death, he felt his strongest ties to home had been broken.

Albert was able to speak German well enough to get by, but he didn't understand English at all. When the freighter arrived in New York, he left the ship and wandered the streets of the city wondering how he could exchange a little of the money in his pocket for something to eat. Finally a meat market sign in German caught his eye, so he went in the shop hoping to converse in German. This was a lucky find. John Augberg, a young German blacksmith working temporarily in the market, took Albert under his wing. With his help Albert made a start on the English language.

It turned out that his new friend was also interested in going west. Neither of them had much money, so they decided to ride the rails on a freight train. They rode an empty freight car all the way to Nebraska before they were discovered and kicked off.

It was haying time in Nebraska, so the two had no trouble finding work. It was so hot in the fields that Albert claimed ever afterward he 'scalded' his scalp. One day when they came to wash up at the pump, he ran his hand through his hair and it came out by the handful. Before long, he went bald on top, and he blamed it all on the Nebraska weather. Albert and John continued on west in the spring of 1884; once again they hit the rails. They got as far as Rock Springs before they were again discovered. Albert and John apparently went separate ways, as John isn't mentioned in Albert's memories of his later experiences. It was about this time that Albert's incident with the runaway freight cars took place.

Albert was just six or seven weeks away from his twenty-fourth birthday and working in the mines in Rock Springs at the time of the infamous Chinese Massacre on September 2, 1885. Although he had no part in it, he said the Irish miners who started the debacle had a legitimate gripe—they just took it out on the wrong fellows.

The miners were paid by the ton for the coal they mined. Since the Irish miners were much the fastest and cleverest, they were always put to opening up a new vein—much of which was rock and not paid for. When they got into good coal, the bosses would send around a crew of Chinese who were paid much less per ton. This had happened often enough to infuriate the Irish. When one crew of Chinese came around and announced they were to take over a vein that had just been opened up, the Irish crew took after them with their picks. The Chinese fled through the mine and some of them made it to the top. The mine shafts resounded with the conflict. Miners jumped into the fray. Irishmen took after any Chinese who happened to be near. The Chinese had no place to go topside except the wretched hovels made of wood scraps in the Chinese ghetto called Chinatown. Some enraged Irishman set the place afire. Although Albert was there in Rock Springs during the riot, he had no idea of the loss of life. His opinion was that the mine operators influenced the local press to hush the whole affair.

The Rock Springs area knew Albert's footprints for the next ten years—from cowboying in Brown's Hole to gold mining at South Pass City to homesteading on the East Fork of the Green River. Through his railroad car escapade and his subsequent association with the railroad official, Albert became acquainted with many of the important families of the bustling area of Rock Springs. He worked on the Quealy ranch, knew Theodore C. Hays, Archie Blair, and M. S. Kemmerer whom he later guided on hunting trips into the Green River watershed and over the divide into Jackson's Hole. Somewhere along the way he met up with a man of indeterminate age, older by some years than himself, named Billie Bierer. They teamed up together and hunted, trapped, and prospected the east drainages of the Rockies until they took it into their heads to claim some land and settle down.

Their first homestead venture was on the East Fork of Green River in 1888–89. Having built their home cabin on a bench overlooking the stream, they started their fences, and in the fall they had laid in a goodly supply of game meat and had hauled a load of flour and spuds from Rock Springs. They were well situated for what turned out to be the hardest winter ever to hit Wyoming. Not so well prepared were their neighbors.

Settlers had started to homestead along the East Fork; many were families with small children. As storm followed storm it was all the families could do to keep the cabins warm. There was much hardship. Albert and Billie shared their supplies as long as they lasted. When their food ran out, the two men snow-shoed the seventy miles to Rock Springs for supplies, returning with their back packs and two heavy-laden toboggans which they dragged behind them.

In the spring the East Fork lost almost every homesteader. Wagons piled with the pitiful belongings headed toward Rock Springs and civilization—the men to get jobs in the mines to finance a new start, maybe in a gentler climate.

The wild animal herds were severely hit by the severity of that winter. Dead elk dotted the desert, along with cattle and other game animals. The Green River could be crossed dry-footed by stepping on the carcasses of elk which had floated down and hung up on the shallows. Ernest Thompson Seton later wrote that the antelope population of Wyoming may have lost ninety percent of their number that winter.

Along with their other pursuits, Albert and Billie Bierer had mined for gold at South Pass. They decided they were not ready to settle down to homesteading, so they sold the relinquishment to a man named Gilligan. The ranch on the East Fork of the Green is still called the Gilligan Place. The partners went back to prospecting for gold, trapping and guiding.

They prospected streams from South Pass City to Red Lodge, Montana. Once, when they were leaving South Pass City, a mining company representative asked them if they would dispose of some dynamite which he feared was crystallized. The partners packed it carefully on their pack-horses and started away from town. Suddenly it occurred to them it might be fun to give the residents of the town a thrill—a farewell salute. They selected a spot they considered harmless and stacked the powder there. Repairing to the far side of a ridge, they settled themselves behind some huge boulders and shot into the dynamite. The resulting explosion rocked the town of South Pass City and, they later learned, even broke some windows. At the moment, they gathered up their frightened horses and rode on their way, with some speed.

Another tale Albert told with tongue in cheek concerned a band of Indians, few in number, who fell in with Albert and Billie while the two were trapping and prospecting on the Green River. Being hungry, and not inclined to get out and hustle up their own food, the Indians began begging food from Albert and Billie. This went on for some time and the two trappers were getting irked. One day they had just returned to camp and were wearily setting about the preparation of their supper when the Indians descended upon them with their usual pleas. Albert was about to throw out a pan of left-over beans which had soured. The two men looked at each other, shrugged, looked away. What the hell! Why not? They gave the beans to the Indians who then withdrew to their own camp. Albert and Billie had their supper, cleaned up the camp and turned in for the night. The Indians never begged from them again.

Because of his preference for outdoor life and his knowledge of the area and its wildlife, Albert gravitated toward any opportunities to make a living in outdoor pursuits. Soon, guiding big game hunters became one of his sources of income. From this he slipped naturally into taxidermy, a skill which was to later become his profession. It was difficult to get trophy heads mounted, so Albert sent off for books on the subject and taught himself the taxidermist trade. (Sending off for books and teaching himself was characteristic of Albert's approach to the unknown.) He began in Rock Springs by practicing upon his own kills and those of his friends, progressed to doing the trophies of his hunters, and by the time he had settled in Jackson's Hole he had as much work as he cared to do.

In the winter of 1894-95, Albert and Billie came into the Jackson's Hole country to trap. They built a half-dugout, half-log cabin on the upper reaches of Little Gros Ventre Creek (now Flat Creek). It may have measured ten by ten, with a sod roof and a rock-and-clay fireplace. Its only drawback was a shorter-than-normal doorway, the top of which was one of the transverse logs of the hut. Inside, the men had all the comforts of their camp gear plus a book or two and a stack of well-read newspapers to help wile away the long winter days.

One evening while Albert and Billie were completing their routine chores, a mountain lion following the scent of meat came down the slope to investigate. Sensing the strange presence of man, the lion stopped on the sod roof and gave a challenging screech. The piercing scream right over their heads electrified the men; they rushed through the door to see what was happening. Billie, being quite short, cleared the doorway easily. But Albert forgot to duck as he went through and peeled his scalp back on the cut-away half log that was the top of the doorway. The sudden emergence of the men startled the lion and he ran. After checking the horses to make sure they were all right, the men went back to the cabin to repair the damage to Albert's head. They had no first aid supplies, so they simply rearranged his peeled-back scalp and plastered it in place with several layers of damp newspaper—which were allowed to stay there until they wore off.

On another occasion, a soggy day when Albert had slogged his trap line on his snow shoes in wet snow, he came in, built up a fire and put his shoes to dry with the soles turned to the blaze. He sat down to rest a few minutes before starting supper and dozed off on the bunk. When he awoke his shoes were curled up—shrunken and crisp and useless. Jackson's Hole, one hundred miles from the nearest market, was no place to be in the middle of winter without shoes.

Necessity prompting, Albert went outside to the meat locker (the shady north side of the cabin) and skinned out the hocks of the moose which made up a part of their winter's meat. He fleshed out the skins, shaped a pair of moccasins and sewed up the toe. Thinking he would shape them to his feet by wearing them while they dried, he laced them up and wore them around wet. This was fine all evening, and he wore them to bed. During the night, the hides really started to dry and shrink. He woke up with pins and needles in his feet and his ankles swollen. For a few minutes he struggled with the lacings but the knot had dried hard and fast also. Albert knew a quicker way to relieve the pains: he waded through the snow to the near-by creek and, finding a spot of open water, he waded up and down until the leather stretched again. Drying, a little at a time, with Albert applying much bear grease the moose-hock shoes dried to a fine fit and lasted out the winter.

❧ *Albert T. Nelson loved the outdoors, whether he was working as a taxidermist, serving as Wyoming's first State Game Warden, or homesteading.* (Stimson Collection, Wyoming State Museum)

In early spring, having decided to return later and homestead in the valley, the men moved out of their winter camp in Jackson's Hole and took their winter's catch to trade for goods and supplies.

In June of 1895, Albert and Billie packed up their seventeen head of horses and headed up the Green River to cross over into the Gros Ventre drainage and thus back into Jackson's Hole—this time with the intention of homesteading. But there were Indian troubles in Jackson's Hole in the summer of 1895—stemming from the settlers' concern to save the elk "from wanton killing." The Indians, for their part, were convinced they had every right to kill game animals on unoccupied lands according to the so-called Connor Treaty signed at Green River County, Utah, on July 3, 1868.

One small group of Indians had been arrested in the latter part of June. They had been tried in Marysvale (the settlement's name before the post office name was changed to Jackson) by Justice of the Peace Frank H. Rhodes. They had been fined seventy-five dollars apiece and allowed "to escape"—for lack of a jail or any suitable place to hold or care for them. Those who couldn't pay the fine had their horses and equipment confiscated.

On July 5, as Nelson and Bierer were camped at the red cliffs on the Gros Ventre, a big group of settlers led by Bill Manning rode up the other bank of the river, forded and approached their camp. The partners soon learned that these men were a posse, made up of settlers of the valley, and formed with the sanction of Governor William A. Richards. They were out to enforce the new hunting statutes according to the laws passed by the young state which, as yet, lacked enforcement officers. The Indians of the Fort Hall Reservation in Idaho, as well as some from the Wind River Reservation east of the Wind River Range, had been killing elk in great numbers for the hides. With the June incident fresh in the their minds, the posse expected that the Indians they were presently seeking were likely to be disagreeable.

The posse made a determined effort to deputize Nelson and Bierer. However, someone had to stay with the outfit and the seventeen head of horses, so Billie stayed with the camp while Albert joined the posse.

Traveling up Crystal Creek, over the divide and onto a tributary of the Green, the posse came upon the Indians' camp. They rode up to a group of Indians at the camp's edge and proceeded to arrest them, following a plan they had decided beforehand that every member of the posse should have his gun loaded and ready to fire if ordered to do so. Confident this display of power would quickly win the day, the posse was rattled when the Indians objected to the arrest and stated they wouldn't go.

While the argument was on, Vic Gustaveson, his gun pointed down toward the ground, fired accidentally. Poor Gus was so excited when the gun went off that he rushed out in front of the crowd with his hand raised, shouting, "It vass an occident! It vass an occident!" At the same time the Indians were dismounting, offering their weapons, and saying, "Me heap good Indian!"

The arrested Indians were put under guard and their camp was searched. The posse found 211 hides, the hair scraped and hides ready for tanning. No like amount of meat was found, indicating that the elk had been slaughtered for the hides alone.

This party of Indians was taken to Marysvale, and after a pre-liminary hearing, four of them were taken to Evanston, the county seat, to stand trial. At Evanston, both the Fort Hall agent and the Army Commander were greatly disturbed by the arrests. They held that the Wyoming Game Laws did not provide for arrest without warrant unless the offense was committed in full view of the arrest-ing officer. Also they believed the Connor Treaty protected the Indi-ans. The Indians were set free. The agents of the two reservations were notified to check that the Indians were back on the reservations and the Ninth Cavalry of the Army was dispatched to "protect" the "law abiding" citizens of Jackson's Hole. (The Federal agencies were of the opinion that the posse was made up of the "famous Jackson's Hole outlaws...many of whom make their living taking wealthy Easterners and Europeans out to slaughter the wild game.")

Albert was present at the conclusion of another sortie made by the posse, when, their numbers greatly reduced, they brought in a party of Bannocks who were off their reservation illegally. (The pre-viously arrested Shoshones had been a detached group of these Indi-ans.) This time the posse's action resulted in the arrest of a big group of Indians, their escape as they were being moved along the Hoback drainage, and the killing of one Indian for which Bill Man-ning stood trial.

During this action an Indian infant of approximately two years was riding behind his mother when a low limb scraped them both off the horse. The mother jumped up and ran away afoot. The baby was picked up by one of the posse and carried back to the valley. He was cared for by Mrs. Martin Nelson until the troops returned him to Fort Hall some months later.

The Indians were rounded up in small groups and brought to a makeshift compound near Battle Mountain. Albert was at this camp when one of the prisoners pointed toward him then rubbed his belly muttering "Ingle-moot-chee-tie-vo [Red Whiskers], him heap son-of-a-bitch." Albert figured he must have been one of the Indi-ans who got the sour beans that time down on the Green River.

Jackson's Indian troubles pointed up a general lack of clear understanding concerning the rights of the state to protect the ani-mals with game laws, as well as the rights of the Indians according to the treaty. After conferring with Attorney General Benjamin Fowler, Governor Richards decided to make a test case in court in order to settle for all time the jurisdiction of the wild game within the state. Charges were still pending against Chief Race Horse, of the Bannocks, for killing seven head of elk in Uinta County. A trial of Race Horse was held in the circuit court at Cheyenne in November, and Chief Race Horse was acquitted under the Connor Treaty of 1868.

Governor Richards urged an appeal, and on May 25, 1896, the United States Supreme Court reversed the decision, deciding in favor of the State of Wyoming. In delivering the opinion, Justice White said, "The power of a state to control and regulate the taking of game cannot be questioned.... According to the act admitting Wyoming to statehood on July 10, 1890, 'Wyoming...is hereby declared to be admitted into the Union on an equal footing with the original States in all respects whatever,' the act which admitted Wyoming made no reservation whatever in favor of the Indians."

Since the posse had been operating under sanction and with orders of the Governor, charges against Bill Manning for the killing of the Indian Se-we-agat were dropped. Race Horse was not required to serve any prison time but was discharged also. The "troubles" paved the way for the state legislature to pass more comprehensive game laws and establish the Wyoming Game and Fish Commission to work out enforcement procedures.

At last the position of State Game Warden was created by the Fifth Wyoming Legislature in 1899. The act read in part: "Section 1, The Governor shall appoint a suitable person to serve as State Game Warden, whose duty it shall be to protect the game and fish of this state and to enforce the laws relating thereto." With the recommendation of Dan Nowlin, Uinta County's representative and Jackson resident, and with added recommendations from many important men of the state, in 1899, Governor DeForest Richards appointed Albert Theophil Nelson as the first Wyoming Game Warden—the lone guardian of the entire state's wildlife.

While the state had been enmeshed in court cases to determine legal rights, Albert and Billie had been working to prove up on the two homesteads they had taken along the Gros Ventre in 1896. Billie's homestead at the mouth of the creek later named for him is now partially covered by the Gros Ventre slide. Billie had predicted that the ground would some day slide down the mountain. He said that when he laid his ear to the ground along that slope he could hear underground water running. Due to health problems in later years, Billie sold his ranch. He was not in the valley when his prediction came true.

Albert's homestead entry lay along the Gros Ventre River where it emerged from the canyon, just above the present town of Kelly. His domestic water right was the first out of Ditch Creek—he simply dug a ditch from Ditch Creek with a team and a moldboard plow, his eye and the running water as a level. He filed for his irrigation water right out of the Gros Ventre River. If he had filed for his irrigation water from the same source as his domestic water, his water problems would have been simplified. Getting a ditch from the Gros Ventre onto his acres turned out to be a terrific drain upon his time and resources.

Albert built well; the buildings on the ranch were of log with dove-tailed corners, willows were used for stripping and the cracks daubed with mud. A shingle mill had been set up in the valley, so the house boasted a shingled roof, instead of the more common sod roof. A devoted gardener, Albert planted the first crabapple and cherry trees and lilac bushes in Jackson's Hole. He continued to take out hunting and fishing parties and soon started up his taxidermy business once more.

Many notable persons were among his customers. He did work for the Harrimans, John D. Rockefeller, Jr., and Ernest Thompson Seton. It was Seton who interested a large firm of New York taxidermists in Albert, and he was offered a position with them in 1899. He refused because at the time he was about to be married. And anyway, he did not want to leave the west.

Some of Albert's most enjoyable work involved taking Carl Rungius, one of America's foremost animal artists, on painting-location pack trips into the mountains of the area. Beautiful Rungius paintings grace the interior of Jackson Lake Lodge. Over the years Albert and Rungius became firm friends, and Rungius usually arranged his trips to coincide with the time Albert could take from his working schedule.

Rungius packed into the mountains with other friends as well, and it was during one such pack trip into the Green River mountains with another guide that Rungius broke his leg. Since the party was on the headwaters of Green River when the accident occurred, it was decided that the nearest doctor was in Jackson's Hole. Rungius was taken as far as Bill Manning's cabin in South Park. A rider was sent on to Jackson to fetch the doctor.

The doctor arrived, as did Albert Nelson. The doctor, the men noticed, was under the influence of alcohol when he arrived. The comforts and discomforts of alcohol were well known in the valley and no one sought to deny anyone its use, but the men were watchful as the doctor prepared to set the leg. After offering Rungius a fortifying swig from his bottle — Rungius declined the gesture — the doctor set the leg in a haphazard way, nodded with satisfaction and gathered up his tools. The men were relieved when the doctor went on his way.

No sooner had the doctor gone, than Rungius began to worry about the break making him permanently crippled.

He put the query to his companions, "Do you think the doctor got the bone back into place?" They had to admit it had not looked straight to them.

Rungius told them, "If you fellows think you can manage the traction necessary to pull those bones apart until the ends can come together right, I promise you I can stand it."

Albert was a taxidermist, so he knew something about bones, and much about plaster-of-paris casts. Bill Manning and Albert sawed the cast off and ground it into powder again. With a steady pressure they stretched the leg until Albert could feel a clean and even replacement of the bone edges. They encased the leg in a clean sock and soaked and reapplied the plaster-of-paris.

Rungius stood the ordeal with only a grunt or two, adding directions and encouragement to his friends when he thought it necessary. Nelson and Manning were dubious about the outcome of their non-professional job.

"Don't worry. It feels all right this time," Rungius reassured them. "My uncle is a surgeon. When I get back east I'll have it examined. If it isn't straight, it can be rebroken and reset."

To get "back east" at that time, Rungius had to endure a painfully slow and rough wagon trip out of the valley.

Some months later a letter arrived informing Albert that upon examination the leg was found to have a perfect set. Albert was happy at this news. In the same mail was a roll which he assumed to be a large calendar.

Since Albert had snowshoed the fourteen miles from Kelly to Antelope Pass (the Y junction one mile west of present Jackson), he left the bulky roll until another trip. The long rolled package stood in the corner of the post office room for most of the winter.

Months later, when he came on another snowshoe trip to the post office, Mrs. Anderson asked, "Aren't you going to take your package this time?"

Albert picked it up and ran a knife edge unceremoniously along the tube, thinking that if he didn't like the calendar, it wasn't worth packing all that way to Kelly.

The canvas which emerged was a beautiful oil painting of a bull elk polishing the velvet from his antlers on a convenient spruce— Rungius's thank you for the medical service. The Rungius painting was treasured.

Another of Albert's favorite clients was J. E. Stimson, an artist and photographer who came often to Jackson for scenic trips. Albert took him out on pack trips for picture taking and fishing. While they were at the business of camping and shooting pictures, Stimson taught Albert photographic techniques and the film developing process. At the ranch Albert set up a darkroom and did his own film developing, but photography was a skill he did not pursue very diligently.

During the time Albert was establishing himself as a rancher, he became acquainted with Sarah Avilla Allen, a young lady whose interests matched his own. With her parents, Charles J. and Maria Allen, and her six brothers and sisters—Orpha, Mary Ann, Cassie, Valdez, Marion and Neal, she had come to Jackson's Hole in 1896. She loved to hunt, to ride, and to dance. The hard work of pioneer life held no fears for her.

No longer the penniless young immigrant whose home was whatever camp he made for the night, Albert, at thirty-nine, was a man of property, a homesteader, a taxidermist, a guide and outfitter, a man with many friends. He was the State Game Warden. Satisfied he could support a family, he courted Sarah Avilla Allen and on February 8, 1900, married her. Avilla was just two months short of her twenty-first birthday. Children born to this union were: Josephine Marie (m. Roice), Mabel Carrie (m. Osborn, Hokanson), Charles Myron, Otto Marion, Anna Avilla (m. Ferrin), Neal Valdez, and Albert William.

After serving three years of the four-year appointment as State Game Warden, Albert resigned. The growing responsibilities of family, ranching, outfitting and taxidermy made it difficult to keep up the long trips throughout the state. The pay was one hundred dollars a month. The first month's wage went to pay for having the game laws printed. Any deputy he hired was paid from his own pocket, as were all travel expenses. Any apprehended culprit was smart enough to ask for a jury trial, which meant Albert had to travel to the county seat of whatever county the offense had occurred in. At this time the state was divided into thirteen counties. Albert had to go as far as Cheyenne for a few trials.

The new game laws were very unpopular anyway. No one wanted to be restricted in freedom to use the game as it always had been used. Though Albert made many arrests, his convictions in court were zero. When looked upon in comparison with the force now used to enforce the game laws of the state, and the stricter view of the laws, it does look like an impossible and discouraging commitment for one man to shoulder. Albert turned over all his records to Dan Nowlin who replaced him and filed the first report. Consequently it is Dan Nowlin who is sometimes referred to as being the first game warden of the state.

During the next few years Albert concentrated on increasing the productivity of his land and building up a small herd of cattle. His life once again centered on ranching, guiding and taxidermy.

At about this time Albert and Avilla had to go through an experience few parents have been called on to withstand. Otto, a curious three-and-a-half or four-year-old, was caught playing with matches. His mother took the matches away and put them high up in the cupboard. But when she went outside, Otto locked the doors, climbed up and got the matches, and ran to the bedroom. Anna, just one and a half, and determined not to be left behind, tagged along after Otto. For added concealment, the two crawled under the bed. There Otto took a match and lighting it, gave it to his sister. Anna was quite fascinated with the match until it burned her finger. She dropped it. The flame caught in her dress and flared upward. Terrified, she crawled from under the bed and ran screaming from the room.

Avilla was working outside the house. Hearing the screams, she rushed to the house but couldn't get in the locked door. Frantically she broke a window and climbed in. After grabbing up Anna, Avilla rolled her in "something" to put out the fire. (In the confusion and tension of the moment, how the fire was extinguished became a forgotten incident.) Carrying Anna in her arms, Avilla rushed out of the house to the big gravel bank overlooking the meadowlands where Albert, their son Charlie, and Fred Carlton were working. When they recognized the urgency of her screaming, they abandoned their work and came quickly to the house. Someone was sent the ten miles to Jackson to bring back Dr. Reese.

After he arrived and examined the burn covering Anna's chest, arms, neck and face, he prescribed the application of linseed oil over the entire afflicted area. He said there wasn't much else that he could do and returned to Jackson. About a week later infection set in and "proud flesh" started to form. The doctor regretfully pronounced he could do no more for Anna.

As Anna's condition grew worse, Albert and Avilla cast about desperately for something they could do to help. Neighbors came to comfort and to help. Albert had read somewhere that by blowing powdered alum into an infected open wound in an animal, the infection could be cleared up. Knowing no other alternative to take, he sterilized one of the knives from his taxidermy equipment and prepared to cut away as much infection and proud flesh as he could from the small body of his daughter.

Avilla's sister Nan Budge, Mrs. Lew Royer, and Hattie May tried to assist by holding Anna motionless while her father worked over her arms, chest, neck and face. During the tense, slow process, first one woman then another and another got sick and had to leave.

Finally Avilla was left alone holding her daughter while her husband delicately carved away the shrunken flesh.

As he gently blew the powdered alum onto the raw wounds, Anna convulsed violently and became unconscious. Her parents, having done all in their power to do, put her to bed and prayed that she would live through the night.

Slowly Anna recovered. She was up and about in about a month, but it was much longer before the skin fully healed. She was scarred from her ordeal, but her father's efforts apparently kept her from being deformed by angry, shrunken flesh.

Avilla's life ended December 4, 1913, just a little less than two months short of her fourteenth wedding anniversary. She was thirty-four when she died of complications of pregnancy. The children ranged in age from Josephine, who was almost twelve, to baby Albert, nineteen months. Relatives, neighbors and friends gathered around Albert to give comfort and assistance to the family. Many offered to take a child or two to raise. Albert allowed the children to spend time with relatives, but he refused to have the seven children permanently split up. He never remarried. The measure of his success as a parent is evidenced by the love and respect in which he was held by all his children, as well as by the citizens of the valley. The death of his wife changed the course of Albert's life again. With the added responsibility of caring for the children, Albert decided to sell the ranch and to establish his home and taxidermy shop in the nearby town of Kelly.

By the year 1927, with the youngest child, Albert Jr., a strapping fifteen year old, and with the two older girls married, it seemed that life would begin to smooth the path for Albert Sr. Instead it pulled another blockbuster from its bag of tricks.

The landslide which Uncle Billie Bierer had predicted had happened in May 1925. *[See other accounts in this volume.]* The slide dammed the Gros Ventre and formed Lower Slide Lake behind the dam. There had been a general unease concerning the great earthen dam dumped by the slide into the canyon of the Gros Ventre. Although the rock and debris filled the riverbed for about a half mile, and although the army engineers had pronounced that it would never wash out, still the river was seeping through the packed rocks and earth. The river was not cutting a new channel from the top down as had been expected.

On May 18, 1927, this dam gave way. The resulting flood completely wiped out the town of Kelly and all of the ranches along the streambed from the dam to the confluence of the Gros Ventre with the Snake, some eight miles below.

Fortunately for the people along the Gros Ventre, the dam gave way in the daytime. Also fortunately, the Forest Service ranger living at Kelly, Charlie Dibble, had been watching the extremely high water and the dam "situation." He was on his way to check on them when he saw a barn which he knew to have been above the dam, floating along on the downstream side. He raced ahead of the flood water to a telephone and alerted all the residents of Kelly and the ranchers along the stream.

When the softened dam gave way, the stored waters in the lake forced huge boulders and trees down through the canyon like a monstrous V-plow gouging out the streambed. While confined in the canyon with no place to spread out, the water crested high in the middle, gathering power.

Earlier that morning, the residents of Kelly had been aware that the river was high and rising. Many of them were concerned about the bridge at the edge of town. They guided the driftwood past the piers, trying to keep the high water from doing damage. A mill pond and sawmill stood on the bank of the river. Albert Sr. was helping the owner, Joe Kneedy, dismantle and take in his saw so that it would not be damaged in case of high water.

Everyone feared that the dam might go out and that the river would flood. But no one dreamed that it would come like a tidal wave with a face of granite.

When the word was flashed about the little settlement that everyone should get out immediately, Albert Sr. went to his own home and looked about to decide what to save and how to evacuate his family. Neal and Otto, who had been outside and had seen the flood break out of the canyon, rushed in and grabbed him, each at an arm. Albert, temporarily nonplused, said something to the effect of "If the good Lord wants to take this place, He might as well take me, too!"

Urging that they didn't have time to argue, his sons dragged him along through the door. With the thought of saving something, anything, Anna grabbed the rolled up canvas—the painting sent to Albert by Carl Rungius. Albert had never found a suitable frame for the picture. If he had, it probably would have been lost to the flood, as were all the rest of their possessions.

The flood bulldozed the town of Kelly from the river bank, leaving only the church and schoolhouse standing. Both of these buildings were back from the river on a rise, a previous riverbank of an earlier age of the river.

Mr. and Mrs. Kneedy and their adopted son, Little Joe, were the only victims of the flood in the town of Kelly. But at one ranch downstream, Mrs. Lovejoy and her sister Miss Smith took too long to load a wagon and were caught by the flood. At the Edick home the same thing happened to Mr. Edick and his hired man Clint Stevens. Mr. Edick caught in a tree which stood while all its neighbors were swept away. Clint rode the hayrack until it tipped over and was swept from view. In all, the flood took six victims. Had it not been for Dibble's early warning, there might have been a hundred.

When the cataclysm subsided and only rushing muddy waters marked the site of Kelly, the residents gathered together to compare notes and to check themselves to see if any were missing. They had to make new plans for their lives, at least for the next few hours. Albert suggested that they offer a prayer to thank the Lord for sparing their lives and to ask for strength and guidance for the time ahead.

The raging river had cut off help from Jackson, at least for that day. Many of the refugees were taken to the homes of friends and relatives throughout the valley bordering the north bank of the Gros Ventre. The rest made a camp at Antelope Springs, a few miles north of Kelly, where they kept the campfires burning all night.

In the days that followed, help and supplies flowed in from the residents of Jackson and from the Red Cross. None of this could replace the homes that were lost. Even the earth was gouged away from the bedrock, making rebuilding on the land impossible.

Search for the missing victims and salvage work along the river began as soon as the water subsided. As Albert and young Albert were plowing the drift piles, Albert Sr. spotted Mr. Kneedy's wrist above the sand and he sent young Albert on some trumped up errand so that he would not be present to help uncover the corpse.

It was a time of communal sorrow, heartache and help—the village of Kelly never recovered.

For the third time, Albert set about establishing a home. The Nelson family decided to rebuild their home and business in the town of Jackson. The older boys already had firm reputations as excellent carpenters and log men. Charlie and Otto also helped with the taxidermy. Soon the family was well established in their new home, with more work than they could keep up with.

Albert Sr. was a hale and hearty sixty-six years young when the move to Jackson was made. He had no thought of retiring, or even of slacking off on the hard work, although he had young men eager to help. In a few years he had again built up a lovely yard, with lilacs that had managed to survive the flood at the old homestead and crabapple trees ordered from the nurseries. Tiger lilies, peonies and gladiolus burst into bloom for him, and soon his strawberry and raspberry patches bore so heavily that the family could not use all the fruit and had to seek a market among the neighbors.

In Jackson, with five young people at home approaching marrying age, the Nelson place became a scene of social activity. Dances, picnics, skating, toboggan and sleigh rides soon had the usual effect. Nineteen thirty-two, the "year of the weddings," brought three daughters-in-law and one son-in-law into the family as Charlie, Anna, Neal, and Albert married. Still, it was a close-knit family group with all the children (except Mabel who was at Ashton) living not more than seven miles from their father's house. The boys worked together as carpenter contractors in summer and helped at the taxidermy work in the winters. A new generation of Nelsons sprang up in the various households.

Aside from getting a little arthritic, Albert was as active as any of his sons. There always seemed to be time for a "family picnic" when all or most of the clan gathered to go fishing. During hunting season all of the families that could get away from the press of work packed their camping gear and went down on the Sweetwater, or the Green River, or Muddy Gap, or some remote place Albert kept fond memories of. The families filled their game licenses, hunted arrowheads and weather-beaten relics, and Albert told of his experiences when he and Uncle Billie and their pack string made their way through the area in the 1880s and 90s.

Happy and productive, these were the good years and there is little to note until World War II. The younger sons, Neal and Albert, had three children each and work which was classified as vital. Consequently their draft status was 1C. Having no family, Otto was drafted right away, and Charlie, his marriage ending, volunteered. So the two men who had been the most help with the taxidermy shop, the ones who were actually living at home with their father, went off to the war. Neal and Young Albert also left the valley to help with the war effort—helping to build air force bases in Utah and Mountain Home, Idaho.

There was still plenty of family at home in Jackson to keep Albert Sr. company. Naturally, taxidermy work was curtailed somewhat by the war. However, Albert worked steadily at his craft through the war years. Since he read widely and unfailingly listened to the news broadcasts, he kept himself thoroughly briefed on all military engagements. Through a Swedish newspaper he subscribed to, he also kept up with the northern European view of the war and its progress. Many people of the valley relied on him for news of how things were "gettin' along."

During the war, Albert was in his mid-eighties—the oldest working taxidermist in the U.S. While his family was disrupted and two of his sons served on the front lines, Albert worked in anxious solitude in his shop. His customers still received high quality work on time, his garden never suffered (in this time of scarcity, it was expanded and put to greater use), his bachelor quarters were kept tidy, and he was his own cook and secretary. He never failed to buy a bond of the largest denomination he could afford each month, putting it in the name of a daughter or daughter-in-law each time.

In spite of his self-sufficient character, he was very glad to have his two soldiers come marching safely home and to welcome the returning families who had spent the war years outside the valley on war-related construction.

What can one say of his last years except that they were filled with the love and honor of family, friends and acquaintances?

Albert died March 14, 1957, at the age of ninety-five, surrounded by all of his children. He was fortunate to be active and mentally alert up to his last short illness. It is safe to say that no pioneer of Jackson's Hole, or of Wyoming, has commanded more respect for the honesty and fairness of his character, the high quality of his workmanship and his calm acceptance of adversity.

Profoundly affected by his father's death, Albert W. Nelson described his experience in a letter to his daughter Dorothy (in Lakeland, Florida, attending Florida Southern College), informing her of her grandfather's death:

> ...Now, Din, I'm going to tell you how I am going to remember.... Dad said, "Son, Billie has come to guide me across the Buffalo Range....
>
> I said "Then you're going to leave us, Dad?" Dad looked at me, then smiled. He said, "Son, can't tell you much about this now, as what it's like, but Billie told me that they had sent him here to take me to this place of rest and contentment; where no one ever grows old or weary; where peace is eternal and love everlasting...." He said Uncle Billie told him that all men who love the outdoors, the game, the good clean living, and the campfire smoke, the ringing of a horse bell at night, the bright stars, the rustle of the breeze in the pines, the mountains, and many other things that nature has given us to use and enjoy, always go to that place of rest through the Buffalo Range; and that they always send an old friend to guide you over. He said he wasn't leaving us for long, and that he would be there waiting with Mamma for us to come after our work here was done and we had earned our place up there with our loved ones.
>
> By then it was light and I could hear Uncle Billie say, "Well, Al, it's daylight. Reckon maybe we had better start. We'll see lots of buffalo today." Dad said, "I'm ready, Bill." They got on their horses, started the pack string and rode away. Dad turned in his saddle and waved. He called back and said, "I'll see you, Son." They both looked so young and happy. Dad was wanting to see what was over the next ridge...

ᏚHEEPMAN'S ᎠREAM

THE EARLIEST SETTLERS IN JACKSON'S Hole brought no sheep. Instead they brought cattle. The cattlemen were convinced that sheep graze mountain pasture too closely, and any cattleman living in Jackson's Hole was most anxious to "conserve" the lush mountain grazing, especially since the sheep herds threatening it were based either far down the Green River or over in Idaho. For these "foreigners" to come into the valley in the summertime and graze off the best ranges was an intolerable trespass.

Albert T. Nelson told of finding a wide sheep trail coming up the Green River and down the Crystal Creek fork of the Gros Ventre when he was guiding a hunting party sometime before 1895. Other early settlers told of at least two occasions when bands of sheep were brought into the country, either through Snake River Canyon or over Teton or Mosquito Creek Pass, and trailed up the west side of the valley before crossing the river on Menor's Ferry.

About 1901, some of the settlers held a meeting and decided to do something about this. At least two separate bands of sheep were intercepted, sheep, dogs and horses killed, and herders roughed up and sent away with a warning never to come back. B.W. Driggs' account of one incident, in his *History of Teton Valley, Idaho* relates:

> During August of 1901, some of the sheep of Smart and Webster Sheep Co. of Rexburg, Idaho, got a little over the divide on the Jackson side of the range, on the upper part of Mosquito Creek. The stockmen of Jackson Hole, using the excuse that the sheep were encroaching on the elk range, began the extermination of the sheep over which John Palmer was foreman, and Nean Christianson was herder of

one flock. Nean was in his camp just starting to get breakfast when three masked men crept upon him with leveled guns. They tied him to a tree, gave him a few lashes, then fired a shot which was a signal for the other men to start the slaughter of the sheep. The firing and stampeding resulted in the death of about 300 animals.

Nean witnessed them kill his horse and dog and the burning of the camp equipment. He then begged for his life, promising the raiders that he would leave. They threatened to take him to Jackson, but upon his promising to get out with the sheep they finally let him go, first taking his gun. He took the remaining sheep to safer quarters.

The second incident, according to local oral history, entailed the roughing up of two herders, destruction of their camp, killing of their horses, killing and scattering of the sheep herd and a warning.

Albert Nelson told of coming upon two graves, somewhere on the pass between Wilson and Victor. The mounds didn't look too real, though he didn't excavate them to check for authenticity, and the inscription on the headboard bore the message, "Here lies the sheepmen's hopes." Since he had never heard of a killing in these sheep incidents, he took it to be a practical joke, or a warning.

The identity of the settlers who scared the sheepmen out of the "Hole" has been pretty well known through the years, but since I don't know *all* of them, I won't reveal any.

This somewhat territorial conservation program of the cattlemen probably saved the elk range. The whole west was anyone's range who could claim it, and when the Forest Service was established and grazing permit areas allotted around 1905, they granted permits *in situ* to the stockmen who had been using the various areas. The administrators of the Teton Forest Reserve incorporated the same reasoning that the cattlemen had used, that sheep stripped the range of the same forage the elk use, and they restricted permit leases to cattle on the Teton Forest.

Through good management, the elk and the cattle have coexisted pretty well in the ninety-some years since.

So died the sheepmen's hopes.

TOOTH FOR TOOTH

BOUT THE TIME OF THE "SHEEP WAR" there was another conservation problem which was giving the natives an outraged feeling in the midriff. A small group of hunter-trappers was killing bull elk for their teeth. Tusk hunters killed elk just to extract the two ivory incisors.

Elk have two pure ivory teeth which are valued as items of jewelry and decorative baubles. When elk are irritated they click their upper teeth against their lower teeth making a warning sound. These ivory teeth seem to have no purpose other than to enhance this clicking. At that time, the members of the Elk's Club were enthusiastic customers of tusk hunters. I hasten to add that the Elk's Club members stopped buying elk teeth for ornaments when they learned that animals were being killed only for their teeth. However, at the turn of the century, when conservation was in its infancy and very few regulations of any kind were in force, anything a man could turn a penny at was fair game—or so he thought.

Every man in the valley had his little hoard of elk teeth tucked away in his tobacco sack, with a little tobacco left in it to darken them nicely. These were mostly gathered from legally licensed kills in the fall. Teeth were also pulled from any carcass of winter-killed elk one happened to find.

But these tusk hunters deliberately killed elk and left the whole carcass. They took only the teeth. Especially did they kill the prime bulls, which were likely to have the biggest darkest teeth. If the wanton destruction continued, guides would have a hard time finding a prime head for hunters in the fall. And what Jackson's Hole homesteader didn't earn part of his living off the dude hunters each autumn?

It was pretty well known, or suspected, who the tusk hunters were. They were clever poachers, and game wardens had trouble obtaining the evidence to pin the killings to the culprits. If the simple possession of elk teeth were a crime, it was likely every man in the county could have been found guilty.

The tuskers preferred to locate and follow a herd when a light snowstorm was starting, masking their deed as it was committed, as well as covering their tracks. Another ploy they used was a pair of elk-track stilts.

Eventually game wardens back-tracking from some elk carcasses left on Slate Creek, found in the trail what looked like the mark of the edge of a board. They made a sneak on the Fred Koerner cabin where Charlie Purdy, one of the suspects, was batching and trapping. Hung on the side of the cabin was a pair of boards like small webs, with elk feet nailed to the bottom. The stilts, or webs, were confiscated and sent to the State Game and Fish Office.

The Jacksonites knew what the game department was up against. Insufficient evidence was only a part of the problem. If an arrest was made, the case had to be tried way down in Evanston, the County seat, and juries were not noted for handing out guilty verdicts on Wyoming's game cases. Word was passed around the valley that some concerned citizens should meet at the Henshew ranch on the Gros Ventre below Kelly, to discuss the situation. Ben Goe, Cal Carrington and Guy Germain, three young men who hadn't been invited, sneaked up and listened outside the window.

It was the consensus of opinion at the meeting that running certain men out of the country would be the most effective way to be entirely rid of the problem. If they could be told forcibly enough to leave and not come back, it was thought that they would comply—and it would save the county a lot of money, too, it was further rationalized.

The suspected tusk hunters who were to be ordered to leave were: Charlie Purdy, an old trapper who lived on the Fish Creek Fork of the Gros Ventre (Purdy Basin is named for him); Isbel, also a trapper and wolf hunter; William Binkley, who had a place on the south side of the river at Kelly; and Bill Merritt, homesteading near Kelly and the son-in-law of Binkley.

❧This posse caught the elk tooth poachers and traveled to California to testify against the tusk hunters. Kneeling are Charles Harvey, Rube Tuttle, and Si Ferrin. Among those in the back row are Mr. and Mrs. Pierce Cunningham and Charles Deloney. (JHM&HC and Faye Deloney)

Purdy and Isbel, trapping for the bounty, had just about cleared the valley of wolves and mountain lion. Charlie Purdy was a slow-moving man. Jim Budge, Sr., always said of him that when he went out to hunt a wolf, he could usually get him because the wolf thought he was a stump and would come right up to smell him.

Binkley and Merritt were men with families who were going through the usual homesteading struggle.

The three eavesdroppers got on their horses and rode off to warn the tuskers.

Allen Budge told of the long evening of worry and strain Aunt Nan Budge and her children experienced the night the tusk hunters were ordered to leave. Jim Budge, Sr., Aunt Nan's husband, Otho Williams, Tom Henshew, Bill Sebaum and Jim May had been the ones chosen by lot to go and order the tuskers to leave. They met at the Henshew place and made the rounds of the tuskers' homes.

Merritt's wife was pregnant, so they were given an extra day to vacate. The others were ordered to be gone in twenty-four hours. Not one of the committee members ever told what was said to the tuskers. But it must have been effective because they met the deadline.

Whether because of the timely warning from the eavesdroppers, or because they were getting ready to make a sale anyway, the tuskers departed from Ashton, Idaho, on the train, in an emigrant car loaded with their possessions.

The Wyoming game wardens knew the group had hides and scalps of elk but could not link these items to illegal killing. Idaho had no law to stop them. However, they could be apprehended under a Federal Law if they were transporting unlicensed game across state lines. The tuskers were stopped when the train reached California, and the car was searched.

Si Ferrin, game warden in Jackson at the time, D. C. Nowlin, Jacksonite and State Game Warden at the time, plus Charlie Harvey, a deputy game warden, and Pierce Cunningham, *maybe* a deputy, had been busily stirring up all this pursuit and arrived in California on a later train. When the car was searched, no elk teeth were found. Charlie Harvey was sharp enough to ask the California officers if they could furnish a policewoman to search the women. The corsets of the ladies were found to be padded with elk teeth.

The case was tried by a Federal Judge in Pocatello. The charge—transporting contraband across a state line. The evidence was confiscated by the federal government and shipped off to Washington, D.C., where it probably reposes in some dim ghostly forgotten nook to this day.

The Wyoming Game and Fish Department thought they should have it back but got no action for all their requests.

For some reason, Charlie Purdy was the only one to be sentenced to a prison term for the charge. When he had served his time in the federal pen, he returned, not quite to Jackson, but nearby. He spent his last years trapping near Loon Lake, up near Squirrel Meadows at the north end of the Tetons.

I was curious about the deserted homesteads after the tuskers packed up and left.

"What happened to their places?" I asked Allen. "Did the fellows get to come back and sell their houses, their homestead relinquishments? Or did they sell them to someone outside who came in to claim them?"

"Come to think of it," Allen answered, "Sebaum got Binkley's place. It's the Teton Valley Ranch now, you know. Merritt's homestead was right next to it and Sebaum got that too. I don't know how Sebaum got them, whether he paid the men anything, or not."

Since Binkley, Merritt and Sebaum are all gone we may never know.

FEUD OVER THE FORMER OPEN RANGE

WHEN THE NEWLY CREATED Forest Service Department started administering its domain, sometime around 1901, the restrictions at first were so slight that they passed almost unnoticed. The settlers who had been cutting trees for house logs, fencing and lumber at will now were requested to let the Forest Service know their requirements, and they would help find and mark a suitable site.

The same held true for the ranchers who had been grazing cattle on land that was now set aside as "forest preserve." Ranchers were requested to let the Forest Service know where and how many cattle they grazed and a permit would be issued for the same. No fees were charged at first. Generally the range the rancher had been using was assigned to him by permit.

The ranchers were irritated with even these mild beginnings of control. Some of them made no effort to comply, although they continued to turn their cattle out onto the wide open spaces they had always used. (After all, they had been there before the Forest Service.) One of the non-compliers was the LP&O Ranch, owned by the Shives.

Josiah D. (Si) Ferrin, of the JF Ranch, was one of the ranchers who had complied with the requirements, received his permit for the Spread Creek drainage and made his arrangements accordingly.

Si and his boys were building up a sizable spread stretching from the mouth of the Buffalo south toward Spread Creek, and he and neighbors Otto Kusche, Pierce Cunningham and Dick Olds had received a Forest Service permit to go further up the creek with this combined herd. (Kusche's place and the JF were a part of what is now called the Elk Ranch.)

Over on the Buffalo meadows near the foot of Togwotee Pass, Jack and Lucy Shives were putting together a large ranch with quite a few head of cattle. Jack Shives and John Cherry had homesteaded adjoining claims by squatters right in 1892. They raised some cattle and took out hunting parties.

In 1897 Jack married widow Lucy Nesbitt. This broke up the Cherry-Shives partnership. John moved to the north end of the East Gros Ventre Butte, where he ranched for the remainder of his life. Lucy and Jack continued to run cattle and a hunting camp on the Buffalo. Lucy Nesbitt Shives was an excellent horsewoman who loved the outdoor life. She was as at home on the range as her husband.

In 1911 her mother, Mary Wadams, over eighty years of age at the time, homesteaded adjoining acreage to the Shives. She was a rugged pioneer type who refused to move to her daughter's house in the winter, staying in her own homestead cabin until she received the final proof and patent on the claim. With the addition in 1915 of a homestead filed by Lucy's daughter, Carrie Nesbitt Dunn, and one filed by a Ben Kilky, who worked for the Shives while homesteading, these claims made up the ranch known as the Hatchet Ranch.

Before the feud developed, Lucy and Jack were busily building up their joint holdings. They called it the LP&O. Most everybody else called it the Shives place.

Every spring the Shives had always just opened their gates and let their cattle out. They herded them loosely by putting salt out in good areas and riding out occasionally to check. Over the ridge onto the Spread Creek drainage was a natural drift for the cattle that the Shives allowed to continue. They refused to notify the Forest Service and obtain a permit, since they had always run cattle like this.

Si and his sons, and neighbors Cunningham, Kusche and Olds pushed their cattle up the Spread Creek drainage, spread their salt and went on home. Almost before they could unsaddle, bunches of cattle were hanging along the fenced fields again. As soon as they could get around to it, the Ferrins gathered up the cows and took them up the creek again. Again they wouldn't stay.

It seemed bunches of cattle were coming down the trails returning to the ranch headquarters every time anyone looked out.

One day when one of the men was putting out more salt, he spotted a herd of cows actually running down the creek. He spurred over to a good lookout spot in time to see a dog disappear up the creek.

When this was related to Si, he became hopping mad. He rightly surmised that it was Shives dogging his cattle out of Spread Creek, because they were the only others with cattle on it. Si took to riding the ridges every time he had a spare minute.

One day Si and Otto Kusche were riding the range together when they came in sight of two other riders, accompanied by a couple of dogs, approaching a little herd of cattle the men knew to be JF stock.

While Si and Kusche watched, the other riders turned the cattle down the trail and "let" the dogs give them a good chase along the way. Si was fuming as he made tracks over to the offenders.

As he and Kusche galloped nearer, Si saw that one of the pair was Lucy Shives and the other was Rudolph Rosencrans, an ex-military man from Germany who was a newcomer to the valley. (Rosie had not yet started his long career as a Forest Service ranger in Teton Forest and was at this time working as a hired man for the Shives.)

Si pulled up, roaring that they had better call their god-damn dogs off before he shot every god-damned son-of-a-bitch right there. And what did they think they were doing running his cows off his range anyway? The tirade continued, liberally clothed in down-to-earth terms.

Lucy was all ready to start yelling that it was her range when Rosencrans interrupted (the proper military gentleman; trying to shame Si).

"Mr. Ferrin, you shouldn't talk dat vay in front of a lady. Haven't you got any manners?"

Just what Si wanted! Someone to vent his rage on. He jumped off his horse, yelling blasphemies as he hopped around trying to get out of his chaps.

"Get down off-a that horse you little Dutch son-of-a-bitch. I'll be glad to talk to you instead of the lady." Arms akimbo, he braced his belly up to Rosie's horse.

Since Si was about twice Rosie's size and had the added advantage of being twice as mad, Rosie let caution be the better part of valor and stayed on his horse.

With some more swearing on the one side and some conciliatory statements on the other, the range war subsided to bluff and bluster, arm waving and finger pointing. The cattle of the Spread Creek permittees were allowed to graze unmolested, and the LP&O cattle continued to graze there, too. Without permit.

A sequel to the range dispute happened sometime later when Otto Kusche and Rudolph Rosencrans, both fairly recent German immigrants, were having a sociable beer in the bar. They got to talking about the event and laughing about the action of the day. A silence came upon them and each reviewed private thoughts about the rough and ready ways of the valley.

Otto shifted a little on his seat and shrugged. "Rudolph," he said to Rosie. "I don't tink I'd let anybody talk to me like dat. He called you a little Dutch son-of-a-bitch. I tink you should-a got down and fought him. To protect your honor."

Rosie thought about this for awhile, then squinted at Otto out of the corner of his eye. With a tight little smile, he jabbed. "Vell, vy didn't you get down and fight him? Ain't you a Dutch son-of-a-bitch, too?"

TETON PASS: LIFELINE TO THE VALLEY

J OHN COLTER IS GIVEN CREDIT FOR using Teton Pass on his long circle to advertise Manual Lisa's trading post to the Indians in the winter of 1807–08. Trappers under the leadership of Andrew Henry used the pass in the trapping season of 1810–11. Some of these trappers, John Hoback, Edward Robinson and Jacob Reznor, led the Wilson Price Hunt party of Astorians over the pass in 1811 when their efforts to float the Snake River Canyon were unsuccessful. Other white trappers may have used the pass earlier, but these are the first on record.

The Indian trails the trappers followed were no doubt first made by the big herds of game animals who trailed into Jackson's Hole for summer grazing. Invariably animals choose the quickest but easiest grade over a mountain. This early trail over Teton Pass did not go up Trail Creek on the west side, as the road does now, but started up the Moose Creek drainage, climbed the ridge between Moose Creek and Trail Creek, then crossed over to the Trail Creek drainage near the pass. This trail was used until the settlers of the late 1880s felt the need to bring wagons over the pass.

The earliest settlers of Jackson's Hole came in with pack outfits. They dismantled essential machinery, like a mower or wagon, and packed it in on horses. However, when the Sylvester Wilson party moved several families to the valley in 1889, they brought their womenfolk and several wagons full of all their household goods. The men cut out a wide enough track for a wagon to pass and corduroyed the swampy places with cut poles. The job took several weeks, but the effort was worthwhile.

Now all the settlers could haul in bigger loads of supplies from the nearest market—St. Anthony, Idaho. The new road followed Trail

Creek from the valley floor on the west side, up to the pass, then down the middle of the draw into Black Canyon on the east side.

No great effort was made to improve upon this set of tracks until Harris Dunn & Company, needed to freight heavy equipment and a sawmill to its mining claims on Whetstone Creek, a stream on the Pacific Creek drainage. In 1895 this company put a crew to work on the road, widening the cuts, making dugways in some places, bridging some water crossings and corduroying "the blue mudhole" and other bog holes.

They constructed a ferry over the Snake about a mile below the outlet of Jackson Lake and set up their sawmill on Pacific Creek. They sawed some big timbers in which they bored holes about two inches deep. These timbers formed the bottom of their sluice boxes, which they set up near the mine. They diverted water from the creek and washed their ore, expecting at least some gold for their $50,000 investment and expenses.

The poor showing of the light flower gold they recovered made further financing impossible. The company folded in 1897. A workman named Conrad, who had been caretaking the mines and running the ferry, was left without a job. He continued to run the ferry until the fares were not sufficient enough to keep him in supplies. He packed up, leaving the ferry to run itself.

The sawmill was sold to Steven Leek. J.H. Uhl bought the lumber that was on hand. The timbers used on the flumes and sluice boxes were gratefully salvaged by various ranchers who cared to take the time to tear them down and haul them home. Charlie Allen built a saddle shed out of some of the holey timber. By putting the smooth side of the boards outside and the holes inside he could drive a wooden peg into the wall at any spot convenient for hanging saddles, harness, collars or bridles. It was a giant wall-to-wall peg board.

The road over the pass was still a steep and miserable drag up the creek valley on the west side and down the steep sidehill and creek bottom on the east. Double teams had to be used to get up the mountain, and usually the drivers drug a big log, besides rough-locking the wheels, to ease the descent. Wagon travel over the pass was discontinued each fall after the snow became too deep to wade.

❦ These teams and sleighs freighted materials over Teton Pass for the Rainbow Building in the winter of 1928-29. (Author's collection)

The handful of settlers were careful to have their winter supplies laid in before this. Mail was carried into the valley on snowshoe trips out to Victor.

After 1895 the country on both sides of the mountain experienced a population explosion. Homesteaders began settling and filing on all of the open land. Regular mail delivery contracts were demanded by the increasing population.

During the summer and fall months, when the road over the pass was open, dudes came for elaborate pack and hunting trips. This created increased demand for food and material goods; enough to support a new service-oriented business—freighting.

By 1905, the road over the pass was used enough to keep the snow road "broke out" all winter. This meant the road was mostly just packed and tramped down snow, as teams wallowed through each new snowfall, with portions of the deeper drifts shoveled by hand when necessary.

But winter brought the ever present fear of snowslides; the tragedy of being caught in them; and the labor of digging a road over or through them. Springtime always brought the disintegration of the packed snow road, causing frequent tip-overs. As the firmly packed base broke up, the sleigh runners would sink, drag, or skid from side to side, making a much harder pull for the teams. Footing for the teams would become unstable and treacherous. In spite of the difficulties, Teton Pass became the lifeline into Jackson's Hole, the only year-around traveled road.

With the completion of the Oregon Short Line Railroad spur track to Victor, Idaho, in 1912, travel over the pass was given another boost. The spur connected Victor to Idaho Falls and Pocatello, connecting with the Union Pacific at Ogden. Teton Pass did away with some fifty to sixty miles of stage travel.

Up to that point any improvements made on the pass had been made out of necessity, by citizens who were in immediate need of the improvement. In 1913, they got a sponsor. The road traversed land which had just recently been set aside as the nation's first National Forest Preserve. Some of the revenue coming from timber sales and grazing permits was allotted to road improvement on the forest land. Starting in 1913, the Teton Pass road began to benefit from these moneys.

Forest Ranger Al Austin sent a crew to survey a graded roadway up the mountain side. From 1913 to 1917, crews labored with horse-drawn equipment.

The eight switchbacks on the east side of the mountain and the five draws plus the figure eight switchback on the west side eased and smoothed the struggle of crossing Teton Pass. The earliest cars started coming over about this time. (See *First Car Over Teton Pass*) With frequent stops for water, they steamed their way to the top. Then they smoked their brake linings all the way to the bottom. The pass was still no boulevard.

To take care of the sleeping and eating needs of the travelers, two hotels, one in Victor and one in Jackson, were started, and two roadhouses were started, one on each side of the pass. John Bircher kept the roadhouse and livery accommodations, as well as operating a sawmill, on the west side.

John Lockwood started roadhouse facilities at his ranch at the foot of the hill on the east side of the mountain. Mr. Lockwood died of pneumonia following overexertions at snow shoveling. His widow then married Charlie Harvey. The place later passed to John Miller, who sold to Tom Lee, who sold it to Frank Crandell. Mr. Crandell was a mail carrier as well as innkeeper. Nate Davis was the last to operate the ranch as a roadhouse. It is now Betty

Woolsey's Trail Creek Ranch, one of the most successful dude ranches of the valley.

Ed T. Blair was one of those who carried the mail by horseback and webs before the road was used all winter. When in Victor he would stay over at the home of John Eynon. Everybody always figured this practice resulted from his attraction to Effie, one of John's daughters. While Ed was courting Effie, he must have been the most enthusiastic mail carrier in the West. They were married in 1893, and rode over the hill with another newlywed couple, Robert and Grace Miller. Ed had homesteaded on the east bank of the Snake River (where the highway now crosses at the Wilson bridge). There he started a ferry. Ed was soon running the afore-mentioned sawmill for Steve Leek. He helped Steve move it to the foot of Teton Pass, about a half mile above the roadhouse, where he continued to operate it. Ed went on to purchase and operate other mills for himself, both in Jackson Hole and Teton Basin.

While Harry Scott held the mail contract from Victor to Jackson (from approximately 1919 through the 1920s), there was a roadhouse on the top of the pass. The Scotts leased it from the Forest Service. Harry drove the mail and also had a passenger service in summer. His wife Blanche, or daughter Evalyn, drove a nine-passenger car. The pass road was still narrow and rough and surely no drive for an amateur.

In 1923, the Bureau of Public Roads assumed responsibility for the pass. State highway funds were allocated to widen and gravel Teton Pass. The grade that the Forest Service had surveyed in 1913 was not changed. The old switch-backs on the east, and the white dugway figure eight on the west were used until the modernizing job started by the state highway department in 1961.

Now a wide, sweeping oiled highway crosses Teton Pass. It is an easier grade with very few curves. The Mount Glory slide still proves to be a problem. It runs nearly every year. Efforts by the highway department to build a bridge over the slide area proved impractical when a slide swept the bridge away. Even though the pass road is now a pleasure to drive, traffic thereon can still be tied up by snowslides in the wintertime.

BOB PRICE: JNDEPENDENT THINKER

A CERTAIN INDEPENDENCE OF THOUGHT and action was characteristic of all men in the early days of the west. It is a disappearing quality as people live closer together and become interdependent for livelihood and decisions. Occasionally, we still find a person who does his own thinking. Just such a one is Bob Price, lifetime resident of Jackson's Hole when I interviewed him in 1972.

A sample of his thinking:

Question: "How do you feel about the Grand Teton Park taking over the valley?"

Answer: "I think it was a good thing to preserve the west side in a natural state for a scenic park, but they didn't need the east side."

"And the timber?"

"I said a long time ago that Smokey Bear would cost them their forest by stopping forest fires. They just can't seem to accept a death loss. Trees as well as animals. If fire doesn't clean 'em up once in awhile, the bugs get in. It is hard to start a fire in a good healthy stand of timber, but it could go like mad in this bug-killed stuff. It just makes you sick to ride around the west and look at all that sick timber."

Bob was born in Jackson's Hole about 1902. When I asked how the present compares to the old days, he said, "The Tetons and Snake River are still there. They're about the only thing that's the same.... Come to think about it, Snake River is not the same. That dike they've put along both sides—the silliest thing I ever heard of, keeping a river from making its own course; it's agin nature."

"How does the fishing and hunting compare with when you were a boy?" I asked.

"In the real early days, the Territory first imposed a limit. That was when my grandparents had been here awhile. I think the limit was six elk per person. When the state was organized and they got some game laws, they put on a limit of one elk per person, and you had to use the carcass, not just the hide or teeth.

"The fishing was good all over then. We caught lots of fish in Flat Creek, but even in those days they tasted muddy if they were caught out there in the flat. There was whitefish in Flat Creek then, but not in the other streams. I don't know when they got scattered around in all the streams in the country.

"The size of the fish? Oh, they'd most of them weigh five or six pounds. You'd straddle 'em to get the hook out, and they could just about drag you back in the water!

"Yeah..." Bob sighed and checked the tamp in his pipe bowl. "That dike sure ruined the fishing along the Snake River. It used to meander back and forth and have a pool at every turn. Now it's just a mill stream. But," cynicism colored his voice, "look at all that land they saved!"

Bob was raised in the area called Zenith. Zenith is a place name that is no longer in use. It referred to that area north of the confluence of the Gros Ventre River and the Snake, northward along the riverbottom lands of the Snake River almost to Moose. The grade school and post office were in the vicinity of the present-day golf club's main buildings. The post office was in the Price's home. Mail came from Jackson twice a week, Wednesdays and Saturdays. It was carried by Boyd Wilson on horseback or driving a sleigh or wagon.

The Price children went to the Zenith grade school. The largest enrollment that Bob remembers in the Zenith school was thirty-seven. It was a lonesome country, back when Bob was growing up. The deep snow and unplowed roads made travel difficult. Visiting was kept to a minimum.

The long winter season was broken by an occasional party at the school or a visit to a neighboring ranch. The boys got together to ski cross-country. They made sails out of pieces of canvas nailed to a frame, and this gave them a good ride downwind. But it was pretty tough to carry the sail back.

One July 4th, the Prices decided to celebrate with a camping trip to Jenny Lake. They hooked up the team and wagon, drove to the lake, camped overnight and came back late the next day. Aside from Bill Menor at the ferry, they didn't see another soul on the two-day trip.

Mention of the Menor's Ferry brought forth a story from Bob's memory....

"Once when Grandpa 'Slough Grass' Nelson was working for Bill Menor on the ferry, a big log floated down and swiped the ferryboat, breaking the cable. The ferry was carrying passengers, as well as Bill and Nelson, when it came loose from the cable and went floating down the river.

"Bill Menor commenced yelling and ran the length of the platform, jumped as far as he could toward the shore, thrashing and struggling in the water, 'Come and get me! Come and get me! I can't swim!' he yelled."

Bob chortled quietly around his pipe and took a short drag as he contemplated Bill's plight. "One of the passengers jumped in and pulled him to shore...."

"Bill and his brother Holiday didn't get along very good, did they?" I asked.

"They got along pretty good," Bob drawled, "with the river between them. You knew Holiday had a lime kiln on the east side, and Bill ran the ferry from the other? Long as they didn't have to keep house together, they got along okay."

The long lonesome winters up country were conducive to a lot of reading. Bob ignored the high school, which was down at Jackson, but he signed up for a correspondence course in electronic engineering. As early as 1918-19 he had constructed crystal sets and may have had the first radio reception in the valley.

By 1926-28 he had constructed a broadcasting set and, for those hep enough to have a radio, Bob broadcast news, commentary and some phonograph music right into their homes. In 1930, Bob was required to get a ham license, have a shortwave number, or else quit broadcasting.

When the town advanced to the civilized state provided by Benson's power plant, Bob conducted a radio and appliance repair business. From 1952 until it was replaced by Lower Valley Power and Light, he operated the generator which Benson had installed up Flat Creek.

This do-it-yourself attitude of Bob's recalls a story told around the country years ago about his grandfather....

It seems that Mr. Price had a good hay crop one year and put up much more hay than he needed. One of the neighbors was not so fortunate and had more cattle than he had hay for. He approached Price with an offer to buy hay.

"No," said Mr. Price, "I haven't got any hay to sell."

The neighbor raised the price he was willing to pay.

"No," came the short reply. "I haven't got any hay I want to sell."

Knowing darn well that Price didn't need all the hay he had, the neighbor nevertheless had to go further afield to buy hay, with a longer hauling problem.

A neighbor who had heard the whole transaction asked Bob's grandfather, "Why didn't ya sell him some hay? You got plenty."

"If he needs that much hay," said Mr. Price, "let him raise that much hay."

$\mathcal{D}$ISAPPEARANCE OF $\mathcal{J}$UDGE $\mathcal{W}$HITE

W HEN JACKSON'S HOLE WAS STILL only the northern portion of Uinta County, a justice of the peace for the area was appointed by the name of White. After his appointment, everyone called him "Judge" White. So now, even those who knew him well cannot remember his first name.

Judge White built a cabin at the mouth of Cache Creek canyon but never homesteaded the land. He lived in a one room cabin with only his dog for a companion. He took most of his meals at the Jackson Hotel, owned at the time by Pete Nelson and his family.

Pearl Nelson Deyo and Almer Nelson remember Judge White as a steady and respectable fellow, fortyish, a carpenter by trade. He had, in fact, helped Pete build the first home the Nelsons had in Jackson (many years later called the Charlie Wilson home, or the Gib Scott place).

He helped build the Jackson Hotel and many other of the town's first buildings. He had to be a well-known and steady type to have been appointed justice of the peace.

After hunting season one year, Judge White didn't show up at the hotel for meals for several days, but no one noticed or commented until his dog came to the hotel, looking lean and lonesome. Pete took the dog back to the cabin and found Judge White was gone. Only a few carpenter tools, a few clothes and his sparse furniture remained in the cabin.

Pete asked everyone who came to the hotel if they knew the Judge's whereabouts. Finally, someone from Wilson told that White had been over there awhile back wanting to get a horse, by loan or rent, to go down the trail through Snake River Canyon to Star Valley.

Someone else told that Rastus Brown had borrowed a horse from his brother, Harold Brown, and escorted White down Snake River Canyon. The three Brown brothers had homesteaded just below Wilson on land that is now the Crescent H Ranch. (Some of the Rass Brown buildings are still standing on the ranch.)

These bits of gossip satisfied Pete. He took care of the dog and supposed that Judge White would come back when his business "outside" was finished.

But questions niggled at the back of folks' minds. Why would he leave the dog without care? And why hadn't he mentioned his trip at the hotel, the place where he had most of his meals?

Judge White was still "outside" when D. C. Nowlin, State Game Warden and a former Jackson resident, showed up from Cheyenne looking for him. Hunting season was closed and the fees collected for hunting licenses should have been sent in. Judge White was the only one in Jackson's Hole permitted to sell the state hunting licenses.

According to the state bookkeepers, he should have collected $2,700 that season. No one at state headquarters had heard anything from him, in spite of letters demanding explanation. Nowlin had come all this way to force an accounting.

A new interest was taken in the disappearance of Judge White. It looked suspiciously like he had absconded with the license fees, plus whatever he had collected in civil case fines over several months' time.

Rass Brown, the last man to see him, was not available for questioning. He had packed up his wife and kids and moved to somewhere in Montana.

The State Game Department brought action against the bondsmen, so Pete Nelson, Rube Tuttle, and Charles Deloney had to shell out nine hundred dollars apiece of their hard-earned money to cover the license discrepancy. Naturally the trio of bondsmen did what they could to try to find the culprit by notifying sheriffs' offices and so forth.

A report was received that Judge White had been seen in Ely, Nevada. Pete Nelson shaved off his mustache, as a token disguise, and traveled to Nevada to investigate. The suspect was not Judge White.

Months went by, then someone found a bare human skull along the trail which led down the west side of Snake River Canyon. The skull had a bullet hole in it and the bullet was still inside. There was not a shred of other remains where the skull was found.

The sheriff and his deputies searched the west side of the river from Wilson to Alpine. Other non-deputized individuals also searched over a long period of time. No further body remains, clothing or money were ever found, but the skull was generally believed to be Judge White's. The circumstantial evidence now seemed to point to murder instead of grand larceny. How to prove the skull was Judge White's was a problem.

The dentist who took care of White's teeth was located and the evidence was presented for his study. He decided that the teeth were, in fact, those he had worked on for Judge White.

So why wasn't the last person to see Judge White alive brought in for questioning? Could the law not locate him? Or didn't they try? Was the evidence too circumstantial?

The fact is that Rass Brown was never brought to trial. He died of natural causes in California in 1933.

So the mystery remains just that.

Questions still niggle at the back of old-timers' minds. Is the skull really that of Judge White? Was he trying to make off with the money, and did he get "done in" by a greater rascal? Was it Rass Brown or another? Was Rass Brown's coming back honestly and returning the borrowed horse, then moving innocently out of the valley just a natural train of events? Or did the Judge get away with the money? If that's the case, then who got killed?

The object of speculation, the skull, which reposed on a shelf at Roy VanVleck's Mercantile for years and years, is now a part of the collection of the Jackson Hole Museum and Historical Center. The bullet still rattles around inside.

$\mathscr{F}$ROM $\mathcal{N}$OTHING $\mathcal{T}$O $\mathcal{N}$OW

PEARL NELSON DEYO MOVED TO the Jackson valley in 1902. It was early in 1972 that I caught her when she had time to visit with me about her early memories of Jackson's Hole. Her recollections multiplied as we compared early experiences; one memory sparked others. Her brother Almer joined us and added a few of his recollections. Their combined knowledge contributes to a fuller account of the early history of Jackson's Hole.

"There was nothing here then." Pearl, like many old timers, her brother included, is an enthusiastic raconteur. "Nothing! No electricity, no running water, no indoor toilets, no telephone, no sidewalks, no streets, just roads that went just about where they wanted to. We didn't even have a road to come over the hill [Teton Pass]. We had to ride in on horseback over a trail that had just been broke out through the snow the day or so before. The snow came clear up to the saddle skirts. We girls had never ridden before but we soon learned.

"There was nothing much here when we got here, but oh, we had fun. I'd like to live that time over again. We came from Menominee, Michigan. All of us kids were born there, or across the state line in Marinette, Wisconsin, where my dad had relatives. Dad and Mother [Pete and Katrina Nelson] met there in Wisconsin.

"I'll have to tell you a little story about Mother. She was engaged to another man back in Denmark. They decided that he would go to the United States and work until he had enough money to send for her. He did his part, but when she got over here, she decided she didn't love him that much after all. She wouldn't marry him, but she insisted upon working to pay him back for her ticket. The place where she went to work as a hired girl was for my father's family. That was how they met.

175

"We lived in a big house on Pembine farm, on the Menominee River in Michigan. It must have had a dozen rooms. Dad cleared and farmed 320 acres but it didn't belong to him. He got to live there and farm it just for the taxes and clearing it and keeping it in good shape. He logged in the winter. Everyone there logged in the winter.

"There was lots of deer and smaller game around our place. Dad was a great one to hunt, and many businessmen from the cities came there to hunt with him. William Mosser, a Pennsylvania man, was especially fond of Dad. He paid Dad's expenses to come out to Jackson's Hole with him to hunt elk one fall.

"That's how Dad came to fall in love with this country. They stayed with Frank Peterson and hunted with him.

"Mr. Mosser bought four head of horses out west and had Frank bring them back to Pennsylvania. Frank stopped at our place on that trip, so we knew him, too, before we started west. Dad couldn't rest until he arranged his business so he could move us to Jackson's Hole.

"We started out on the train, of course. There was Dad and Mother and five of us children. I'm the oldest—I was fourteen, then Emily, Asker, Aktor and Almer. Almer was only six.

"We arrived in St. Anthony, which was as far as the railroad came. Frank Peterson was supposed to meet us there, but we learned that the Teton Pass was still snowed up. No one had been 'out' yet, so we settled down in the St. Anthony Hotel for awhile. From a porch of the hotel Dad watched some workers digging a basement with teams and slip scrapers. Dad said, 'If that man with the gray team will sell, I'm going to buy them.' Pretty soon he came back and reported he had bought them. When he had found a wagon and the rest of an outfit, he loaded us and our stuff and we started across the rolling hills toward Victor, Idaho.

"It took us two days to get to Victor. We couldn't cross Canyon Creek where the highway is now. It was too steep and rugged. No bridges, no anything. We had to go way downstream to get across. But, we had a good time along the way, and Dad liked his team.

"When we got to Victor we still had to wait. Irma Jones' father had the Hotel there then. We stayed several days with him, then we came up the canyon about five miles and camped on Trail Creek.

That was fun too. Finally Frank Peterson broke a trail out over Teton Pass and came to meet us.

"We all got on the saddle horses, put our things on the pack horses and started over the mountain. Dad left the wagon in Victor and went back after it later in the summer. Mother and we girls hadn't ridden much, but we *couldn't* have walked. The snow was up to the saddle skirts, and, even though they had wallowed out the trail the day before, it was hard on the horses.

"We had a meal at the Bircher roadhouse on the west side of the mountain. Some people named Lockwood had the roadhouse at the foot of the hill on the east side. We stayed at the Lockwoods another week while Dad went with Frank Peterson to try to find someplace for us to live. There was just nothing for anyone to live in in those days. Frank and another bachelor were living up on Flat Creek and the Miners and Coffins had moved in with them until they could get something built to live in.

"Finally they squeezed over so we could cook and eat in with them for two nights. We pitched a tent on Flat Creek and lived and camped in that most of the summer. From there we moved into a one-room cabin north of the springs at Botcher Hill," near where the fish hatchery now stands. "I don't know who it belonged to, but a man named Jack Gray and his wife had been living there. They went back to Colorado and we moved in. I shouldn't be admitting this, but the first night we just couldn't sleep—bed bugs! Ohh! my dad was allergic to bed bugs. If there was one around anywhere it would find him.

"Next morning he moved everything out and we scrubbed while he went to get some lime. He whitewashed every bit of the inside—every crack and cranny. It sure worked, because we never saw another one.

"Dad and mother fixed up that one room cabin until it was pretty cute. They hung a flowered curtain across the middle to make two rooms, a living room-kitchen on one side and bedroom on the other. We lived there until late fall, because I remember our first school was near the north end of what is now called Miller Butte. The Goe boys were in school then, I don't remember the others. We walked across the creek flats. A long walk I can tell you.

"Mr. Mosser and my Dad and another man named Trexlor had been busy buying some land near Jackson to start a ranch. They bought the land from Stephen Adams, now called the Poodle Ranch, and from Webb La Plant" [the big field which stretches from The Virginian to the Kmart shopping mall]. "That place had a big house, and we were sure relieved to move in there. Mr. and Mrs. Charlie Wort were our first visitors. My goodness, I thought Mrs. Wort was the most beautiful woman I ever saw. They had John with them, and he was just a baby.

"Dad, Mosser and Trexlor bought some cattle at Cora, so Dad took Guy Germain with him to ride down there to drive them home. Emily and I didn't think about the long hard drive Dad had. We were just worried that he wouldn't get back in time to take us to the Fourth of July dance. I suppose we were too young to have dates. He made it, and we got to go to the dance.

"I don't remember the cattle or the men working them, but I can see the brand they put on them as plain as can be. It was the JPN, my dad's brand.

"While we lived on that ranch, I used to ride over to the Snake River and fish from horseback. We always caught a nice mess of fish, two and three pounders.

"Mrs. Mosser used to come out and stay at the ranch. She was just as nice as she could be. She would come out even if Mr. Mosser didn't, bringing her maid with her. They would go on pack trips.

"I helped in the hay field one year. It was *so* hot. I was running a hay rake and I almost got a heat stroke. That put an end to my working in the fields.

"The boys used to fish in Flat Creek, near the house. They would use a line with three hooks attached. They never thought of pulling the line in until they felt three strikes and knew they had three fish on the line. They were big ones too.

"We lived there three years or so. I know that my dad bought the Jackson Hotel from John Anderson sometime about 1905. He didn't like the cattle business too well, so Nelson, Mosser and Trexler dissolved their partnership on good terms. They still came out to go hunting with Dad, and we kept our horses down at the ranch. Mr. Mosser was on his way out west to go hunting with Dad when he

When Sarah McCain got the post office, she moved it to her house on the south side of the square. (JHM&HC)

died. We felt bad about that, he was still quite a young man.

"Those years at the hotel were the fun time. I wish I could live them over. Everyone was so happy and friendly, young and old were all the same—happy-go-lucky.

"If there was a celebration of any kind, folks would come from up the Gros Ventre, the Buffalo Rivers, and Moran and just stay in town two or three days. I don't know how we fed them all, or put them up. I remember the first Fourth of July we had at the hotel. We rented out all our own rooms, and we slept on the floor in the kitchen and shed.

"Many people were musical. Mrs. Jack Shives would play at the dances, also the Miners, Peck and his father and sister, and Mrs. Cunningham played the violin. Lee Lucas, his brother Woods and his sister, Mrs. Seelamire, would play at the dances. We even had a little orchestra our family played in. Asker and I, and Dick Myers, Peck Miner, Lucy Miner and Emily Coffin. Aktor and Almer took turns playing triangle. We played at dances all one winter.

"The dances were held in the Clubhouse, but sometimes the guests here at the hotel would get together for a good time, and we would just shove the tables together in the dining room. The orchestra would get on top of the tables to play, and we could use the rest of the floor to dance on. There was no drinking, everybody just liked to have a good time.

"We acquired the Post Office along with the hotel, but Dad soon got rid of that. It was in a lean-to built onto the hotel, and boy! was it ever cold in the winter! The stamp pad was frozen every morning, and we had to take it to the kitchen and thaw it out before we could stamp the letters. I always helped with that job.

"Sarah McCain got the Post Office from us and moved it to her house on the south side of the square. I think Mr. and Mrs. Baxter had it next. Ethal Baxter was a lot of fun. I've got a picture of her and me, you'll never guess who it is. I worked for Baxters in the Post Office later, during the First World War.

"We went to school in the little brick building on the south corner of our street. I don't know what was in it first, but it served a lot of uses—a dentist's office, a lunch room—before it became the first Jackson State Bank."

Here Almer Nelson joined the conversation to describe two early businessmen. Parker and Mullen had a plaster, lime and brick kiln out west of town at Antelope Pass. They built a good many brick buildings in town, including the brick facing of the Jackson Hotel which no longer stands. They built the brick building on the corner (later to become the first bank), the Charles Deloney home, and the Mormon Church, all buildings which are gone now. They also built the Deloney store, a parking lot and the first brick schoolhouse, which burned in 1915 and stood at Broadway and Jackson Street.

It seemed the town was going to be mostly brick, but when they finished all of their current jobs and went away, the brick business languished. Billie Cowan later had a kiln east of town, up the draw which is north of Government Ranch Springs. However, building with brick was replaced with log construction and now very few of the brick buildings have survived the expansion changes.

I happened to hit Almer in a good mood to reminisce, and he continued to relive the past—

"My father bought those lots the hotel was on for fifteen dollars per lot. Trouble was there wasn't any money. I suppose you could have bought all the lots around the square for a hundred dollars, but nobody had the hundred dollars. If you borrowed money it

❧ *This timbering cart is thought to have been built by Johnny Carnes and is shown in Roy VanVleck's yard.* (JHM&HC)

cost you twelve percent interest. That put a lot of the early old timers out of business.

"For the most part people got along on what they had or could make for themselves. Some of them got started on very little, the way the VanVleck brothers did. Roy and Frank VanVleck came out to Encampment, Wyoming, from Michigan. They tried to get a start there, but wound up with nothing but a crop of potatoes. They loaded up a ton of potatoes on their wagon and brought them to Jackson's Hole in 1906. They rented a part of the downstairs of the Clubhouse and set up business with a ton of potatoes. That was how they got their start. Before long they were selling all kinds of general mercantile goods and built a store of their own next to the Clubhouse. They lived in the back of the store, but took their meals at the hotel. That's how Pearl met Frank. It turned out she married him later."

"Yes, but that was after we sold the Hotel, you're getting ahead of the story," Pearl admonished.

I asked, "Was the drugstore in the Clubhouse then?"

"I don't remember if it was there then, or later," Pearl replied. "Doc Steel had a drugstore on Glenwood Street. It looked like that was going to be the main street of Jackson. Pap Deloney's store was there, and Doc Steel's drugstore and the Episcopal Church faced west on that street. A Miss Moon and a Mr. Robinson had a drugstore in the Clubhouse before Jimmy Simpson got it.

"Oh, the exciting thing that happened while we had the hotel was Fred Lovejoy's telephone line. Mose Giltner must have been the first hook-up, because I remember a group of us in Fred's office taking turns talking to Mose to try out the new line. That was in 1907 or 08.

"Rodebeck started the newspaper, the *Jackson's Hole Courier,* in 1909. His building was along Cache Street," now part of St. John's Episcopal Church property. "The first store in the town was in the Simpson building, which stood where the Anvil Motel now stands. There was a saloon along there, too, owned by Walt Spicer and T. Lloyd. But that may have been a little later."

When I asked if there was another hotel in town, one at Crabtree Corner, Pearl answered, "I don't think so. Dr. Palmer and his wife lived there, they may have rented rooms. Ma Reed had a hotel there before the Crabtrees came along." Doctor Palmer ran what he called "an insanitorium." He may have had boarders or other guests.

Almer said, "It was while we were in the hotel that you won that beauty contest. Tell them about that."

"Oh, that," Pearl scoffed. "That wasn't a beauty contest. It was just something the *Cheyenne Tribune* was promoting, to build up their circulation. I won this contest and was named Most Popular Girl in Uinta County. It wasn't anything, but they had my name and picture and a big write-up in the *Cheyenne Tribune.* I received a lovely solid gold watch for a prize."

That reminded Pearl of another bit of Jackson history shared by old timers. "I've lived in three counties and never moved from Jackson Hole. Uinta, and then Lincoln, and now Teton.

"Anyway," Pearl continued. "In the winter of 1908-09, Pierce Cunningham and Pete Nelson made a business swap. We moved to the Cunningham place on Spread Creek in the spring of 1909. The Cunninghams became the owners of the Jackson Hotel."

With not so much need of the girls' help, father Nelson reminded Pearl that she was twenty-one now and probably ought to get a job.

"I got a job all right," Pearl said. "I got married. Frank Van-Vleck and I were married at the Cunningham place in October of that year. At first we lived in part of the house Dr. and Mrs. Palmer had in town (Crabtree Hotel). Then Frank and Roy dissolved their partnership. Roy took the store and Frank took the V Bar V Ranch

❧ *Pat Reed built the Reed Hotel which included a widow's walk. When Dr. Palmer owned it, he called it the "insanitorium."* (JHM&HC)

which they had bought in the Hoback Basin, and we moved down there. Our son, Clinton, was born in Jackson in 1910.

"Emily [Pearl's sister] met Billie Thompson at the Cunningham place, too. Maybe she knew him before, but he was a neighbor there. He was the son of Mrs. J.H. Uhl who lived up Spread Creek, a little way from us. They got married but I don't remember the date. They named their only daughter after me, we called her 'Little Pearl'" [the late Pearl Johnson].

One odd incident happened to Pearl's younger brothers, Aktor and Almer, at the Cunningham place. They were out playing along the road that ran past the place. They had been told that the road went right over the graves of the two horse thieves who had been killed nearby, so they were not too surprised to see a human skull lying out in the road.

It was evident that a badger had been digging. The hole he had dug and the pile of dirt were right there. "What'll we do?" was the first reaction. They talked it over and decided they didn't need any help. They just dug the hole a little bigger, stuffed the skull back in and filled the hole in. They stamped in the dirt and went on down the road, their good deed done for the day.

Asker was stricken with diabetes, and insulin treatment had not yet been developed. Two or three trips to hospitals in Salt Lake City did no good. The only treatment known was the withdrawal of sugar. He was a bright and winning boy, whom everyone loved. The Nelson family lost their first son at the age of seventeen.

Pete took the mail contract to haul the mail from Kelly to Moran. While he had this contract, Aktor, who was only sixteen, did much of the driving. He never forgot the winter day he had a breakdown and had to walk sixteen miles to the ranch, carrying the first class mail, which he was afraid to leave with the sleigh.

Aktor and Vivian Smith had met when they were school kids. The Nelsons still lived in the hotel when Vivian's folks came to the country. Vivian and her sister Maude were sent to town to live with Mrs. Josh Adams in the little brick building on the corner. (It was evidently not the year it was used as a school.)

Aktor and Vivian started going together when they were both grown and Aktor worked near the Smith ranch at Blacktail Butte. They were married in 1922, and spent their first years together at the Ferry ranch, owned by Mrs. Noble, at Moose. Their daughter Echo [now Echo Taylor] was born in Jackson in 1927.

Almer met his future bride, Loleta Thomas, when she helped Aktor care for the family during the flu epidemic following the First World War. Aktor and Loleta seemed to be immune themselves, as they cared for one after another of the stricken families. Loleta had come into the valley to teach.

After their marriage, Almer was appointed supervisor of what the natives have always called "The Government Ranch." He held this post until retirement in 1956. They had one daughter, Alma Ruth, born in 1926.

Pierce Cunningham bought the Cunningham place back from the Nelsons after a few years. Pete then filed on some opened Forest Service land nearby for another ranch, which he called The Moosehead Ranch. Pete built cabins on this place and continued to take hunters out in the fall.

The Nelsons lived on this place until 1929, when they sold to the Snake River Land Company and the ranch is now part of Grand Teton National Park. They acquired still another Forest Service acreage across the road. There they built another home where they lived until Pete's death. Mrs. Nelson then moved into a small home next door to Pearl on Cache Avenue. In this home, Katrina enjoyed the calm years of retirement near her children and grandchildren.

Pearl and Frank VanVleck had separated and Pearl married Fred Deyo. To this marriage were born Erma, John, Clifford and Tommy.

Fred and Pearl both enjoyed a great love of life and fun. A book would be required to count off some of Fred's pranks which have become legend. Just one short story about him is included here.

During the Second World War, Fred was game warden over Teton County. Hunting season opened in the fall as usual, even though all goods were rationed. Fellows from all over the state saved their precious gas coupons and bullet rations to come hunting in Jackson Hole.

In a rough bit of country along the Antelope Flat road, Fred planted a mounted, whole elk. He stood it upright, fastened to a sturdy post, with a big, round timber saw wired behind it.

The elk was visible from the road, but if a hunter took time enough to get far enough off the road to be legal to shoot it, he could see there was something wrong. (You *know* not many would take that much time!)

A hunter (or a whole carload of hunters) would come cruising along, spy the elk at the edge of the timber, throw on the brakes, back up to get a good clear line, jump out of the car with gun in hand and start blazing away.

Pretty soon, when the elk wouldn't fall, the hunter would slow up a bit. When he fired slowly enough to hear the Pin-n-ng! Pin-n-ng! after every shot, he definitely got suspicious. When his precious ammunition was gone and the elk still stood, he'd finally go over and take a look. Whether that stand-in elk soon became too tattered to stand up and pass as the real thing, no one knows. However, no hunter was ever mad enough to tear the mounted elk down.

"Let the next S.O.B. waste his ammunition, too!"

EARLY FAMILIES CONTRIBUTE TO "EMPIRE"

JACK EYNON BROUGHT HIS FAMILY into Jackson's Hole in 1905. He had purchased the Blodget place in Spring Gulch—now a part of the Hansen ranches. This was their first home in Jackson's Hole.

Before coming into Jackson's Hole, Jack had already pioneered in Teton Basin, being among the first settlers of Victor. With eight other men, their families and goods, the Jack Eynons arrived in what was then called Pierre's Hole on April 22, 1889.

Six of the families established homes there. They were the Jack Lewises and the Rufus Eynons; Jack Eynon and his brother-in-law, Lysander Curtis; Ed Rico and David R. Sinclair. Since the land was unsurveyed, the families established squatter's rights upon adjoining claims.

They built homes along the north side of their properties in order to have near neighbors and proceeded with improvements. Later, when the land was surveyed they filed and proved up on their claims on the same day.

One of the first things the homesteaders did was to scout the streams south of their places for an irrigation water supply. Up Warm Creek they found the skeletal hand of a man caught in a bear trap. This so unnerved some of the party that the scouting was ended for the day. They named the creek Skull Creek.

At first the settlers called their community Alpine. In 1892, they changed the name to Raymond. On September 9, 1900, it was again changed—this time to Victor to honor Claude Victor, a man "who showed great courage by carrying the mail to Jackson during the Indian scare."

Other families moved to the community bringing brothers Arthur and T. W. Porter, who started a store. The original group of

186

homesteaders purchased this store and organized the Victor Mercantile Company. Jack became the storekeeper for the company.

By this time Jack's family consisted of his wife Lois Ann Curtis Eynon, sons Lester, Horace and Curtis, and daughters Irene, Laverna and Edith. In April 1904, Lois Ann passed away, leaving Jack with very small children. Life in the home in Victor suddenly seemed intolerable to Jack. He sold his interests there and came to Jackson for a new start at the Blodget place. He married a young lady, Mary Turner of Morgan, Utah, a sister of the late, longtime Jackson resident John Turner of Turpin Meadows and Jackson.

Mary was affectionately received by Jack's children and was always called "Aunt Mary" by them and close family friends. The first two winters the Eynons had to leave the ranch so that the children could attend school at St. Anthony. After that there were schools at Jackson, eight miles from their home, or Zenith, about three miles away.

Jackson's Hole was first a part of Uinta County, then county boundaries were reorganized and the valley was a part of Lincoln County from 1911 to 1920. In 1921, Teton County was formed, encompassing Jackson Hole. Jack Enyon served in the state legislature representing Uinta County in 1911 and representing Lincoln County in 1913.

The Eynons moved from the Spring Gulch ranch to one in South Park, then purchased and operated the Jackson Hotel for a few years. Mary and Jack had one boy and four girls to add to the first family. The boy, Joe, died in 1913. The girls were Leona, Maxine, Joella, and Gertrude.

The older children were at the center of community activities, especially the fun things. When Jack combined money and talents with Roy VanVleck, Pierce Cunningham and T. Lloyd to create the Jackson Hole Frontier Days Company, Lester, Horace, Curt, and even Verna were right in there participating. Irene says she was right in there helping, too, but she wasn't allowed to play cowboy.

Jack had acquired a big army tent which was set up in the Pete Karns place, and there the crowds were served sandwiches and cold drinks. Irene's most vivid memory is of making forty or fifty loaves of bread a day.

The Eynons continued to play a vital role in the development of Jackson's Hole. Jack and Mary ranched at Elk just before selling out to retire in 1931, when they moved to Idaho Falls. The boys have been active in almost every major project of the valley's growth. They worked on the Moran dam, carried the mail on various routes, freighted, operated hunting camps and ranches.

Besides the Eynon name of the descendants, there are the girls' married names; the Hodges, Stilsons, Taylors and Birchers. These are family names which have been on the rolls of "those present" since the land was opened up to settling. Families like these were the Jackson's Hole contribution to "Empire Building."

"What's the Difference? It All Has to Be Plowed."

To get to be a "character," one only has to be consistently different from the ordinary run-of-the-mill human. The *difference* can take many forms: genius, prankster, loner, liar, misogynist, prophet or bum. Or just...*different*. The moniker eventually comes to be used on the human who consistently takes the independent, non-conforming course in life.

In the early days, Jackson's Hole attracted many settlers who qualified for the title "character." A person had to be an independent type to live in this isolated, rugged, economically stringent part of the world. Settlers to the valley cherished all their "characters." Indeed, with only occasional mail and newspapers from the "outside," it was the Jackson's Hole "characters" who provided a good portion of the entertainment and neighborly exchange in the valley.

One young man who started life as a strict conformist, then lived out his long life as one of Jackson's most popular "characters," was John L. Dodge.

John was born into one of America's notable families at Council Bluffs, Iowa, on December 12, 1867. His father, Nathan P. Dodge, was a pioneer realtor and his uncle was General Grenville M. Dodge, of Union Pacific Railway fame. John himself was filled with his family's urge toward achievement; this urge which leads us to outdo our fellow man.

As a law student at Harvard, he was outstanding both scholastically and in athletics. He served with Teddy Roosevelt's Rough Riders in the Spanish American War. He was well on his way to fulfilling his potential and becoming a Very Important Person when he suffered a nervous breakdown—possibly incurred by his pursuit of excellence.

189

While convalescing, he was sent on a tour of the west to regain strength of body and peace of mind. When he discovered Jackson's Hole, he decided to remain here.

John homesteaded the ranch he named "The Wilderness Ranch" in 1905. This is a beautiful spot, with a large flowing spring, located on the west side of Snake River, about five miles above the Wilson bridge. Since he received a regular check from his family—a remittance man, that alone being enough to set him apart from the other settlers—he was able to hire help whenever he needed it.

He built the usual two-room log cabin, with a dog-trot between that and a storage room. The whole was roofed with poles and sod. A large, cobblestone, mud-chinked fireplace filled one side of the larger room. It was a comfortable homestead cabin by local standards.

Gradually it became apparent, first to his neighbors and then to the rest of the valley, that John never did anything the urgent, hard way. Even so, he was not lazy. He kept things up. But if there was an easy way to keep things going, John found it.

While most men spent a great deal of their time sawing and splitting wood for the house, John dragged a length of log through the cabin to the fireplace, poked in the one end and let it burn. As the end charred away he advanced the log until he had used it up. Sometimes the log extended into the kitchen, and occasionally he even had to leave the outside door open a bit until the log got shorter.

He set the house afire once or twice but always managed to put out the blaze without burning down the place.

His housekeeping was indifferent, but he always had a good supply of books and newspapers—usually scattered all over the floor where he dropped them as he finished reading. He was better informed about world events than any of his neighbors and always was delighted to converse with anyone about anything. He knew so much, but his neighbors worried because the man was just not practical, a prime and necessary virtue in a homesteader. Take his plowing as an example....

A neighbor rode by one day and saw John out in the field, riding his plow, the lines looped over his arm while both hands held up a newspaper he was reading. The team meandered around the field wherever they felt like going. The neighbor couldn't stand it. He stopped by the fence, and when the team brought the plow and John near, he called out a greeting. John glanced over the top of his newspaper and pulled up nearby, happy to pause for a neighborly visit.

After some small talk about the weather, John's neighbor noted, "I see you're getting your field ready to plant?"

"Yeah," John agreed. "I might get some grass seed in this year. It's been in oats long enough. Say," John said pointing to the news column he'd been studying, "I see the stock market is hitting lows on everything. Factories are closing. There's a real panic back east."

"What kind of grass seed you puttin' in?" Immediate, hardscrabble existence in the valley being more important to settlers than nebulous *outside* conditions, the neighbor persisted, intending to be helpful. "I planted bluegrass and redtop and some alsike clover. Alsike does real good in this country."

"I dunno. I'll get the seed when I get the plowing done.... I see here in the paper where the Interstate Commerce Commission has been given jurisdiction over the telephone and telegraph companies."

"When Fred Lovejoy gets his telephone line strung up this side of the river, *he* can worry about who has jurisdiction over it," the neighbor said. Clearly, helping John was an exercise in futility. "Why don't *you* keep that near horse in the furrow and make him plow a straight line?"

"What's the difference?" John shrugged. "It all has to be plowed." Tipping his head in farewell, he settled into the plow seat, braced his feet against the plow, and popped the reins to start the team off. He spread the newspaper and began to read.

So the men parted, each still sunk in his own train of thought and major interest. Of course, the neighbor repeated John's remark until it became a Jackson cliché. "What's the difference? It's all got to be plowed."

When John got older he built a house in Wilson, where he lived with several goats, some cats and dogs and a corral for his horses when they weren't pasturing out on the ranch. He had a barn with a long sloping shed roof which the goats used for their own private mountain. They scampered up and down, jumping from the ground to the low eaves, from the roof of the barn to roofs of other sheds. They had a joyful life.

Neighbors shook their heads. Each new story about John circulated around the valley. John and I once shared the outcome of an incident at Jackson's Frontier Days. I was not of an age or disposition to appreciate it at the time.

A Yellowstone Park stagecoach was parked in the lean-to of John's barn. The stage rolled out every Frontier Days. John hooked four head of horses to it and drove to Jackson. If any other teamsters could produce a stagecoach, there would be a stagecoach race at the Frontier Celebration. Dodge usually lost.

He always rode one of the horses in the cow pony free-for-all race, too. And he always wore his tan duster—a type of coat no cowboy was caught dead in at that time—the coat tails flapping out behind him as he came dashing around the track. Always last.

One year when I was very young, barely in my teens, I borrowed my brother-in-law's cow pony to enter this race.

Henry told me, "Old Prince may not come in first, but I'll bet he can't be beat at second." He continued bracingly, "When he sets out after anything he won't let it get away from him."

Well, Old Prince hadn't been used to chase cows, much less race trained horses, for two or three years, so Prince and I came thundering along last. Well, to my mind, just as good as last. John Dodge, his long tan duster coattails flapping in the wind, came loping along behind me. I suffered absolute, total embarrassment.

I was nearly in tears as we pulled up after crossing the finish line. John reined up beside me, grinning and talkative, "That was a fine race! A fine bunch of horses, a lot of fun!"

"*I* don't think it's much fun to come in last!" I huffed. "How can you stand it? Why do you race all the time, when you never win?"

This ungracious thrust was my own reaction to losing. I never meant to be unkind. Fortunately, John didn't take it as an insult, merely a question that needed answering.

"Who cares about winning?" he warbled. "It's fun to get out here and race. It's exhilarating. Somebody has to lose. If I come in last, that just keeps someone else from feeling bad about being last. That makes me feel good."

I wasn't comforted then, but I've often thought of, and admired, his philosophy since. How or when John Dodge got switched off from the human desire to win, I don't know. He lived to the age of ninety, leaving Jackson to return to Council Bluffs only when he was unable to live alone and care for himself. His life here was spent accepting and savoring each day as it came along, with no effort whatever to change the world.

"What's the difference? It's all got to be plowed anyway."

WHEN A WOMAN CHOOSES A HUSBAND

T HE RISING SUN SPOTLIGHTED A TALL, very thin young
woman walking along the frozen and rutted wagon tracks
that hugged the bottom lands of the north end of the East
Gros Ventre Butte. She carried a big fat baby boy just under one
year old. The long skirts and petticoats that swished around her
ankles further impeded her progress, while a steel boned corset kept
needed air from the bottom of tubercular-scarred lungs. Sometimes
the baby rode one hip then was changed to the other, then for a
change and a rest he was carried piggy-back.

If you have built a sympathetic mental picture of a pitiful, over-
burdened young woman, wipe it out. Eva Lucas was a young lady
who loved every beautiful moment, every energetic motion, and
every challenge of the hard life and country she had chosen.

Each Monday morning she readied the baby and herself for the
six-mile walk from the homestead in Spring Gulch, around the end
of the butte, over the Flat Creek flats, to the Curtis home at the
mouth of Curtis Canyon. Here she taught the Curtis, Ferrin, Goe,
and other neighboring children until Friday, when, after dismissing
school, she picked up baby Bob and walked back across the flats,
around the butte to the log cabin, which had so recently become
her home. She had decided she could be well and strong in the west,
and she was a very determined young woman.

As a young teacher in Wichita, Kansas, Eva Phillips had
planned with a group of other young teachers to take a trip through
the exciting wilderness of Yellowstone National Park.

Florence Horton, one of the group, had two brothers homesteading in the nearby Jackson's Hole country. She made arrangements for her brothers to take the party through the Park with buggy

194

and camp outfit. The romantic setting had the effect that Florence had probably anticipated: her brother Lee Lucas and Eva fell in love.

Eva had stayed to teach a session of summer school before returning to Wichita. In December she returned to Jackson to marry Lee. That was in 1905. Now in the late fall of 1907, she was teaching again.

Homesteaders did whatever came handy to make a little cash to tide over the months between scanty crop incomes. As a teacher, Eva had a ready-made job.

Life in the log-cabin homestead was a far cry from the stimulating contacts of the "intelligentsia" teachers and shopkeepers of the growing town of Wichita. Here in Jackson, Eva often walked the three miles south down the Spring Gulch road to the Redmonds, where she browsed in Bill Redmond's ample library and borrowed current periodicals to take home.

Bill's eastern family kept a steady stream of the best in literature coming to this "outlandish" place where Bill had elected to spend his life. Ida Redmond and Eva each bore a son during Eva's second year out west—Ida's third child, the Lucas' first.

Lee and his brother Woods, with their sister Camillia (Mid) Seelamire, often played music at the dances around the valley. Mid also taught at the local school at Zenith and bore a baby girl called Bunny who was near Bob's age.

High spirited and intelligent companionship was not lacking but the distances were far and the work hard and menial. Lee wanted Eva to ride to her teaching job but when the ground was frozen, and Flat Creek had to be crossed on ice, she preferred to trust herself and the baby to her own feet.

Upon arrival at the Curtis home, she turned Bob over to Lucy Curtis in the big warm kitchen. Lucy had already cleared away the breakfast and tidied the house. She was "making over" two little suits of underwear from some of Hyrum's old ones. As Lucy said, "Folks have to make do with what they have." Lucy's cleverness at sewing and cooking and "making do" were a constant source of wonder to Eva.

As baby Bob went into Lucy's arms, he suddenly turned and, with a big smile, held out his arms to Eva to come back. Eva claimed

❧ Children of the valley found fun in "hooky bobbin'" on the milk delivery sleigh operated by Ernest Van Lewen. (JHM&HC)

she was "not the mother type," but at this mark of favor, she suddenly felt constriction in her chest and a rush of blood from her head which almost made her giddy. She knew then that she loved this mite of new humanity more than life itself.

Eva gathered the rowdy boys and the earnest girls of the neighboring families into the living room for classes. She loved them all. No one could stimulate young minds or draw out the plans and dreams of youngsters better, discussing with them ways and means of making dreams come true.

Friday afternoon, with classes dismissed, Eva bundled the baby in his coats, mitts, cap and overshoes and set out across the flats. She noted every color change of the quaking aspen, the tawny crisp-ripened grasses, and the new sprinkling of snow on the peaks.

Eva swung along, full of planning for the two days she would have at home. Two days of cooking and straightening up and washing would get the cabin in shape for another week of absence. Lee was a neat and tidy bachelor in her absence but there was much a man just didn't do.

Soon the school year would close for the worst winter months and she could be home all day. She would have earned enough money for a few luxuries and many necessities, besides paying Lucy Curtis for her board and room and the care of the baby. Thus distributing a little hard cash to the Curtis home also.

At the John Cherry homestead at the north end of the butte, Eva stopped for a rest and a sociable chat. He just yelled "Come in!" without getting up. She found John sitting by the cook stove with his leg propped up on the oven door.

Seeing bandages around John's knee, Eva put Bob down and came to John with some concern.

"Whatever happened to you, John? Are you all right here by yourself? Can you get around to get what you need?"

"I'm all right now," John grumbled through his beard. "It was that colt I'm trying to break to lead. He kicked me on the leg and knocked my knee-cap clean down to my ankle! I thought I'd never git it back up."

"My goodness! What did you ever do, here all by yourself?"

"Well, it hurt like hell, but I jest took aholt of my leg with both hands and kep workin' it around." With his hands hovering a safe distance above the injury, he demonstrated the procedure. "It hurt a-plenty, I can tell you. But I got it back up where it belongs." Sighing mightily, he finished the tale. "I hung onto it while I hobbled into the house, then I wrapped it in these here rags. They've held it up there pretty good every since."

"You had better let me soak it in some hot Epsom salts water. Have you got some?" Eva asked.

"No, that ain't necessary. I rubbed it with some horse liniment. That'll fix it up all right. Don't you worry none."

Eva fixed John a meal before taking the baby up and starting on around the butte. The evening had grown dark and the air crisp. The silhouette of the Tetons reared like a jagged-edged wall in front of her. A coyote howled his evening serenade. As she came in sight of the lights of home, Eva was overwhelmed with a feeling of fulfillment. Surely this was pay enough for any labor—beauty, home, loved ones and a satisfying occupation.

She laughed to herself as she thought how Lee would appreciate the latest John Cherry exaggeration.

A statement Lee often quoted came to her mind, "When a woman chooses a husband, or when a man chooses a homestead, they had better be darned sure it is what they want, because they are going to be giving it their life's work for a long, long time."

Two-Man Land Rush

Jackson's Hole witnessed a land rush back about 1907. While it did not have the scope, the multitudes, nor the national (or local) publicity that occurred at the Oklahoma Panhandle, still it was quite as important to the two fellows who participated.

"Si" (Josiah David) Ferrin came to Jackson's Hole first in 1898. He was the top hand drover for a cattle buyer named John Wilson.

Wilson and his cowboys went into the back country far removed from a railway, then they started back toward a shipping point, buying cattle as they went along. In addition to his own droving business, Wilson also was trusted to collect tithing for the Mormon Church. Ranchers paid in the form of so many head of cattle, which Wilson delivered to market, sending the receipts to church headquarters.

They trailed cattle they bought in Jackson's Hole and held them on Bryant Flat until they had bought all available cattle in the "Hole." Then they trailed up over Willow Creek, up Greys River, through Salt River Pass and down to Cokeville to load and ship.

Si fell in love with the Buffalo Bench area in Jackson's Hole and vowed to come back and homestead a cattle ranch there.

Back home in the Ogden Valley, it took Si two years to get squared away for the move to Jackson's Hole. By that time he had talked about it so eloquently that some fifteen families started the trek to the greener pastures.

April 1900 was a very wet month. In Marsh Valley, Utah, the ground was so soft the men found that the only way they could make progress was to fasten big cottonwood logs under the wagons. When the wheels sank the logs became skids. The teams were doubled up as far as needed to bring a wagon through.

Most of the families decided that the area around St. Anthony and Egin Bench, Idaho, looked good enough and stopped there. Si, his two brothers James and Orson, his wife's brother Joe Heninger, and Ralph Tuttle brought their wagons and families along to Jackson's Hole.

When they arrived in the valley, the homesteaders were greeted with bad news. The Buffalo Bench area (and all unfiled land down to approximately the Gros Ventre) had been withdrawn from homesteading when the Teton National Forest Preserve was created from the southern portions of what had been the Yellowstone National Forest Preserve plus some additional acreage.

Si's brothers could not find a suitable location, so they returned to the Egin Bench-Twin Groves area. The Heningers and Si Ferrins decided to stay.

A movement to have the arable lands of the upper valley released from Forest Service jurisdiction was under way, and it was expected to gain Congressional favor.

Si sent his Wyoming Congressman a letter asking that he be notified the minute the land was open. While waiting, Si rented the Dan Nowlin place east of Jackson. Nowlin moved his family to the Green River valley where he had taken a job as superintendent of the old 67 Ranch, one of the first big ranches of Wyoming. Uncle Joe Heninger freighted the Nowlin possessions up the Gros Ventre and down the Green River to their new location.

The waiting period dragged on several years. While on the Nowlin place, Emma Ferrin, who already had three sturdy young boys, Curtis, Leonard and Ray, gave birth to Glenn and later, Bob. Emma died when Bob was born. Si was left alone with his family and a newborn baby.

Neighbors and relatives helped out. A young girl, Edith McInelly, had been caring for Emma, the house and children. When Emma died, Edith took the baby home to Teton Basin. The other boys were taken to grandparents in Ogden. Soon Edith and Si married, and the family was reunited on the ranch near Jackson.

At this time, Si filed on a desert claim along Flat Creek. Loading a plow on his wagon, he went to the claim to start improvements. Soon he came home. "Hell, I hooked the team on the plow and tried to make a furrow. It was so rocky I couldn't even get the plow into the ground. I just looked around and couldn't see a place that wasn't rocky, so I loaded the plow up and came home." He never proved up on this land.

To make ends meet, homesteaders usually took on additional work when they could get it. In the spring of 1907, Si and Ralph Spencer, a good friend of his, were working for the Game Department. Camped on the shores of String Lake, they had been trying to catch some beaver trappers who were "working" the area illegally.

One evening Oscar Hoagland arrived at the camp with two special delivery letters, one for each of the men. They scanned the return address and stuck them in their pockets, unopened. The long-awaited official notification had finally arrived. The trappers they were stalking were forgotten.

By this time many men were interested in the land to be opened for filing. Both fellows knew what the other had his sights on—the same parcel of land. Many miles to the northeast, not far above the mouth of the Buffalo River, was a nice open spring. Nearby some trapper, or possibly homesteader, had built a cabin. It was abandoned. The spring and adjacent acres were the choice site in the newly opened area.

Next morning the two men were up and had their camp packed on the pack horses bright and early. As they mounted up Ralph said, "Well, which way're you goin'? Down to the ferry or up to Moran?"

"I ain't goin' neither place," Si said. "I'm goin' right straight across."

"You big fool," Ralph snorted. "I hope you drown." They parted ways to start their rides.

There was a toll bridge at Moran, just below the present dam site. It washed out in the spring of 1910, but in 1907 Ralph could cross the bank-full Snake River on this bridge. He made the best speed his horses could sustain. He still had to cross the raging Buffalo above its mouth.

Si headed due east past Burnt Ridge and the Potholes. Finding a ford that was good in late summertime, he urged his horses off into it. The strong muddy current immediately swept the horses off their feet. Si knew they were strong swimmers. Knowing his packhorse would follow along, Si reined his saddle horse only slightly, to keep him headed across. They angled downstream, coming out far below where he had intended, but still on a good graveled bank. Si immediately resumed his grueling pace.

When Ralph came riding up to the spring, Si already had his stakes firmly pounded into the corners of his claim. His camp was set up and Si was getting supper.

"Well, you made it across the river I see. I knew I couldn't beat you if you got through that."

"You might as well get down and eat," Si answered. "After that we can go out and stake you a second-best claim. Tomorrow we'll ride down to Pedigrew's [the land commissioner] and file on 'em 'fore anybody else gets up here."

The Ferrins moved to the Buffalo in 1908. Edith and Si welcomed Merritt, Emily, Harvey, Edith and Ada (twins), Howard, June, Luella, and Tobe (Harold), the second family of babies to come to join the first five boys. The JF ranch came to be known as the Elk Ranch. Si made his dream of a big cattle and hay ranch come true on the Buffalo Bench. It was the dearly loved home of the Ferrin family until its sale to the Snake River Land Company in the 1930s.

Now that the Elk Ranch is a part of the Grand Teton National Park, it still supports herds of cattle in the summertime. These cattle belong to ranchers who had forest grazing permits before the park was created. The permit area included the Potholes, Burnt Ridge, Pilgrim and Arizona Creeks, and all the ridges north of Moran. These permit areas had to be honored by GTNP when it was created.

✳ Roy VanVleck used this photo to lure his bride to Jackson. It is taken looking up Cache Creek in 1907 and shows the Simpson Ranch in the center background as well as the town buildings described by VanVleck. (JHM&HC)

BAIT FOR A BRIDE

Roy VanVleck sent a photograph of Jackson, taken in 1907, to his childhood sweetheart, Genevieve Lawton.

Miss Lawton lived in Lawton, Michigan, and Roy, hoping to marry her and entice her to move to Jackson's Hole, wrote the following on the back of the photo:

"Jackson, Wyo., the center and outfitting point of the famous Jackson's Hole, the greatest big game country in the world. Nearly one hundred miles from the nearest railroad point, it is one of the few typical frontier towns left in the great west.

"The square two-story building standing in the background is the Club House, which we have leased for two years. Our store is on the first floor and we let the hall for dances, lodge meetings, etc.

"The two story brick building is the Jackson Hotel, where we board. Several houses are not shown in the picture.

"The last building to the right is the Mormon Church. They use it for dances and picnics as well as a place of worship.

"Away back, some twelve or fifteen miles, is the Cache Creek Divide. June 1st, 1907, when this picture was taken, the snow was ten to fifteen feet deep up there. The little lumps or knobs all over the ground are bunches of sage brush. The down timber at the right is where we get our wood."

The fact that the town was "one hundred miles from the nearest railroad point" or that on June 1 there was ten to fifteen feet of snow on the ground above town, did not seem to deter Miss Lawton. In 1911 she married Roy, and moved to the frontier town of Jackson with him.

WHERE THERE'S A WILL

MARK ANDERSON VERY NEARLY DID not make it to adulthood. The saga of his escape from early death is one of a stubborn spirit in a strong body—helped in an emergency by loving family and friends.

Mark was just five years old when he and his brother Oliver and sister Myrtle arrived with their parents in Jackson's Hole in 1895. His father, John Anderson, homesteaded at the north end of Spring Gulch (a part of what is now the Hansen ranch, for many years known as the lower Bar BC). Since the nearest school was approximately ten miles away in South Park, Mrs. Anderson had John build a house at Antelope Pass (now called the Y) at the south end of Spring Gulch, shortening the distance to school by several miles.

Antelope Pass is a natural junction, sitting like the hub of a wheel whose spokes reach out to Jackson, South Park, Wilson, and Spring Gulch. Travelers going most anywhere passed by Mary Anderson's door. The house had only two bedrooms plus kitchen and living room, but there were so few accommodations in the valley that Mary was constantly being called upon to put people up. Her home did not start as a hotel, but it soon became one as Mary's entrepreneurial instincts blossomed and she provided travelers with a room and meals.

To help further with family income, she acquired the Post Office commission in 1900 and moved the post office from the Simpson ranch to her Antelope Pass home.

When the town of Jackson was platted and lots became available in 1901, John purchased the lot across from the northwest corner of the square, the southeast corner of Cache and Deloney Streets, and moved the house from Antelope Pass into town. It was jacked onto skids and, dragged by horses, rolled along on log rollers from Antelope Pass into Jackson. Getting it across Flat Creek was the biggest problem.

Situated in the brand new little village, the Anderson home/post office was remodeled into a two-story hotel with a dining room and a lobby which held the post office. The building was faced with brick, then given a veranda, and a sign was hung from the veranda stating Jackson Hotel.

Mark had the usual interesting boyhood pursuits of the country —hunting and fishing with his father, cowboying for his dad and other ranchers, helping to break colts, in addition to lending a hand at the hotel. His first schooling was at South Park ten miles from their ranch. His brother and sister had boarded with the Tom Estes family who lived about half a mile from the school.

A school was finally started in Jackson about 1902. Classes were held in the Clubhouse and in the small brick building near the hotel. A young medical student, a man named Melton, just out of school came to visit the country in the summer of 1903 and stayed to teach the winter of 1903–04.

Mark had become severely ill while with his father at the ranch, and when a little rest in bed only seemed to increase the misery, he was brought to town to his mother's care. The abdominal misery and temperature increased alarmingly, so young Dr. Melton was consulted.

The little town of Jackson had no hospital. Edgar A. Melton was not a surgeon trained to operate and feared the case was an appendix condition. About the only relief he could give was pain-relieving laudanum. He pronounced that there was no hope for fourteen-year-old Mark.

Relatives in Idaho were notified. An aunt, Anna Hansen, a trained nurse, came. Under the constant care of Mark's mother, Dr. Melton, and Anna, he was never without an attendant at call. Terribly ill, he refused to die.

Other relatives who had come expecting to console the family and attend the funeral, spent their time fishing in the summer and hunting with John in the fall, before they had to go back to their several businesses.

❧ *Mary and John Anderson moved their home from Antelope Pass into Jackson, remodeled it and called it the Jackson Hotel. Shown here are Robert Miller, Pierce Cunningham (owner at the time of the photo), Long Tom Imeson, and Butch Robinson.* (JHM&HC)

Mark was in constant pain and very low spirits, but still he lingered on. In late fall he told his mother, "If you can just get me out of here to a hospital, I'll try to live." With great determination, Mrs. Anderson began to plan to "get him out."

A purse of one hundred dollars was raised, a good-sized amount in those days, by Charles Deloney, Dr. Melton, Rube Tuttle, Pete Karns, George Goe, Walt Nickles, Arthur Mullen, and Henry Parker—all friends who wanted to help share the expenses.

Dr. Melton was sure that the rough jouncing of a buggy or wagon would be the death of Mark. By now he was taking large doses of morphine derivatives and was in such agony he was doubled up like a jackknife all the time. Four men volunteered to carry Mark by hand on a stretcher the seventy-five miles to the railway.

At that time the rails ended at St. Anthony, Idaho. Mrs. Anderson prepared camp equipment and food for a trip of several days, then, driving the white-topped buggy, she accompanied the stretcher bearers. Mark's father, along with Hyrum Deloney (who had been foremost in planning the trip), Ben Goe and Art Mullen were the four who carried Mark from Jackson to St. Anthony.

At the Snake River, John and Hyrum found a riffle and waded the river, holding the stretcher high. The onlookers held their breath as the men felt for good footing in the always-strong and often treacherous current.

The men took short turns carrying and resting by riding in the buggy between turns. Wherever a ranch home happened to coincide with the night's stop, they were given comfort and good meals. The road over Teton Pass was steeper then, going right up the draw on the Jackson side, right down the draw on the Victor side. The wagon had to have a "rough lock" (a pole or chain in the wheels), and the men had to use extreme caution.

Finally, the long march was accomplished. Mark was taken to Dr. Horsburger in St. Anthony. There was no hospital in St. Anthony in those days either, so after a short rest for the patient, Dr. Horsburger sent mother and son on the train to St. Mark's hospital in Salt Lake City. There Doctors Pinkerton and Landenberger examined him. Mark was so weak that the doctors were appalled. They were sure he could not live through an operation. In addition, he had become addicted to painkilling drugs.

They sent him back to St. Anthony to build up his strength under Dr. Horsberger's care. Withdrawal from the addicting drugs was the most difficult part of the process.

The next spring Dr. Landenberger operated and, with a brilliant piece of surgery, was able to rectify the mess that the ruptured appendix and consequent peritonitis had wreaked in Mark's insides.

With Mark's recovery, Mary once again directed her energies toward a long-cherished goal of better schooling for the children. So the hotel was sold to Peter Nelson (about 1905 according to Peter Nelson's daughter Pearl). Mrs. Anderson moved with her children to Pocatello where there was a high school and junior college. John stayed at the ranch as he had no interest in city life.

Mark continued to spend time at his father's ranch, walking like a half-opened jackknife for a year or two, but he rode and punched cows on the long drives over Union Pass and down the Wind River to Hudson.

There he helped load them on the railroad and traveled with them to Omaha. It was on one of these trips, as his journal reveals below, that he decided to go back to school and try to find a different life's work than ranching.

It was October 1908. I was eighteen years of age. We were trailing cattle to market from Jackson's Hole up over the Continental Divide over Union Pass, down the Wind River, across the reservation to Hudson, Wyoming. Here we would load them on the railroad cars for shipment to stockyards at Omaha, Nebraska. We were three weeks on the trail. The feed was good on the open range of the mountains so, "Drive them slow and easy. That fat is worth money, don't knock it off," warned the boss.

It was on this trip to Omaha that I decided to go back to school. I had then been out of school for five years. I now recall some of the incidents of the trip.

We were night herding on the upper Gros Ventre. The cattle had bedded down on an open sage flat near the mouth of Fish Creek. Ollie Smith and I took the herd from midnight on, the graveyard shift. It was the first time I had witnessed the Aurora Borealis. The streams of color rolled up from the northern horizon at intervals, sometimes reaching the zenith, soon the whole heavenly bowl was lighted.

The colors, cool green and blue hues at first, soon ran into the warmer hues. While the northern horizon remained the brightest, the other horizons were glowing soon, the south remaining palest. Perhaps it presaged the great storm which struck us on the Wind River side of the divide a few days later.

How quiet and contented a big herd of cattle can be on a still night. With full bellies they are free from worry and know nothing of the destination we are steering them toward each day. Only an occasional sigh here, a nose blowing there, to mar the silence of the night. You ride around slowly until you meet the other rider, you chat a few minutes then ride back. If it is chilly you ride out a ways, get off your horse and walk a wider circle. The cattle are used to a horse but might spook at a man afoot. You keep a respectable distance.

We had crossed over the Continental Divide on the old Fish Creek-Wind River trail. As though to live up to its name, when we arrived on the Wind River drainage the wind began to blow, we decided to make camp for the night. The heretofore clear sky grew cloudy and dark, it began snowing and the cattle grew restless.

The midnight shift came, and as Ollie and I rolled out, the snow rolled in. The cowboys from the earlier shift said they were having trouble holding the cattle in the driving snow storm. The rest of the crew was rousted out and there was no sleep for anybody the balance of the night, and for all the next day and night. The cattle wanted to drift with the storm. It was hard to hold them together, little bunches were always trying to quit the herd and duck into the timber or down a gully. If we should let them get away they would be hard to find in the timbered, broken country on the top of the mountains. Their tracks would soon be snowed under, so we tried to keep them together, and in sight while they were making the tracks.

What a relief when we came to the fences of the Rocking Chair outfit on the afternoon of the second day of the storm. We were welcomed in and the owners allowed us to put the herd in a fenced field. The men enjoyed the comfort of the bunkhouse for a couple of days while the storm blew itself out. A count of the cattle showed we had lost only two head, one of them a "canner."

The eighty mile trip from Dubois down the Wind, across the reservation [unfenced at that time] and on to Hudson and the railroad, was long but not hard. Not hard except as all cowboy work is hard, physical action from daylight to dark. There were no stampedes and the chuck wagon kept up, bringing our grub and beds at the regular times.

When we arrived in Omaha and the cattle were auctioned off and we had received our checks from Clay-Robinson Co., we, of course, felt pretty rich. My father had given me two steers for which I got a personal check. I went to Brandie's Store and bought a complete outfit of city clothes. I got my hair cut, took off my range Levis and boots, took a bath and really dressed up, I even had a new overcoat. The old sheepskin coat, Levis and boots went into a sack to be shipped home. Instantly I was treated like a stranger by my own buddies. When I told them I was headed for Pocatello to go to school they thought for sure I was a bunchquitter. I guess they were about right. There were eight of us in that group that took the herd to Omaha. I am the only one of the eight living today [1958]. Ranch life is not too healthy for most people after all.

His fine spirit was lost to Jackson's Hole soon afterward, but Provo, Utah, gained a productive, useful citizen.

The list of honors accorded Mark Anderson in his adult life included: Student Body President at the College of Southern Idaho, the winning of two scholarships, and his appointment as Range Investigator over all districts of the Forest Service (an appointment which he resigned because he and his wife could not stand the big city atmosphere of Washington, D.C.).

Mark is the author of *Range Investigation Studies*, a text used by the Forest Service. He wrote it while he served as range manager of the Ogden Supervisory District in the Forest Service,

Upon entering the business world as owner-manager of the Roberts Hotel in Provo, Utah, Mark served his community as president of the Utah State Game and Fish Commission and as mayor of Provo for many years, during which time he arranged the municipal power and electric company which serves the city. The grateful community named the Mark Anderson Utility Center for him.

CHARLIE FOX: BUILDER

MOST EARLY SETTLERS TO THE VALLEY had enough carpentry skills to construct their own homes. But as the population grew and local business became more diversified, demand for housing and business structures grew apace.

By 1910, a regular building contractor, in the person of Charlie Fox, arrived in the valley. Until his death in 1936, Fox was the most active builder in Jackson's Hole, and the number of business buildings, homes, dude ranches, churches and other buildings in the valley bearing the mark of his industry would be hard to enumerate. Almost every man who needed a job and had any skill at building, worked for Charlie Fox on some project during those years.

Charlie was a rather short and stocky man with a round head and thick neck. He gave you a straightforward look from honest blue eyes. Not a man of high temper or blustery speech, he still expected a good day's work from his men. He was born in Hamm, Germany, in 1858, and had emigrated to the United States when he was seventeen years old. Among other jobs, he worked for the Pullman Company, of Chicago, as a cabinet maker. He enlisted in the Seventh Infantry Regiment of the Regular Army on February 19, 1884. He happened to be stationed in Rock Springs at the time of the massacre of Chinese miners by others miners. The Army was called upon to quell the disturbance. If he related his part in the army action to stop the violence, it hasn't become part of Jackson's Hole oral history.

Following his Army discharge, he engaged in construction in the Rock Springs area, sometimes in the mines. When the Spanish American war broke out, he reenlisted in the Army, serving in the First Battalion of Wyoming Volunteers. This was the same division in which Will Deloney and Fred Price (two Jackson's Hole boys) served.

Enrolled on April 19, 1898, he served for the duration of the war (two years) and was discharged at the Presidio in San Francisco September 21, 1899. He was Quarter Master Sergeant of his company. When World War I broke out, he was living in Jackson and once more tried to enlist. He failed to be accepted but served without pay as drill sergeant for the volunteer company sent from here.

Charlie Fox remained a bachelor. He took most of his meals at Ma Reed's Hotel. In 1912, young Dr. Huff arrived in the country—and the Jacksonites were *so* glad to have him! He also took his meals at Ma Reed's Hotel and even did some of his first operations on her big kitchen table. He wanted to stay in Jackson's Hole but as yet had no place to live and no office for his practice.

Ma Reed got right after Charlie Fox. "Look here, we're going to lose that young doctor if he doesn't get some place to live. Why don't you get busy and build a house for him?"

So Charlie did. And Dr. Huff went back to Baltimore to marry his sweetheart and bring her west.

They rented the house from Charlie and set up housekeeping, creating a little office and emergency room on one end. Everything was rosy until Si Ferrin came down from the Buffalo River area looking for a house in town. His large family of children were getting old enough to need a high school education, and Si needed a big house. Charlie Fox sold the house to him.

Si wanted it right away, so the young Huffs had to move into a one-room cabin, partition it off, and have living quarters, plus office, plus emergency room altogether until they could get enough money for a home of their own. They didn't hold it against Charlie; he later built the big white house on Broadway for Dr. Huff and Edna.

In 1921–22, Fox built a large frame house on the northeast corner of Cache and Pearl streets. It was planned and built as a family residence—which was how he intended to sell it. Before he got it sold, Teton County was formed.

Newly elected as County Superintendent of Schools, Eva Lucas rented the house. Mrs. Lucas lived with her family on a ranch in Spring Gulch, some seven or so miles from town—long, cold, troublesome miles. She decided it would be easier to organize the work of her new office if she had a residence in town and had decided she would move to town to get the office working. (Besides, it would be advantageous for her boys to be in the town school for the winter, instead of the country school at Zenith.) The house was large —three stories counting the full basement. It was probably the first house in town to be fully modern with an electric generator in the basement to run an electric pump and, of course, the lights. It even had modern plumbing!

By spring the other county officers were needing a place to conduct business. The house was large; it could be remodeled to accommodate offices—even have the jail in the basement. The county rented it from Charlie, but Mrs. Lucas was allowed to stay in residence until the roads had thawed, dried up, and been packed down enough that she could get back and forth to the ranch. What was Charlie's wrath when he found Eva had used the basement for a convenient chicken coop for her hens all winter. Probably not near as much wrath as sheriff Jim Francis and his deputy felt when they had to clean it and deodorize it before it was a fit place for jail cells.

This house served as the courthouse until 1930, when the second Teton County courthouse was built about a block south on Cache Avenue. It was also constructed by Charlie Fox. The family home that had served almost ten years as a courthouse was bought and converted to a hotel in 1932 by Frank and Jack Childs. They didn't keep it long. Jack and Hazel Smith had it next. They renamed it the Smith Hotel. Charlie and Rilla Hedrick had a turn at running a hotel in the building before Lyman Richman got it, when it was named the Commercial Hotel.

Abi Garriman purchased the building, mainly because he wanted the town lots which went with it. He sold the old house to Shriver and LaPreath who moved the building downtown in 1975, from its corner on Pearl and Cache to the corner of Milward and Mercill Streets. There it served as a rather rundown rooming house until a tragic fire gutted it in 1980s. The remains were torn down and the lot restored. A sad ending of Teton County's first courthouse.

The Fox shop and lumberyard was located on the south side of Cache Avenue at Pearl Street. His personal cabin was nearby. Charlie spent many of his winters in California.

Charlie Fox's most famous, most photographed work is no doubt the little Church of Transfiguration at Moose, built in 1925. The lot for the building was donated by Maud Noble; the building costs donated by the summer dudes of the surrounding ranches. For years the great Sunday treat was to ride to the scenic Episcopal church—horseback or in stagecoaches—which were tied to hitching racks or parked at the rear of the church while it was in session.

Charlie Fox died at age seventy-eight in L.D.S. Hospital in Salt Lake City, where he had gone for surgery. His grave is in the Aspen Cemetery, in Jackson, among friends; many monuments to his industry fill the town and the valley.

TINSY

ONE OF THE MOST COLORFUL characters to live up the river was a lady whose name was—and I never heard any other—Tinsy.

This woman of rather dubious fame and mysterious background lived with an interesting character named Walter Plumber. This arrangement was never graced with a marriage ceremony, but the couple seemed quite congenial.

But maybe I'd better backtrack to the arrival of Walter on the Gros Ventre scene. The Lemon place was so labeled because a man named Lemon homesteaded it. Like so many other ranches in the valley, the name identifies the place long after the original owner has been forgotten. The Lemon place was one of those abandoned homesteads. The Fish Creek grazing permit-holders paid taxes on it for many years, thinking they could get it for a tax title.

Suddenly one year, the back taxes were paid. The heirs of Mr. Lemon, whoever they were, had been paid a sum sufficient to satisfy them, and a new owner appeared on the river—Walter Plumber.

Walter Plumber had been a druggist in Lander on the east side of the Wind River Range. Although he was a well-educated man, he became quite a recluse and one of the most eccentric people in a rather eccentric neighborhood. He scorned the cattle business (which most residents of that time considered the prime occupation). Instead, he started a big game outfitters business.

This was a well-respected business in the valley, but none of the established outfitters thought he was qualified to be a big game guide and outfitter.

His clients must have shared this conclusion because the Wyoming Game and Fish wardens received more complaints over the years concerning his accommodations than on all other outfitters combined. Even so, the warden's hands were tied because no out-of-state hunter could spare the time to stay and pursue a legal action against Mr. Plumber.

The gist of the complaints was that the accommodations did not coincide with his advertising brochure. For instance, he advertised cabins with running water (there was water running—in the ditch just outside the door), and electric lights (he had a wind battery charger which seldom worked, so the lights were the kerosene lamp or lantern). Guests said the food was poor, and guides other than Walter non-existent, no matter how many hunters in the party. But since they didn't stay to follow up their complaints, and since the Jackson's Hole country continued to grow in popularity, Walter's hunting business continued to prosper. He put out a beautiful brochure.

Ranchers with grazing permits on the Fish Creek watershed had an altogether different problem with Plumber. The ranch lay astraddle the Fish Creek fork of the Gros Ventre, controlling a mile or so of the stream and the access to the upper reaches of Fish Creek. Access upstream for their cattle was the reason the cattlemen who grazed the upper Fish had wanted to obtain the place.

After Plumber's arrival the trailing of the herds to the range past the Lemon place was always full of excitement. If the cowboys got the herd stringing past the place before daylight, Walter suddenly appeared in his nightshirt somewhere up in front of the herd and started a stampede backward down the trail.

If they got permission from him to use the road (it *did* go through his ranch—which *was* fenced—but the road had been in use since the country was opened) they thought they were placating him or even being neighborly. But his dogs mysteriously got loose and came yapping through the herd. The cows with new calves gave chase, creating a milling, thundering mess and all the pairs would become unmothered.

There was great relief when the Forest Service constructed a bypass trail from the Cottonwood watershed over to Fish Creek above the Lemon place. The new trail was steep and the cows didn't like it, but they traveled it without harassment from Plumber.

So Plumber wasn't neighborly, and he wasn't neighbored with. His mother came to live with him. For many years she carried on the hard work of cooking for hunters and keeping the house and cabins—more-or-less. When she became unable to carry on, Walter advertised in the big city papers for a cook for a dude ranch. This was when Tinsy appeared.

Tinsy was a dancer whose face had traveled far—and signs of the trip were engraved upon it. She came out to cook for the hunting season and stayed on...and on. She was a native of Sweden and may at one time have been good at her trade. She danced for, and with, the native bachelors every time she had the chance. It was rumored the hunters were also entertained.

After Walter's mother died, Tinsy shared Walter's secluded existence for the rest of their years up the river. She went to Sweden once or twice, and speculation ran high in the neighborhood about whether she would come back. She always, *always* did.

Once she even got married, but not to Walter.

Late one autumn, when the cattle were shipped and the hunters gone, some of the neighbors up the river got together to drive to Jackson for business. It was late enough that snow might be a problem so they agreed to leave horse-drawn sleighs at the Dew place, ready for the return trip, and all go to town in Plumber's car. Hence Walter and Tinsy, Butch and Eddie Robinson, and Billy Lafferty journeyed off to town together.

After business affairs were finished came a period of relaxing. They relaxed in the various bars around town until it became evident that a period of serious celebration was due. After all, the work year was at an end, it was the last trip to town before winter set in, and so forth.

Sometime during the celebration Billy Lafferty proposed to Tinsy, and since the general mood was so agreeable, she accepted. The night had worn away, and it was not too long until the Justice of the Peace would be available, so everyone made ready for the ceremony.

Making ready required little more than another drink to celebrate the coming event, a general washing up in cold water—desirable for the astringent effects upon one's equilibrium—and a trip to the courthouse for a license.

This was before the days of blood tests and the waiting period which might cool the ardor of the concerned parties. In due time the wedding was performed, with Walter and the Robinsons as attendants and witnesses.

The bride and groom kissed, and the wedding party had a big dinner, courtesy of the bridegroom, then they loaded in the car and started up the river.

Tinsy and Billy slept most of the way. In fact, all of them slept, except Walter, who had his problems trying to drive the twisty, narrow dirt road. When they arrived at the "Y" at the Dew place, where Plumber would take the Fish Creek fork and Lafferty would go on up the Gros Ventre, Billy went to the barn to make his outfit ready.

When he returned to help Tinsy into his sleigh, he found her all snuggled down with Plumber and ready to start in the opposite direction.

"Tinsy, what are you doing? You're my wife now. Come on, get in this sleigh."

"Vy Billy, dat vas shust a fun."

"The hell it was in fun, that was a legal marriage. You're supposed to come home with me now."

"So vat iss? I go home, I go home vit Valter."

Billy Lafferty was not exactly the type to drag his mate home by the bleached-blond hair of her head, so Walter drove off with Billy's new wife, and Billy drove up the river alone, as usual.

This marital state was not only humiliating and intolerable to Billy, but legally risky as well, so far as his property was concerned. So, as soon as possible, he sued for an annulment. When his day in court arrived, Billy appeared before the judge in his best suit, shined and sober. The judge was dignified, a trifle pompous on this occasion to hide his amusement, but kindly.

"Mr. Lafferty," the judge began, "let us have this perfectly clear. I am sure, from the circumstance of your wife's living separated from you, that a legal separation can be arranged. However, you and I must come to a common understanding concerning the facts regarding an annulment. Now…If you had no marital relations with this woman—that is to say, Mr. Lafferty—if you did not cohabit—you may have an annulment. Otherwise you had best sue for divorce."

"Yes sir, Judge," Billy answered. "I guess I know what you mean. I'm not sure about 'co habit' and 'marital relations.' But, in cowman's language, if you mean did I ever 'service' her, why no, sir, I never had that pleasure."

Billy got his annulment, and went back, a legal bachelor, to the bachelor herd up the river.

THE SHEFFIELDS OF MORAN

THE SHEFFIELD HOTEL AT MORAN was an important part of the development of the valley.

Here Frank Crowe, on one of his first engineering projects, received experience on the Jackson Lake dam which helped him to become America's number one dam engineer.

Here King Gustav, then Crown Prince of Sweden, stayed, and other VIPs too numerous to mention enjoyed the early western hospitality, the fine hunting, good fishing and magnificent scenery to be had at the Sheffield Place.

About 1895, Benjamin David Sheffield, thinking that good hunting was on the way out in Montana, moved to Moran, Wyoming. As a young lad, Ben had left his home near Walla Walla, Washington, where his father was Agent of Indian Affairs, to work his way to Montana.

He helped to trail a band of sheep; the job took two years. Their first winter was spent near Boise, Idaho. In Montana, Ben worked at many jobs; he killed wild game to supply the railroad crews when the railroad came through, broke wild horses at Salesville (the Gallatin Gateway), hauled buffalo hides to Fort Benton to be sold, and was undersheriff of Livingston for twelve years.

He filed on the island in the Yellowstone River at Livingston, but since he was under age to prove up on it, he had to spend more than the usual time on the claim. When Billie Sheart perfected the gold bead front gun sight, Ben advertised it through sharp-shooting demonstrations all over the West.

It was natural for Ben, with his hunting talents, to work into the pack trip and hunting business. His first customers were wealthy international hunters from Germany and England who came to America's West to spend several months in the wilds.

It was at this time he extended his trips through the Yellowstone and into Jackson's Hole. The shores of Jackson Lake appealed to him as an ideal location for a hunting lodge.

With Marion Lambert (of Listerine toothpaste) as financial partner, Ben purchased the Cap Smith and Frank Lovell properties near the outlet of the lake. A few other homesteaders were strung along the river at the time.

Charles and Maria Allen, who had homesteaded at the Oxbow Bend in 1896, had the first Moran Post Office at their ranch in 1902. It was run by one or another of the family until 1907. Arch Kimall and Herb Whiteman had homesteads nearby. To cross the river, the settlers used a ferry at the Cunnard place (where the cattle bridge was built in 1953).

Ben worked at building up his lodge in the summers; in the autumns, he was busy with hunting; in the winters, he went to Chicago where one of his clients allowed him a desk in the V.L.A. Sporting Goods store. From there he made contracts for his hunting and outfitting business. (He also sheared sheep in the Chicago Stockyards to keep himself in funds.)

In Chicago, in May 1906, Ben married Margaret Canon Rice, of Wilton, Wisconsin. They had met in Moran the previous summer, where Margaret had accompanied the Fotheringhams as governess for their children. After the wedding, they set out for Moran and the excitement of a dam under construction at the outlet of Jackson Lake.

This first dam was a log rip-rap and dirt-fill affair which raised the waters of the lake only a few feet. However, it made a stirring community out of Moran, which had not even had a store before. The contractors established stables for the teams, bunkhouses for the men, and a commissary for necessities.

Sylvia (Mrs. Pete) Hansen remembers cooking for nine boarders while Pete worked his teams on the dam. Work continued until the first of January 1907, and reopened early the next spring. The job kept the Hansens and many other early settlers in cash while they were trying to prove up on their homesteads.

☙ *The first wooden dam at the outlet of Jackson Lake raised the waters of the lake a few feet. The Sheffield Lodge buildings are in the foreground.* (Grand Teton National Park Collection)

The Sheffields built more cabins and tried to keep up with the demands upon their facilities. They added the Charlie Allen and Arch Kimall places to their holdings. In 1907, with the Allen Place, they acquired the post office, which they kept until 1929.

While the dam was being built, the Sheffields had a fire which destroyed the post office, the dining rooms, their living quarters and kitchen. Margaret Sheffield had wanted a bath tub so badly, and had finally gotten one just a short time before the fire. Someone tried to save it for her, jerked it loose from the pipes and got it stuck in the door, blocking the doorway so they couldn't get much else out.

Bennie, Jr., remembers when the log dam went out in 1910. Ben and Margaret controlled a half mile of lake front and a half mile of river bank with their Moran property. At that time they had the only deeded acres on the shores of Jackson Lake, aside from the John Sargent place. The flood washed out the toll bridge in use below the dam and raised the water around Moran high enough that Herb Whiteman brought a boat and tied it to the Sheffield porch in case they had to evacuate over water.

Edward S. Sheffield, Ben's older brother, came to Moran from Ashton about 1910 and operated a pool hall where Fesler later had his store. Ed also did shoe repair work on the side.

❧ *This photo shows the second dam during the 1930s. This dam is still in use, although in 1993 it underwent a major upgrade. Some of the same landmarks and buildings can be identified.* (JHM&HC)

The second, and present, dam across the river was started in 1911 and completed in 1916. It rather overwhelmed the townsite and didn't do much for their view either, but Moran was still one of the beauty spots of the nation. In 1993, that dam was upgraded at a cost of eighty-two million dollars.

Ben also started a roadhouse at the Snake River crossing south of the Yellowstone Park entrance. Ed and his wife Lillie took charge of that. He tried to homestead the site but the Forest Service had been created by then and had charge over the area. They decreed that the land was not suitable for farming. Instead they gave the Sheffields a lease. The river crossing was a busy place also, as all the materials and supplies for the dam and Moran were freighted from Ashton, Idaho, over the Squirrel Meadows road.

Where nowadays a gas station has to be provided, at that time a livery stable had to be available—with human accommodations for rest, recreation, and nourishment. The Sheffields put up some hay on the meadows along the river and Pole Cat Creek to supply the teams and cattle. Ed dug out the hot springs on Pole Cat Creek and made them into a usable bathing and swimming spot. The free use of these hot springs continued up to 1960, when the Forest Service offered the spot for lease for commercial development.

❧ *Phil Smith (left), first ranger of newly-created Grand Teton National Park, with Ben Sheffield at Sheffield Lodge, Moran.* (JHM&HC)

After Ed Sheffield's death in 1927, Lillie sold the roadhouse to Ray Linch and Neil Dougherty who built it into a dude ranch/motel business which comprises the present Flagg Ranch.

From the turn of the century to 1929 is only thirty years, but thirty years equals a generation. The Ben Sheffields raised two sons on the shores of Jackson Lake, Bennie, Jr., and William Morrow.

Two of Margaret's sisters were at the lodge for several years. Mary Rice was desk clerk from 1922 until the lodge was sold. Nana Rice Thomson and son Jim came to Moran about 1922.

After the Sheffields sold, Jim continued with the Grand Teton Lodge and Transportation Company until 1966. He then moved to Death Valley, California.

This generation saw the big leap from horse-drawn transportation to motorized automation. Everyone who could own a car set out to see the USA, especially Yellowstone National Park. Soon a highway replaced the dirt roads of the valley. And travelers crossed the river on bridges—instead of ferries—at Moose and Wilson, and crossed the river on the new dam at Moran.

During this time the Sheffields started the first boat accommodations on Jackson Lake with a big twelve-passenger launch for fishing and sightseeing trips.

A rumored proposal to extend the wonders of Yellowstone Park
to include the beauties of Jackson's Hole became the talk and con-
tention of the Twenties.

At first the purchases of The Snake River Land Company were
accepted as just another corporation buying and consolidating
many small ranches to make one big one. It had been done before
in the valley.

Even so, it did seem strange that they paid so much more for
the nonproductive lands on the Jenny Lake flats than they paid for
the good hay meadows in the southern and eastern parts of the valley. By the time the secret was out that these lands were destined to
become another park, most of the scenic western side of the valley
under private ownership had been purchased by the Rockefeller-
sponsored corporation.

The story of the creation of Grand Teton National Park is
another book. It is pertinent here because this was the beginning of
the end of the town of Moran.

The Sheffields sold to the Snake River Land Company in 1928;
they gave possession in 1929. They retained some land along the
lake shore and built a home on it in 1930. Ben served as fire guard
at the Signal Mountain lookout station in the 1930s, just as something to keep him interested and active. They used this home in the
summers until Ben Senior's death in 1946.

Margaret sold the home to the McConaughys later that year.

The village of Moran became a corporate structure. The services
the Sheffields had built up continued under the title of Teton Lodge
and Transportation Company until the present Jackson Lake Lodge
facilities were completed.

With this new and beautiful site ready to care for the tourist
demands, the cabins of the old Teton Lodge were moved and nes-
tled into the lodge pole pines surrounding Colter Bay. The larger
buildings were leveled and hauled away, and the site of the town
relandscaped.

Not much is left of the original Moran. The obliteration, changes and relandscaping have left no nook or cranny in which a ghost might linger. In fact, it takes the sharpest memory of the oldest oldtimers to remember how Moran looked before the dam; the rest of us can hardly remember how it looked before Grand Teton National Park.

But some of us know where there is a patch of rhubarb, a stubborn (if civilized) plant, which refuses to give up its home in Moran, even though the hands that planted it fail to return for the harvest.

Moran's Ghost—the rhubarb patch which marks the spot of the kitchen garden of the old Sheffield Lodge.

*M*OST *B*EAUTIFUL *D*OLL

OR THE ALBERT NELSON, SR., family, the Christmas of 1913 had to be faced without Mama. Sarah Avilla, the happy, capable, brimming-with-health Mama had died suddenly earlier in the season.

Several relatives and friends kindly offered to take some of the seven motherless children into their homes to raise, but Albert was determined to keep the family together. Josephine and Mabel, eleven and ten, tried to fill the place of their mother by keeping house and caring for the younger boys—Neal, three-and-a-half, and Albert, one-and-a-half years old.

Charlie (eight) and Otto (seven), the older boys, helped by carrying wood and water and getting themselves ready for school. Only the five-year-old youngest daughter, Anna, was away from the close-knit family circle at Christmas time. She had been staying with Grandma Allen at Moran for awhile and, for some reason lost in the mists of years, she was not sent home to be with the Nelsons for the important day.

In 1913, the Allen homestead, about a mile east of Jackson Lake dam, *was* Moran, so named by postmistress Grandma Allen. The Allen house also accommodated travelers as a roadhouse, one room was a store, a lean-to served liquor at a bar, and the stable housed the travelers' horses. At this "one-home-town" little Anna had aunts, uncles and cousins in abundance, but she missed her home, her brothers and sisters, and most of all, she missed her beloved Mama and Papa.

The school for the district serving the Allen homestead was up the Buffalo Fork about five miles away between the ranches of the Gregorys and the Germanns. All the families of the district made ready to attend the school Christmas party, the big social event of the year. Anna was to go with the Allen family—but would Santa know where to find her?

Yellowstone Park was patrolled by a detachment of U.S. Army cavalry troops and, since Moran was the nearest settlement to South Gate, the troops stationed there used the tiny settlement as "home base." The soldier-rangers furnished the gifts for the Buffalo school Christmas party. They were one hundred percent in attendance to see "their" kids receive presents from Santa.

The schoolhouse was already filled with friends and relatives when the Allen sleigh arrived. The family disentangled themselves and the "covered dishes" of food from the quilts and entered the small, crowded building. The tree, tall as the ceiling would allow, glowed with a blaze of candles.

Trimmings made by the school children and strings of popcorn and cranberries festooned the branches. A heap of presents surrounded the base of the lovely tree. Anna walked up the center aisle a few steps then stopped enchanted. There in the center of the heap of presents was the beautiful, big doll upon which she had set her heart. It was the very doll she had prayed Santa would bring. The very one that had caused her to badger Grandma until she wrote the letter to Santa. She couldn't take her eyes from the doll all through the program.

Santa (Captain Felix Buchenroth) entered the scene at the close of the school program. With a great jangling of real sleigh bells and with authentic snow on his whiskers, he came whooshing through the door, since the building lacked a fireplace.

Santa immediately mingled with the children, greeting them by name and finding out if they had been "good." He often caught them up on this subject, reminding them of some misdeed, which he miraculously seemed to know.

Finally Santa went to the tree and looked over the pile of gifts. "Well, well well," he said, "it looks like Santa's little helpers have been busy. I wonder what lucky little girl gets this beautiful doll?"

There were many other little girls at that Christmas party. Most of them must have wanted that doll too. Anna's small voice was the only one that broke the stillness after the question.

"Me," she said softly.

Santa trotted down the aisle and deposited the doll in Anna's outstretched arms. Hers were the only dry eyes in the assembly. They glowed with the joy of perfect faith rewarded.

The most beautiful doll in the world was cherished not only through Anna's doll-playing childhood, but given a place of honor in her room right on into Anna's nineteenth year. That year "the most beautiful doll in the world" was an unnumbered casualty of the Kelly flood.

JACKSON'S FRONTIER DAYS RODEO

THE WESTERN SHOW NOW CALLED "rodeo" grew with the early settlements of the west. On every occasion when a few fellows got together with a little free time on their hands, horse racing was the order of the day. As ranching spread over the wide open spaces, the skills of working cowboys were introduced into the contests. The cowboys each chipped in an entry fee to make the winning worthwhile. The idea became a standard western event.

The five-mile relay race was the big event of the early meets in Jackson. Charlie Wort of Jackson's Hole, and Keith and Keyes Blair from the other side of the mountain [Teton Pass] kept the race track warm with Roman races (rider standing on two horses), half-mile and quarter-mile races, novelty races (the same horse walks a quarter mile, trots the next quarter mile and runs the last quarter mile), chariot races, and then the five-mile relay.

Ranchers around the country brought their bad horses, and any good rider was welcome, for his ante in the kitty, to try to ride them.

It was all a big community effort usually held to celebrate special days.

In about 1911, four early Jackson settlers, with business and ranch interests, made a business proposition out of what had been casual race-meet, bucking-contest, get-togethers. They called it "Frontier Days." Jack Eynon, Roy VanVleck, Pierce Cunningham and T. Lloyd were the four entrepreneurs. And for a few years, until World War I interfered with their contestants, they put on a show that rivaled the "Daddy of Them All" at Cheyenne. (See chapter: *First Car Over Teton Pass*)

When Frontier Days became an owned and commercial show, it still retained a great deal of this community spirit. The ranchers

❧ One of the events of the three-day Frontier Days celebration in Jackson was chariot races. (JHM&HC)

who owned bucking stock either sold them to the partners or leased them out for the show. The contestants were still local fellows. The spectators were their relatives and friends. It was pretty certain that every spectator had a husband, son, father, beau, horse, cow, bull, steer or calf out there competing. It made for an exciting show.

Frontier Days (shortened by the natives to "Frontier") was held on a field southwest of Jackson which belonged to Bell Flanders. It was a three-day event over Labor Day weekend. Spectators and contestants alike, if they lived far from town, would bring a camp and pitch it along Flat Creek. The two hotels in town were taxed beyond their capacities. Jack Eynon purchased a big army tent which was pitched in the Pete Karns field nearby, and meals were served in it. Irene Eynon Annis says that her contribution to Frontier was to bake forty or fifty loaves of bread a day for this lunchroom.

Corrals were not used for saddling the bucking stock in these early Frontiers. Buckers, either horses or steers, were roped in the big corral, dragged out in the middle of the arena, and once there, blindfolded with a coat, sack or kerchief, and saddled. The bronc rider mounted, got settled, then reached forward and pulled off the blindfold. Cowboys rode the bucking bulls and steers with a saddle.

Old Spot, a bucking bull owned by the partners, was ridden very few times. He was famous all over the area where the partners took their show.

Having so much livestock for the sole purpose of putting on a Western Show created a "expensive, unused asset" the rest of the year, so the partners soon began taking their show to other towns and cities. They traveled over a good bit of Idaho, Wyoming, and Montana in the heyday of their business.

Frontier Days, as a partnership business venture, fell onto difficulties about 1917 or 1918. One of the partners, T. Lloyd, had gone to Alaska; the war took most of the young cowboys; and the partners were involved in other interests. When World War I ended and the boys came marching home, the partners persuaded the newly-formed American Legion to take on the business of running Frontier Days.

The Legion ran a good show, with most of the old-time community involvement, for about ten years. The show never did make much money. If they broke even, the Legionnaires felt pretty good about it. After all, it was, for Jackson, a business-boosting event.

When the returned Legionnaires grew tired of doing all the extra work—gate keepers, ticket sellers, pick-up men, announcers, time keepers, judges, starters and bookkeepers—they hired a Rodeo Company to do all that. The show lost its community feeling. Soon most of the contestants were professionals, the livestock was entirely "outside" raised, and even the name "Frontier Days" got changed to "Rodeo."

For Jacksonites, an old-time affair had bit the dust.

First Car over Teton Pass

Bartha Moulton tells of crossing Teton Pass in the first automobile to make that tortuous journey. According to Bartha (who was Bartha Blanchard in those days), the occasion was the first Jackson's Hole Frontier Days. At the time, she was fourteen years old.

Charles Caughlin, a very close family friend whom the Blanchards called "Uncle Charlie," bought two wagon-loads of soda pop, some concession dolls, balls, games and knick-knacks, and a new car, an EM&F, in Idaho Falls. He planned to take all this over the hill to the Jackson Frontier Days celebration. He would put up stands for the pop and concessions and rent rides in the new-fangled gas buggy. Uncle Charlie had started the Old Faithful Beverage Company in Idaho Falls, one of the earliest businesses still in operation there.

Bartha and her sister Veleta rode with Uncle Charlie in the automobile. Their brother John drove a team and white-top buggy—for insurance.

The auto had a folded-down top, which could be raised in case of rain, and side curtains, which were snapped on if needed. It had carbide headlights and brass trim. The running boards were great improvements over the steps of a buggy. The wheels were small and wide compared to those of a buggy. That they were not big enough was soon apparent, as the greatest trouble on the trip was high-centering.

Most of the trouble spots on the road were passed by riding the center ridge and the outside edge of the road, thereby straddling the ruts. But frequently the outside edge of the road was too close to tree trunks and branches, endangering the new-car finish, or the edge of the road was too perilous to navigate. When forced to drive in the ruts, the men shoveled down the center ridge to save the car's undercarriage.

The EM&F made it all the way to the Bircher roadhouse (called the Half-Way House) on the west side of the "hill" under its own power. From there on up, the team and buggy lent their horse-power.

Veleta grew weary of the harrowing tippiness of bouncing in and out of the ruts, and the constant delays caused by getting stuck in them. She quit the car at the top and rode on to Jackson with some other Victor visitors. Bartha stayed with the auto and Uncle Charlie.

With the car in the lowest gear, and by occasionally roughlocking the wheels, they made it to the bottom with no more than the usual trouble.

Arriving at Snake River, Uncle Charlie and John were faced with a different problem; the river was too low for the ferry to operate but too deep for the car to ford. Again ingenuity and energy solved the difficulty. They searched up and down the river bank until they found two big timbers. They chained one to the auto on each side, then Johnny and the team pulled the auto across the river. The timbers kept it afloat in the deepest places. After this victory, the rest of the way to Jackson seemed easy.

Jackson was buzzing with activity. Uncle Charlie got rooms for himself and the Blanchard children at the Jackson Hotel, but since most of the Victor visitors were camped in the willows along Cache Creek (on the Smith property just northeast of the Clubhouse), that was where the Blanchard kids spent much of their time. Bartha remembers the families camped along Cache Creek and Flat Creek—cowboys on horses everywhere, lumber wagons full of hay and quilts. Parents and kids came into town from the distant ranches.

We believe this first Frontier Days event was held in 1911. Bartha remembers the time was the first part of September.

At the Frontier grounds—an area that stretched from present Pearl Street to the Snow King slopes and from Cache Avenue to Flat Creek—most of the spectators sat or stood on their wagons to view the events. However, a grandstand had been built for the occasion and was available for those who would pay the extra fee.

Some of the names of riders that Bartha remembers were: Billie Stilson, some of the Si Ferrin boys, some of the Eynons, Dismal Dick Thornton, some of the Seatons, the Clarks and Deyos. Bucking events were interspersed with races. There were quarter- and half-mile free-for-all races, cowpony races, dude races, novelty races, pack-string races, and chuckwagon races, also roping, bull-dogging, clowning, and more races. The Frontier Days show was a three-day affair with the cumulative winners competing on the final day. Of course, there was a dance every evening.

Uncle Charlie did right well with the pop and games concessions. Two wagon-loads of pop were sold before the celebration was a day old. The Kewpie dolls and Teddy bears were gambled for by tossing balls or spinning wheels; they were soon disposed of too.

But the car rides were a failure. What should have been an overwhelming attraction—a ride for two-bits in the first car to come into the valley—was overshadowed by the fact that four other cars came in to Jackson from the north. Whether through Yellowstone Park or over the Ashton/Squirrel Meadows road, Bartha never knew. Those were the only other roads possible for motorized vehicles at the time. Uncle Charlie brought the first car over the mountain to a diluted triumph.

The road back to Victor was a reverse of the trip to Jackson: straddle the ruts back to the river, float the river, straddle the ruts again, horse power up the pass, rough-lock the wheels and straddle the ruts down the canyon.

J.R. JONES:
WINNIN' A BET WITH UNCLE SAM

WHEN JOSEPH REUBEN (J.R.) Jones brought his wife Fidelia and three small children to Jackson's Hole in 1907, it was with the intention of filing on a homestead in the beautiful valley. Unlike so many other settlers coming to the valley, Jones was not a farmer looking for a new location. In fact he had done little actual farming. His life had held plenty of outdoor work, but his background was in the mining fields and at the gambling tables. Dirt farming and cattle raising had not been a part of his experience.

He was born in California in 1873 at a mining camp interestingly named Gouge Eye. His parents had gone there at the urging of his father's brother John who ran a gold camp bar in Dutch Flat. Upon finishing sixth grade, he went prospecting with his father. After working at his uncle's bar and being coached as a dealer at poker, he was allowed to deal at poker.

At age seventeen, he felt competent to strike out on his own. A few years of hard lessons on the vicissitudes of fortune taught him much. He resorted to hard labor in many distasteful jobs to recoup the modest losses he suffered at the gambling tables. He learned early to read character and habits of opponents at cards. Although he learned many of the cheating tricks of the professional gamblers, he noted that card sharps were not welcome in any town for very long and that their natures usually turned to too much drink or to cocaine or other stimulants. He early resolved to play a square game and to keep a reserve fund which did not go to the table with him.

This early bent toward gambling made him consider the homestead in Jackson's Hole as a gamble with Uncle Sam: a sixteen dollar filing fee, plus five years of occupancy, plus $1.25 worth of

❧ Fidelia and J.R. Jones were ill-prepared to be homesteaders, yet they won their bet with Uncle Sam. (JHM&HC)

improvement per acre against 160 acres of Uncle Sam's land, winner keep all. It seemed a sporting chance, and that is what J. R. liked.

Fidelia Humphrey Jones was even less prepared for the life of a homestead pioneer. Orphaned at the age of twelve, she was given a home by a jeweler and his wife. Her schooling had been in the refinements of a young lady. She was a beautiful seamstress, and, at the time she met and fell in love with J. R. Jones, she had her own business—a dress shop where she created her own patterns, sewing the dresses and adding artistic flourishes of her own design. Although she gave up her business to become wife and mother, her creative abilities stood her in good stead throughout her life. She and her daughters were always well dressed.

Nor were her abilities in the practical matters of housekeeping lacking, although many of the problems of homesteading horrified her. She met each with competence and courage—sometimes more accurately characterized as stubbornness and hard work. She accepted, aided, and abetted J.R.'s leadership in life.

J.R. and Fidelia were married in Roseburg, Oregon, in 1899, but soon moved to Sumpter, Oregon, where J.R. had mining interests. They lived there for seven years. Three of their children were born there: Rodney in 1901, Ellen in 1903, and Mildred in 1905. J.R. prospected at various strikes in Oregon, Montana, and Idaho—sometimes making a lucky strike, many times a dry hole. Sometimes claims were sold to try for a better location; sometimes he had to resort to the gambling table to recoup losses or make a new grubstake.

It was while on a prospecting trip to Idaho that he heard of the beautiful valley of Jackson's Hole and that land was still available for homesteading there. J.R. went to take a look and decided that he must return to the valley with his wife and family. He made a deal to buy the improvements and the relinquishment of homestead rights from a man who had run into financial difficulties. Then he returned home to arrange the return journey.

The first thing to try Fidelia's sensibilities was the stagecoach ride from St. Anthony, where she debarked from the train, to Victor. She was sure the driver was just showing off because he thought her a wealthy dude. His reckless driving and lurid cursing caused her to wonder if he were stone drunk (he may well have been!) and would wreck them along the way. Next, the hotel at Victor was dirty, without basin or wash water in the rooms, and, she feared, lousy. To make matters worse, baby Mildred had a high fever, and there was no doctor available. Fidelia sponged the child, gave her what home remedies were available, and prayed for morning. By morning the fever had abated and the family set out on the final leg of their journey.

The trip over Teton Pass was another harrowing experience for Fidelia. The older children—Rodney, six, and Ellen, four—were delighted with the flowers, the opportunity to walk sometimes, and the general feeling of freedom. Fidelia clutched the baby to her and prayed again. At the top of the pass, they stopped to rest the horses and to drink in the beauty of the valley spread below them.

The mail and passenger stage into Jackson from Victor, Idaho, came over Teton Pass. It was in operation until the 1930s. Shown are Clay Seaton, Bob Crisp, and Ray Ferrin in 1924. (JHM&HC and Don Hough)

At the small settlement of Jackson, they spent a night or so at the Nelson Hotel.

The Joneses set off in a hired buggy the next day to inspect the relinquished homestead J.R. had acquired—their future home, the hand he'd been dealt when he took on this bet with Uncle Sam. The land lay on the north bank of the Gros Ventre River, about a mile east of the present highway crossing of the river. Inexperienced at ranching or farming, J.R. wasn't too aware of the potential of the land.

But there awaited another rude shock for Fidelia. A two-room cabin was on the land, but it had been abandoned and cattle had been using it for a fly shed. The dirt roof had shed most of the dirt so the roof leaked. The door was unhinged, and the holes cut for windows were just holes in the walls—not even supported by window frames. There was neither daubing nor chinking between the logs, and there was no floor, just hard-packed dirt. It would take many weeks of work before the cabin was habitable, and winter was coming on.

The homestead sure couldn't be considered a gambler's pat hand by any reading of the lay of the land. J.R. bought a team, wagon, and harness first; paying what he considered too high a price because there was "no opportunity to shop around." He hauled dirt for the roof, dunged out and hauled away the flooring the cows had left, and worked at mud daubing between the logs. Almost everything he needed had to be ordered from Idaho Falls. The windows took weeks to be delivered. J. R. and Fidelia worked into early winter until conditions became impossible, then moved to the Nelson Hotel for the remainder of the winter.

J. R. had started his bet with Uncle Sam with a backlog of $3,000—a pretty good hole card for the times. However, things cost a lot, and the first paying crop might be in the far dim future. J. R. made a little ready money playing cards.

Spring is always late in Jackson's Hole, but when the work could resume, the cabin was made tight, a room added, and the windows put in place. The family moved into their home. It was only the start of the rugged five years it took to win that bet with Uncle Sam.

The children had about six weeks of school in the summer. The first year or so, the Zenith school was held along the Gros Ventre about two-and-a-half miles from the Jones ranch. Rodney and Ellen walked the distance morning and night. In addition, Ellen remembers, an irrigation canal crossed their path, over which she had to be carried. The school was later moved to a place about one mile from their home. Half the walking distance—and with no ditch to cross!

J. R. and Fidelia felt the lack of their own interrupted schooling and hoped to give their children a better education. They spent the long snowed-in days of winter teaching the children at home.

To J. R. and Fidelia, homesteading had sounded fun, neighborhood parties and picnics, neighbors dropping in, maybe sleigh rides to school programs. In actuality, while the men might get out on horseback for mail or supplies—the essentials of life—there was little traveling about after the snow got deep. The weather was severe, and the roads were not kept "broke out" in the deep winter snow. If conditions were too difficult for travel by horse, men snowshoed about the valley on business.

But few women were free of having one or two small children in the home. As a consequence, they were housebound unless a sleigh road was broken out so a team and sleigh could travel. Fidelia missed the companionship of other women.

It was not only in the winter that the isolation caused problems, especially for women. One summer day when J.R. and Rodney had gone to Jackson, Fidelia felt the pains and the rush of blood signaling a miscarriage. Her closest woman neighbor was Mrs. McBride, who lived a mile and a half away. Fidelia could not go herself but she felt she needed help. Six-year-old Ellen was her only messenger.

Fidelia coached the child to walk directly to Mrs. McBride's and to ask her to come as quickly as she could because her mother needed help. The little girl trudged the mile and a half. It was summer, and she was so hot. And she got so thirsty. At last Ellen reached the McBride house. She told the story she had been instructed to repeat, then asked, "Can I have a drink?" Mrs. McBride got her a big drink of water then bustled about, thinking abstractedly of things she needed to do. Apparently there were a great many. Ellen, grateful to be resting yet worried about her mother, watched Mrs. McBride and sipped her water. Finally Mrs. McBride promised to go to Ellen's mother just as soon as she could get the team and buggy ready. "Meantime," she instructed Ellen, "you run home and tell your mama that Mrs. McBride's coming." Ellen put down her glass and started trudging up the road again, wondering why she couldn't just wait and ride with Mrs. McBride.

It took many years to shape up the raw land so that it produced income enough to keep a family. J.R. did as most of the ranchers in the valley did, took on additional work guiding, cooking or wrangling for fishing or hunting parties from the east. In this way he met and became very friendly with author-dude rancher, Struthers Burt.

Burt enjoyed listening to J.R.'s stories about his mining and gambling experiences and encouraged him to put them on paper. This started another facet of J.R.'s career.

Aware that he should have been a bit more attentive to his schooling, J.R. had taken correspondence courses to fill in the gaps in his education. Now he had a reason to make something of it. He wrote stories of mining camps and gaming tables, mostly first person accounts. Struthers was a great help, critiquing and editing for him, and giving advice as to where they could be marketed. The inactive, snowed-in winter days provided J.R. time to concentrate on his stories. He wrote of frontier life.

He wrote about the starving elk and the article found acceptance in the Izaak Walton League magazine *Outdoor America*. A story about stagecoach drivers, "Handlers of Sixes," was purchased and published in *Sunset Magazine*. Perhaps his most widely read story was, "The Bet I Made with Uncle Sam," published in the *Saturday Evening Post*.

"Playing the Gold Camps" was another story for the *Saturday Evening Post*. The *Courier* published a series of historical stories of trapping days, running serially, up to the time of Jones's death.

His article about the starving elk was helpful when the bill to furnish money to feed them was introduced. It also contributed to the enactment to buy "the government ranch"—now the elk refuge.

At the end of the five-year residence required to prove up on their homestead, the Jones family gratefully moved into town. They had won their bet with Uncle Sam but were not at all sure that the worth of their property equaled the money, time, and work they had put into it. J.R. had bought an adjoining place, so their holding was 320 acres. Still, the irrigation water was so chancy that a good crop could not be counted on. The Jones family turned their investment and efforts into property in the town. J.R. opened a tobacco shop on the south side of the town square, with a billiard table and card tables available.

Fidelia was soon involved in all the social activities the village offered. The house was enlarged to accommodate the growing family: Harry, who was born in 1909, Florence in 1911, and Crystal, born in 1913.

In the 1920s, J.R. enlarged the store and changed it into a grocery store. Ellen remembers that she and a friend, Bessie Lloyd, were drafted into the job of making homemade bread each day to sell in the store. (With no bakery in the town, bread shipped in on the mail stage was days old before arrival.) Mrs. Crabtree, who lived in the hotel next door, teased the girls that more bread went out the back door to the trash than went out the front purchased. The dudes said they appreciated the home-baked bread, however, so the girls were mollified.

Through the grocery store, Jones became acquainted with most valley residents. He became involved in community problems and was appointed on the committee to investigate incorporating the town. When this was accomplished, he served on the first town council from 1914 to 1917. In 1921, he served on the school board, and he was an advocate for education. As his children reached high school age, they went to the University Prep School at Laramie, the girls stayed in Ivinson Hall, the boys in the dormitory at the school. Rodney continued his schooling, becoming a doctor of medicine. (He celebrated his ninetieth birthday in 1991 in Denver, Colorado, but is now deceased.) Ellen married Jack Dornan. She is now at 91 (1994) the matriarch of the Dornan enterprises at Moose.

From the time that J.R. Jones first looked upon the beauty and pristine naturalness of Jackson's Hole from the eminence of Teton Pass, he was conscious of a desire to "save it." This urge to "save" Jackson's Hole seems to be the desire of almost everyone who comes to the valley, and their efforts are as varied as their motives. J.R. felt his greatest contribution to the country was his unswerving effort to have the valley set aside as a park, or at least a huge game preserve. In his memoirs of the Park extension, "Some Notes on the Creation of the Grand Teton National Park," he tells of the first time the idea came to him. He thinks he may even have been the first person to verbally propose the park.

The incident occurred on a hunting trip:

It was on a pack trip in the summer of 1909; the dudes were Robert Collier (of *Collier's* magazine) and Owen Waterby. The guides were Billy Lafferty, Otto Lunbeck, and T. Lloyd. Ted Webber was the wrangler and J.R. was the cook. While the men were just gabbing away around the campfire one evening, the question came up, "What would you do with a million dollars?" J.R.'s response came from prior thought, "I'd buy up all of Jackson Hole and make a park and game preserve out of it, and stop this killing of elk for their teeth, and find some way to keep them from starving." This was back in 1909, when nothing had been done about elk or ecology. Collier asked a few questions about the game problems but did not indicate further interest or involvement—thus losing his chance to one-up Mr. Rockefeller.

The idea remained in J.R.'s mind, and in 1919, when Horace Albright, Superintendent of Yellowstone National Park, came to

Jackson with a plan to add some of Jackson's Hole to Yellowstone he was an enthusiastic supporter. The idea was broached by Albright at a public meeting. A goodly crowd was present. Thomas Baxter and Richard Winger were the principal opposition speakers. When a vote for approval of park extension was called, Jones was the only voice raised in favor. The nays were many and vociferous. After that meeting, J. R. was in disfavor locally. He had to defend his position constantly, but never backed down from his pro-park stand.

Albright contacted Jones by letter (the only person in Jackson he felt sympathized with the plan). He contacted Struthers Burt and Horace Carncross back east and won them over to the plan. Here and there in the valley, ranchers who were not making out on their claims were beginning to think it a good idea if the park were to buy out all the valley—if they could get a good price for the land. Support showed up here and there.

Albright called another meeting of people he knew supported the plan. It was held at Maud Noble's cabin at Menor's Ferry, July 26, 1923. Present were Albright, Struthers Burt, Jack Eynon, Horace Carncross, and Dick Winger (who by then had changed his stand).

These men recognized two major obstacles to the plan: local opposition and lack of funding to implement it. Interested parties agreed that the Congress would not be likely to spend the money to buy the private lands—although they might agree to change the public lands in the area from the Forest Department to the Park. (Technically, this would be little more than a transfer of title from the Department of Agriculture to the Department of Interior.)

The small nucleus of park extension proponents determined to raise money to send two representatives to the east to try to interest financing from wealthy philanthropists or corporations. Two thousand dollars was raised, mostly by the efforts of Burt and Albright. Dick Winger and Jack Eynon were delegated to make the trip. This effort was not productive. It was not until Albright persuaded John D. Rockefeller, Jr., to visit the area in 1926 that they found a sponsor willing to back the land acquisition necessary to carry out the plan.

Although J. R. Jones claimed no credit for the final fulfillment of the park plan, he was always proud that he had seen the need for action and had worked for the project from his first acquaintance with the valley. He did not live to see the inclusion of the Jackson Hole National Monument into the plan. But he was on hand when Grand Teton National Park was officially opened.

After suffering a stroke in 1933, J.R. Jones was incapacitated until the time of his death, Friday, January 10, 1936, at St. John's Hospital, in Jackson.

Upper Gros Ventre Slide (1909-1911)

I F ONE HAS LIVED IN JACKSON for an extended period of time, he or she has surely heard all about the sudden creation of Slide Lake on the Gros Ventre River, has seen the huge slide which caused it, and has been told of the devastating flood which happened when the slide-formed dam gave way. For awhile the lake that formed was called "Sudden Lake" because there was already a "Slide Lake" further up the Gros Ventre.

Not so many people know about the upper Slide Lake, nor the slide which created it, although it also happened since the valley was settled by whites.

Far up on the Gros Ventre Mountains, in the vicinity of the headwaters of Burnt Cabin and Goosewing Creeks, was a ridge top which gradually sloughed away. Now it is a denuded, jagged depression, similar to the shoulder of Sheep Mountain from which the 1925 slide ran. This absent ridge top started to slip down slope in 1909.

It was a slow slide, but eventually—by 1911—it had pushed the lower slopes into the river, creating Upper Slide Lake. Al Austin, one of the early Teton Forest rangers, was riding in the slide area during one of its slippages, and told of his experience—along with the comment that he thought the end of the world had come.

Al was traveling leisurely along on horseback on a stretch of ground which was comparatively level for half a mile or so around. Gradually, the sensation crept over him that the earth seemed to be unstable. He got off his horse and held him by the bridle reins while the sensation of instability got more and more acute.

The earth all around him, as far as he could see, began to rise and fall and buckle. Trees pitched and tossed and turned upside down. He did not know which way to go. It was the same wherever

246

❧ Al Austin experienced the Upper Gros Ventre landslide in 1911. Here he wears typical winter travel gear for early valley residents. (JHM&HC)

he looked. He tried to get his horse to go on without him, thinking it might as well save itself if it could, but it would not budge. It stood with all four legs spread and braced, trembling from head to foot.

The earth continued to sway and buckle while terrifying rumbles came from the depths. After some time, the disturbance quieted down. Al, dragging at the reins, got himself and his horse out of the unstable area and to firm ground—which he had thought he would never be able to reach.

It was a long time before the slide area came to rest. Old timers tell of the road tracks periodically being wiped out or slipping way downhill. The Forest Service telephone line was constantly having to be restrung. Deep seemingly bottomless cracks appeared, which travelers had to find a way around.

In the period from 1909 to 1911 the slide was unpredictably and sporadically active.

The two slides which created lakes on the Gros Ventre River are by no means the only evidence of geologic activity in the Gros Ventre Range. There is a large slide on the head of Lafferty Creek, and a fairly large one on a nearby small stream between Lafferty Creek and Cow Creek. Geologists are excited about the earth-shaking activity going on in the Gros Ventre Range. But ranchers, hunters and hikers are somewhat wary.

You can well imagine the early settlers were more excited—and somewhat fearful. Nell Van Dervier, who was researching the slide as a thesis project in 1935, received the following report from an early rancher:

> One day a section of road might be in good condition and the next day there would be a crack several feet deep across it. Or, on other occasions, the whole road bed might slough off to one side. Sometimes a tree, or part of one, would stick up through the surface. It might be the top of the tree or it might be the roots sticking up. Everything seemed to be going topsy turvy.

The Upper Slide Lake is silting up. Before many man-years have passed it will be a grass and willow bottomland again. Just a moment in geologic time.

Snow Slide Buried Elias Wilson

This account was written by Jim Imeson who was present the day in January 1913 when a snowslide on Teton Pass buried Elias Wilson.

WE WERE TRYING TO GET OVER THE PASS to bring my sister's body over for burial in the South Park Cemetery. It was a very bad, stormy period, and a good deal of snow had fallen recently and was continuing to fall. This was during the latter part of January—probably around the 20th to 26th.

Several times we had ascended the pass to or near the twin slides only to be turned back by nightfall. At times there were a good many teams and men in the party.

On the fifth day, it was still snowing and blowing a great gale on the mountain, and at times it was impossible to see more than a few feet. We were just below the twin slides with two covered sleighs and most of the crew were at the slide shoveling a road out. About 3 PM Buster Estes who was carrying the mail came running up the road which had been shoveled out shouting, "Snowslide!"

Of course everyone came to instant attention and started running from the slide which they had been shoveling out. However, the [new] slide was below us on the road at the place of the last water on the east side of the pass [where the sleighs were parked]. My brother Don and Elias Wilson were at the two sleighs shoveling them out so that they could be turned around preparatory to going back that evening.

As soon as it was realized where the slide was, we all ran back. I was the first one onto the slide, and Don was in the middle of the slide pulling his left leg out of the slide. It had been buried midway to a point between his hip and knee.

I said, "Where is Elias?"

249

And Don said, "I don't know."

I continued running over the surface of the slide in an effort to locate him. We had sixteen horses with us and every one of those horses was covered excepting their ears. As I ran by a bay team of my brother Link's, I noticed a slight movement at the hawk joint of one of them. I continued running and suddenly it struck me like a sledge hammer that I had not seen the horse's rear quarter move when I saw the movement.

I raced back, everything was covered with a light snow. Don and Elias had, in shoveling out the sleighs, got their mittens wet, so had put on pairs of grey socks [on their hands], and they blended with the snow covering of everything so that it was almost impossible to recognize the difference between the mitten and the light snow covering on the horse.

Anyway, when I got back to the horse, I saw that it was Elias's hand in the mitten, and he was trying to dig the snow away from his face.

I dropped down and dug as rapidly as possible to his face, which was about 18 inches below the surface, and his face was turning dark from lack of oxygen. I am sure that the horse, in his struggles, must have broken the snow sufficiently to give Elias some air, otherwise he would have smothered.

But regardless of his position and condition, he didn't lose his "cool." I remember as we were digging him out, he looked up—and I can still visualize the snow on his eyebrows—and said, "I thought that the twin slides had run, too, and *there wouldn't be anyone to dig me out.*"

Snow slides do some very queer things. When Elias and Don realized that the slide was coming, they ran to a forked tree on the upper side of the trail, and Elias said, "My God! It's coming over us," and started to climb the tree, while Don was standing behind one fork of it.

Don said [later that] Elias's feet were about up to his [Don's] shoulders when the slide struck. It evidently knocked Elias down and covered him and must have run under Don and threw him up, as he was not covered other than his leg while, Elias was some twenty yards below and covered completely up.

John Wilson was standing behind a fir tree about eighteen inches in diameter, and the slide just covered his feet a little. The sleighs were stationed one before the other in the road, and John said that the one next to him (the upper one) appeared to rise in the air and the slide ran under it. When we got Elias out, we looked around for the one sleigh, and the slide had taken it down the hill about fifty yards and wrapped the box around a tree, completely demolishing it, while the other sleigh box stood on top of the slide as clean as if it had been placed there after the slide had run, and apparently that was what had happened.

We got the last of the horses out at two o'clock that night and returned to the roadhouse at the bottom of the hill. Frank Crandall and family were running it at that time and Lew Knudsen had the mail contract over the hill to Victor, Idaho.

Just one thing more, it developed the next morning that Elias had a well imprinted horseshoe on his back and was very sore.

SIGNED: J. G. IMESON

An additional note by Joyce Imeson Lucas, March 15, 1970:

I heard my Dad [Jim Imeson] tell about this experience several times, and I remember he said on some days during this trip they had as high as forty-eight horses on the hill, trying to get over. On the day they were caught in the slide, they had twelve horses, and in spite of the fact that every horse was caught in the slide and had to be dug out, not one was killed!

Also, another note of interest in regard to another experience: When the road along Bryan Flat was being surveyed many, many years ago, Uncle Elias Wilson was the rod man. He was a great fisherman and sportsman, and as the survey was proceeding, he couldn't resist catching grasshoppers to go fishing that evening. Unbeknownst to the surveyor, he moved the rod a bit as he swatted a grasshopper with his hat, hence there was an unwanted crook in the road; which I think was well worth it because of the history involved and Uncle Elias' love of fishing.

*H*E'S *M*EAN, *B*UT *J*'M *M*ENOR

BILL MENOR CAME TO THE VALLEY IN 1892, homesteading on the west bank of the Snake River, near what is now Moose. Once his basic homestead buildings were completed, he wasted no time in building a ferry across the river.

Menor's Ferry was often the only way to cross the Snake for forty miles. If the river was high and Menor chose not to operate the ferry, travelers had to go eighty miles out of their way—going up the river to cross on the bridge at Moran and following the river back down.

The ferry was a wooden platform attached to shaped wooden rails. It was carried across the river by the current and guided by ropes which where attached to an overhead cable.

The ferry held a four-horse team and later, when gasoline powered vehicles became common, it carried an automobile or a fair-sized truck.

Menor charged twenty-five cents a crossing for a horse and rider and fifty cents for a team. Foot passengers rode free, but they had to wait until the ferry was making a trip with a paying customer aboard.

Bill's younger brother Holiday came to the valley and joined the business in about 1905. Holiday explained both his temperament and the pronunciation of the family name when he said that on a previous job, "My partner's name was Mean, but I was Menor."

Not long after Holiday's arrival in Jackson's Hole, the brothers had a disagreement. Holiday moved to the east side of the river and built a house. For two years the brothers did not speak to each other, although they watched each other across the river. Finally they forgave each other and the feud was forgotten.

252

❧ Bill and Holiday Menor operated a ferry across the Snake River near present-day Moose from 1892 until 1918. (JHM&HC)

In 1918, Bill Menor sold his ranch and the ferry. New owners continued to run it until 1926 when an all-season bridge was completed.

The Menor brothers and the ferry were integral parts of the community. Stories abound concerning the colorful character of the brothers and hazardous episodes on ferry crossings.

❧

AN INTERESTING EVENT RELATING TO Menor's ferry from the life of the late George A. Wilson is portrayed in an early issue of the *Jackson's Hole Courier* under date of Thursday, August 2, 1917. The old newspaper was found in 1972, together with a copy of the issue of June 29, 1917, by Dick Robertson and Bill Jensen of the local sporting goods store while they were going through some old papers. There are not many copies of the *Courier* available preceding the date of the disastrous fire that destroyed the plant in the 1920s.

The June issue, which bears the name of the late Jay Goodrick as the subscriber, tells of the second marriage of Mr. Wilson in the following words: "George Wilson surprised his friends and relatives this week by returning to the valley, after a short trip outside, with a bride.

"It developed that Mr. Wilson had gone out to St. Anthony expressly to meet Mrs. Orah Chambers, his housekeeper, who was returning from a several weeks visit in her former home in California. It was while in St. Anthony that the marriage took place on Tuesday, July 20th.

"Mr. Wilson is one of the most worthy and respected citizens of the valley. He has lived here for many years and has the confidence and good will of all. His bride came to the valley only about a year ago, and, most of the time since she has been here, has been engaged as housekeeper for Mr. Wilson, managing his home and caring for his two children with efficiency and grace, and making friends of all she met. Mr. Wilson is being congratulated by all in having won her for his wife, and both are being showered with well wishes by a host of friends."

The August issue gives an account of an automobile accident at Menor's Ferry with a subheadline "Geo. Wilson and Family have Narrow Escape in Snake River—Wilson Rescues Wife and Daughter" and continues in full as follows: "What might have been a very serious accident occurred last Sunday at Menor's Ferry, when the Geo. Wilson car, in which were Mr. and Mrs. Wilson and thirteen-year-old daughter Mary plunged from the ferry into the swift water of the Snake.

"When the car struck the water Mr. Wilson fought himself free and jerked his wife from the car, holding her in such a way as to hinder him as little as possible; then endeavored to secure the girl, but was unable to locate her and was finally forced to leave the car in order to save his wife, with whom he swam to the bank.

"Mr. Wilson returned at once to the water and tried in vain to reach the car which was now washing rapidly down stream, only the top appearing above the water. He was able to call the girl, who was

🌸 *The Menor Ferry was, at times, the only crossing of the Snake River for forty miles. Here Bill Menor transports a vehicle.* (JHM&HC)

under the top, admonishing her to hang on to the machine. Mr. Wilson made three attempts to swim to the car, but each time the swift water carried him back and washed the car further down stream. The automobile had proceeded in this manner for a quarter of a mile when it turned over and in some mysterious way the girl came up from behind and as she perceived the rear wheel, hooked her foot in the spokes in such a way that she was able to hang on until the current washed her against the back of the machine, when she got a good hold and pulled herself on top of the machine. The machine by this time had lodged on a sand bar. In the meantime Mr. Menor had gone for his boat and he and Mr. Wilson were soon able to get the girl from the top of the machine where she was apparently in the best of spirits. She stated later that she got a black eye out of the mix-up but didn't care about a little thing like that. It was very evident that the little girl's wits were working all of the time or she would never have stayed by the car as she did until help arrived.

"Those who know Snake River say they would have believed it impossible for Mr. Wilson to swim ashore with his wife in the first place, and afterwards to go back into the water three times in an endeavor to reach the car certainly proves that he is some swimmer.

"The family is none the worse for the accident but are thankful it turned out as well as it did. The car suffered a broken top, windshield and steering gear, and was later rescued and brought to Jackson for repairs."

꽃

A TRAGIC STORY involving the hazards of ferry crossings took place at the Nethercott Ferry between Wilson and Jackson, near where the present bridge is located. Sometime around 1913 or 1914, Lewie Fleming and Carl Van Winkle came along the road from Wilson to Jackson, thinking to cross the river on the ferry. When they arrived at the ferry, they found that it was on the wrong side of the river. No one was around the parked ferry, and there was no way to get along to Jackson unless they wished to ford the river. The water was high so they hesitated to do that.

Carl declared that he could "shinny the cable" and bring the ferry back to their side. He reached up and grasped the cable firmly and started swinging hand over hand along the steel rope.

As he neared the center of the cable, the sag put him dangerously near the water. When his feet splashed in the current, he hesitated in his rhythmic swing to look down. This pause allowed the sag of the cable to be more pronounced, and the current caught both of Carl's feet. He pulled his feet free and tried to hook one leg over the cable but missed hooking his heel.

Lewie could see that Carl was in desperate trouble but could do nothing to help.

Carl was tiring. The river caught at his feet again as they came down. Carl doubled and tried once more to raise both feet out of the river, but this effort barely got his feet above the water.

When his feet came down again, the force of the water dragged him into a slanting position. Once again he tried to double at the waist to pull his feet from the water, but the current was too strong. Suddenly his hold failed, and he disappeared in the roiling water of the central channel.

Lewie ran down the riverbank, struggling with dense willow growth and rough terrain, trying to keep sight of the part of the flood tide where Carl might be likely to surface. He knew the current was outrunning him....

He never did see Carl bob up.

Lewie went for help and a search was conducted along the turbulent river. Later Carl's body was found on a sandbar almost as far down river as the mouth of Mosquito Creek.

BEAVER TOOTH NEAL: TOP POACHER

CHARLIE "BEAVER TOOTH" NEAL never ran for a public office that I know of, but he should have. There's no telling how far he would have gone. He was undoubtedly the greatest opportunist that ever lived in Jackson's Hole. His ready wit could turn seemingly impossible situations to his advantage. He was no "city slicker;" his features, manners, speech and clothing were as unpolished as any roughneck in the country. But if there is such a thing as a "country slicker," Beaver Tooth would qualify.

Charlie came to Jackson's Hole around 1900 and spent most of the years from then until the 1930s in the Moran area. His last home was what is now the Heart Six Ranch. For the most part, he made his living trapping. He got his nickname because his incisors were rather prominent and also because of his traffic in beaver.

Since beaver were taken off the legal fur-bearing game list about the time he came to the country, and since it was pretty well known that he still trapped beaver, the game wardens and Beaver Tooth played a cops-and-robbers game every trapping season. Getting the beaver into his traps was simple enough; getting the hides to market with all the game wardens and half the valley residents watching his every move kept Jackson's top poacher in mental exercise.

The schemes Beaver Tooth devised to outwit the law kept the local law enforcement on its toes and the valley folks well entertained. Stories about Beaver Tooth still circulate. For instance, there's the story about Mrs. Neal's periodic trips "out" to see her folks.

Beaver Tooth's wife was a pleasant enough woman. All of the old timers who "knew them when" say that Beaver Tooth and his missus seemed to get along fine. No one ever heard them quarrel. But this didn't stop a periodic disagreement which sent Mrs. Neal, bag and baggage, back to her folks, who lived someplace in the midwest. People figured it was cabin fever, pure and simple.

The story goes that she would arrive at the Crandall Roadhouse at the foot of Teton Pass with her trunks and valises just about every year along in the winter. She would tell a story of Beaver Tooth's "meanness" and shed some restrained tears. The stage-mail drivers and the Crandalls felt sorry for her, of course. Even had they been suspicious, who had authority to search her baggage? Separation apparently had a salubrious effect, for she came back by the time the roads opened up in the spring. Neighbors noted that the Neals always had funds for the summer without too much hard manual labor.

Everyone drew his own conclusions about that string of events.

It was not that the game wardens were lax or lazy in their efforts to catch Charlie that kept him out of jail. Way too much of the wardens' time was spent trailing him around and trying to outguess his methods of getting the hides outside.

The Neals were good neighbors: Mrs. Neal was a sweet and considerate person and Charlie as generous with his time and effort and the loaning of equipment as most settlers. He kept his place up, paid his bills and was never accused of shady dealings with a neighbor. Although Mrs. Neal was loved and respected, her apparent involvement in many of Charlie's evasions of the law could have made her at least an accessory before the fact.

The game wardens devoted so much of their time watching Beaver Tooth that he naturally began to feel they "had it in for him." When Jack Shives was game warden Charlie got mighty tired of being trailed around.

One day as Jack was riding along a tributary of the Buffalo, he spotted a man sitting on the bank of the stream, skinning what looked like a beaver. The guy looked like Charlie Neal.

Jack was so surprised he nearly fell off his horse. He quickly dismounted and tied the animal while he made a big sneak on the trapper. Sure enough, it was Beaver Tooth Neal, and he was skinning a beaver. Jack arrested him on the spot.

Beaver Tooth looked mighty sheepish but submitted to the arrest meekly enough. Jack picked up trap, hide, and knife and took

❦ Beaver Tooth Neal at the trading post on the Buffalo River in about 1914. (JHM&HC)

them along for evidence. Beaver Tooth waived a Justice of the Peace hearing, insisting upon a jury trial. This made it necessary to take him the long way around to Evanston, the county seat at the time.

Beaver Tooth was a model prisoner, in his stay in Jackson jail, on the long trip to the county seat, and while he stayed in Evanston. He refused a lawyer. Said he could plead his own case. The lawyer for the state assembled all the evidence produced by the warden. Beaver Tooth didn't seem to have any.

As the case began, Jack Shives was called to the witness stand. The state's attorney started his questioning.

"Mr. Shives, what transpired to cause you to make this arrest?"

"I saw a man skinning a beaver. Since it is illegal to catch beaver, and I am sworn to protect the game laws, I arrested him."

"Is that man in this courtroom?"

"Yes, sir. Mr. Neal is that man."

"Is this the beaver hide he was skinning?"

"Yes, sir. That is the hide."

"Is this the trap used to catch the beaver?"

"Yes, sir."

"Have these things been out of your possession since you made the arrest?"

"No, sir."

After establishing the place, time and all particulars pertaining to the arrest, the lawyer for the state relinquished his witness to be questioned by Charlie Neal, acting as his own attorney. Charlie strolled from his prisoner's seat to a position in front of the judge.

Ignoring the waiting Shives, Beaver Tooth picked up the trap lying on the table. He examined it, turned it over, squinted his eyes and studied the trap. With the courtroom hushed and expectant, he slowly handed the trap to the judge.

"Your Honor," he said, "the witness has testified that this was the trap which caught the beaver in question. Now, your Honor, I'd like you to examine that trap carefully. That trap isn't just any trap you can buy at a store. It looks to me like that trap is a special trap. If you'll turn it over I think you can see it is stamped with a number.

"Also, your Honor, it is stamped Wyoming Game Department. Now you know it is only the game wardens that get those traps issued to them to trap beaver that's doing too much damage. Now, your Honor, I don't know why Jack Shives would want to bring me in here and cause you all this trouble. Truth of the matter is, he caught that beaver. I was just doing the man a favor, skinning it for him. Everybody knows Jack Shives can't skin a beaver."

Well, Beaver Tooth was acquitted. Was it just because of one man's word against another? Or was it that everyone likes a humorous twist?

Nobody likes to have a red face, the Game Department being no exception. Even though everyone knew that Jack Shives knew how to skin a beaver, and everyone knew Charlie Neal knew how to find and "lift" a government trap, still, Jack Shives' duties with the Department soon terminated.

Beaver Tooth Neal knew how to trap a beaver trapper's trapper.

❧

Before the Oregon Shortline of the Union Pacific Railroad built the spur to Victor, Idaho, in 1912, the residents of Jackson's Hole had a choice of two roads to reach St. Anthony, Ashton, and thence other transfer points along the line.

The first was to go by wagon, stage or horseback up the valley and out by way of the Squirrel Meadows to Ashton, using the freight road which stayed busy supplying materials for the reclamation dam at Moran.

The second route, using the same mode of transportation, was over Teton Pass, through Teton Basin, across Canyon Creek, and on to St. Anthony.

The people living at the north end of the valley usually used the Squirrel Meadows route, while those at the southern end usually went to St. Anthony or Market Lake (which later became Idaho Falls). Either way, every family in the valley, using their own teams and wagons, usually took a few days once or twice a year to go out and stock up. Since it was nice to have help and company along the way, often neighbors got together and formed a wagon train to do their freighting.

On such a trip, Charlie Neal and his neighbor J.H. Uhl, both settlers in the north end of the valley, were making the trek to Ashton. Of course, the wives went along for the shopping.

Charlie made the greater part of his living as a trapper of various fur-bearing animals. The game wardens always suspected that the biggest portion of Charlie's pelts were beaver hides, a protected species. Catching him with the goods was the prime ambition of every warden. At this particular time, Pierce Cunningham was a deputy warden. Friends told him Beaver Tooth Neal planned to go outside. Cunningham made his preparations.

The Uhl wagon and Charlie's wagon, with another neighbor or so in the caravan, stopped to camp for the night at the Porter place, a roadhouse-type ranch near Squirrel Meadows. They hobbled the teams and turned them loose and proceeded with the meals and other chores. Next morning Charlie went out to wrangle the horses.

When he came back to camp he was leading one of his team. The horse was limping along, hardly able to bear weight on one of his legs. The ankle was somewhat swollen below the fetlock. Charlie shook his head and rubbed the leg and just stood around, not knowing just what to do.

Finally he told Uhl, "If you will take my wife and our stuff to Ashton, I think I'd better go along back home and get another horse. I'll be a day behind you getting out there, but I can't go on with this one gimping along."

Uhl agreed and the party split up with Charlie staying behind.

When the wagons reached the state line, the party was surprised to find Pierce Cunningham and another deputy just sitting around, obviously waiting for someone. They offered the customary greetings, talked to all the party, said, "Howdy Ma'am," to Mrs. Neal, and inquired politely, "Isn't Charlie along this trip?"

"One of our horses went lame," she explained. "Charlie had to ride back to the ranch to get another one to take its place. I expect he'll be along tomorrow."

The caravan went on and Pierce and the deputy remained where they were.

"Well, are we goin' back and try to catch up with him, or what?" the deputy questioned.

"He probably cached his stuff and rode back bareback," Pierce reasoned. "We'll just sit tight here. He's got no other way to go with a wagon."

They sat tight, and come the next morning along came the wagon they were waiting for. Beaver Tooth Neal was driving, and although Pierce and the deputy didn't know it, he was driving the same horse he started with two days before.

As soon as Uhl and the others were out of sight he had taken out his knife and cut the horse hair (pulled from the horse's tail) which he'd bound tightly around the horse's ankle. This horse hair loop had caused the swelling and the limp. Then Beaver Tooth had waited around to let the wagon train get a day's march ahead.

Pierce stopped him. "I got a warrant here to search your outfit, Charlie." And this he proceeded to do. Of course, there wasn't much in the wagon but Charlie's bedroll and suitcase and grub box. These were opened and searched thoroughly, every blanket and soogan was unfolded and shaken out. Charlie sat on his wagon seat and watched, grinning his toothy grin. Finally he said, "Whatcha lookin' for if I've got the right to ask?"

"You know damn well what we're lookin' for," Pierce grumbled. "It's time you were takin' your winter's catch out to ship, and I want to see how many beaver hides you got in the pack."

"Oh, that. Well, I sent that bundle on with the missus. Let's see, she oughta be about ready to get on the train by now. Didn't know how long it would take me to get to Ashton, so I just told her to go on and I'd meet her in Salt Lake. Sorry, boy, I guess you'll just have to check my packs next spring."

So one more time the beaver hides got to market.

※

The Model T Ford was careening down the Buffalo Meadows road, driven by Glen Ferrin. Merritt Ferrin was riding passenger. They were two of the Si Ferrin boys, on their way home to the Elk Ranch near the mouth of the Buffalo. On the stretch near the Beaver Tooth Neal store, they spotted old Charlie himself, sitting, with a rifle across his knees on the side of the road. He rose and waved them to a stop.

Glen pulled to a stop beside Beaver Tooth. A prickle of nerves already had iced its way up the back of both boys' necks. Neal looked wild and unkempt, more so than usual, and he was waving the rifle around as he talked. Being stopped at gunpoint was enough to inspire fear, but the way the man rambled and cussed—and the unusual things he said—just about scared the pants off the boys.

"I'm out here to stop you drivin' over this stretch of road. You got to go around. See those marks?" They could see where he had scratched a line across the road with a stick. A one-hundred-foot stretch or so was marked off in the dust and gravel. (There was no blacktop in those days.)

"I got a contract from the Forest Service to count all the rocks in that piece of road. I can't have 'em disturbed."

The boys detoured around Beaver Tooth's stretch of rocks.

At that time, Glen had a contract to build telephone line up to the Blackrock Forest Service Station. The Blackrock cattle herd was being worked for fall roundup at the Hatchet Ranch. There was quite a bit of travel on the road. So Glen and Merritt checked in at the Hatchet Ranch to tell their dad and other neighbors about the scare old Charlie Neal had given them. The news didn't really surprise anybody.

This wasn't the only indication that Neal was going a little off his rocker. Other neighbors cited incidents where Charlie had seemed just not right in his head. The most clinching evidence came from the auctions he had been putting on at his store in Moran and also the store at his home there in Buffalo Meadow. Why, he was selling out his stuff there for whatever anyone would bid—always way below wholesale. Even the town merchants bought at his auctions.

Neighbors talked to Mrs. Neal, and then to the county officers. Soon the sheriff and deputy came up to get Charlie to take him off to the county seat at Evanston. Charlie behaved in a vague and other-worldly way but made no objections. He was given some kind of a hearing and committed to the asylum in Evanston.

After a few months in the asylum, it was noticed that he was as rational as a man ever needed to be. The doctors gave him another batch of tests and found he was the smartest man in the institution. They released him, and he quickly returned to the ranch.

No sooner had he settled down to the various ranch duties, than he was served with an indictment. Scowcrofts and other wholesale suppliers were suing him for non-payment for supplies shipped to his stores over a period of many months—the remainder of which goods he had been auctioning off not so very long ago.

Once again Charlie made the trip to Evanston to appear in the county-seat court.

And this time it was a short stay. The judge threw the case out of court. It was shown that the man was adjudged crazy at the time of the purchases. Therefore he was incompetent and not responsible.

Whatever Charlie made at his auctions turned out to be clear profit. Only some people call that crazy.

⁓

While Charlie "Beaver Tooth" Neal was busy trapping beaver, and other fur bearing animals, his mind entertained the complete picture of the fur industry.

Having experienced difficulty in getting his own pelts to market (at times), it occurred to him that others might have the same problems. The solution was simple. Charlie organized a Trappers' Union.

It was a legal entity—incorporated—and had a board and a chairman: Charlie. For a five dollar membership, a trapper could have his furs sold free of commission fees. It is surprising how many trappers in Jackson, and many surrounding areas, signed up with the Trappers' Union.

Just having a corporation instead of an individual selling furs did not get around that outside broker's payment. Next Charlie organized the Leader Fur Company, another legitimate business enterprise, with Charlie the sole owner.

When the trappers brought in their furs and deposited them in Charlie's warehouse and the trapping season was over, Charlie graded the fur and advertised an auction.

Charlie was the auctioneer. Since there was seldom another fur company representative sent up to Moran for the auction, the Leader Fur Company was usually the only bidder. Each Trappers' Union member got his check for his furs and everything was on the up and up.

Then with his stamped and tagged furs, Charlie set off to the fur markets of the country. He soon became a very sharp bargainer.

If Charlie had confined his efforts to local trappers, the enterprise may have gone unnoticed by the law. But when he advertised to gain members in the Union, it brought on another investigation.

Merritt Ferrin was getting gas at the Gillette Ford Garage, Jackson's busy corner in the early 1930s, when a traveler pulled in to the rear pump. According to Merritt, the driver got out and engaged Wendel Gillette in conversation.

"I'm looking for a man named Charlie Neal," he stated. "Do you have any idea where he lives so you could give me directions?"

"I can tell you where he lived, but Merritt Ferrin there, he can tell you more about him. He has lived neighbors to him all his life." The man turned to Merritt.

"I can tell you a lot about him, all right." Merritt was always a willing conversationalist. "But you're a little late to see him. I just helped bury him about ten days ago. Did you need to see him? Or just know where he lived?"

"I guess I've driven clear up here for nothing," the man said. "I've got some papers to serve on him. We've had him up before the court a couple of other times on his fur deals, but he's got out of it. This time, he advertised through the mails and we have a federal case. It won't do any good now. I can't serve any papers, so I might just as well start back from here." He studied Merritt's face. "You're sure it's the same man?"

"Oh, it's the same guy all right. You can go over to the undertaker over there in the Jackson Mercantile and find that out. Old Beaver Tooth died on the street out in Driggs the other day. He had a heart attack."

After the stranger had gone to verify the death of his man, Merritt turned to Wendel with a fitting epitaph, "Well, old Charlie Neal beat his last rap."

𝒩EWS OF 𝒥EBRUARY 1916

THANKS TO JEAN STEWART, I CAN share with you some excerpts from an old issue of the *Jackson's Hole Courier* that surfaced during some renovations. It is a Thursday, February 10, 1916 issue. Dick Winger was editor. Jackson was in Lincoln County. As you will observe as you read, the folks of the valley were weathering a very bad spell of winter weather.

Some people use newspapers for wrapping paper. Here is a switch when the *Courier* had to use wrapping paper for newsprint:

> Because the Oregon Short Line trains have been unable to get through the snow, and because we were unluckily caught with no supply of paper on hand is not sufficient reason to keep the *Courier* from coming out on time. You will notice this issue is not printed on newsprint but on wrapping paper.
>
> The merchants have come to the rescue with the last bit of wrapping paper in town. In case the mail does not come through before the next issue they have been kind enough to offer several rolls of building paper. We think, however, that there will probably be paper here in time for the next issue, as the drivers from both sides of the pass are making a big effort to get to the top. When you consider that five feet of new snow has fallen on the hill in the past two days their task looks like a hard one.

And other news items from the same issue:

> First news received in Jackson in the past sixteen days. We print below a little news from the outside world for

268

which we are indebted to C. T. Manville, agent for the Oregon Short Line in Victor, Idaho, who transmitted it to us by phone. On account of the storms it has been sixteen days since mail reached even that close to Jackson. The following excerpts were taken from a late edition of *The Salt Lake Republican*, which was brought overland to Victor, and is being closely guarded by residents of that part of the country. We trust *The Salt Lake Republican* will not object to our stealing their front page under the existing circumstances. [Follows news of the German naval activity, notes from Washington with an appeal for unity under "whatever circumstances," by President Woodrow Wilson and an account of a Zeppelin raid over the English countryside, about which the English press remarked, "A number of bombs were dropped but up to the present no considerable damage has been done." Stirring times to be cut off from news.]

The same issue continues with news of the valley:

> Dr. Charles Huff made a trip to the J. P. Nelson ranch on Spread Creek the first of the week on a call stating that Almer Nelson was very ill. The doctor left Tuesday noon but did not reach Nelsons until an early hour Wednesday morning, it being necessary to snowshoe from the Carpenter place on across Antelope Flat. He found Almer very sick and threatened with pneumonia but was able to note much improvement before he left. Dr. Huff snowshoed on to the Coffin and Heninger places where a siege of La Grippe and the mumps is in force.

Also in the same issue of the *Courier*:

> Official City Council proceedings; Present Mayor Harry Wagner, councilmen Jack Eynon and H. W. DeLoney; absent, councilmen J. R. Jones and C. J. Wort. Motion made by councilman Eynon that the marshall's salary be increased to $30.00 per month, seconded by

councilman DeLoney, carried. Received for saloon license, $1250.00, Cowan's pool table license, $10.00, received for dog taxes, $10.00, fine and costs received in the case of Chas. Dann, $7.50, and more on the council proceedings.

And further in the same issue:

Now that the City Fathers have seen fit to increase the salary of the town marshall to the handsome sum of $30.00 per month, and as the season for collecting dog taxes is drawing to a close and this mighty matter lifted from the shoulders of our representative of law and order, we trust that he may be able to give his attention to some of the important ordinances passed by the honorable board. His attention is respectfully called to ordinance No. 18, entitled, "an Ordinance to Prohibit the Running at Large of Horses, Cattle, Mules and Elk in the Town of Jackson." Now we have it from reliable sources that large numbers of elk have for several nights been making themselves at home in the front yard of the mayor of Jackson, at times tramping on his front porch in such numbers as to greatly disturb his rest. Why are not the ordinances of the town of Jackson enforced? At least let's have some action on these important ones....

Ahh—Weren't those the good old days!

$\mathcal{A}$UNT $\mathcal{G}$ERE: $\mathcal{A}$ $\mathcal{C}$HARACTER $\mathcal{A}$LL $\mathcal{R}$IGHT

"SHE'S A CHARACTER ALL RIGHT!" Often this was said of Geraldine Lucas—"Aunt Gere," as she was known to friends and relatives. So what sets one person apart as a "character" when they do the same everyday things as the rest of us do? The dictionary defines a character as: "one with a distinctive behavior or personality different from the norm." Well, yes. This Aunt Gere had. She was an independent thinker, self-sufficient and unafraid—in the days when women were supposed to be timorous, dependent, and a mirror of their men-folks in thinking.

Aunt Gere was born November 5, 1865, at Iowa City, Iowa, the sixth in what became a family of twelve children. Her grandfather, Robert Lucas, had created Iowa City as the first capital of Iowa Territory, when he was appointed Governor of the newly-created Territory. Her father, Robert Lucas, soon moved his family to Nebraska Territory, where he built up a large cattle ranch in the Sand Hills. When Nebraska became a state he was invited to name the county in which he lived. He chose to honor President Franklin Pierce, so it was named Pierce County.

Father Robert Sumner Lucas thought that education for women was a waste of time. Daughter Geraldine wanted to go to college, so go to college she did, working her way to a B.A. degree in Education. She secured work in the school system of New York City, helping her younger sisters with encouragement and money if they also wanted higher education.

While in New York, Geraldine met and married an Irishman named Mike O'Shea. To this union one son was born. They named him Russell L. O'Shea. It must have been a stormy marriage. Aunt Gere would never talk about this period; but she emerged from it with a divorce. It must have been a struggle to divorce a Catholic, and in New York State. She regained the name 'Lucas' for her child and herself, and acquired an abiding hate for all things Irish or Catholic.... She was irreligious to the point of atheism.

She worked hard to provide a home and schooling for her son, so it was a great shock to her pride when he ran away to sea. She said, "If that's all he wants, after my working my fingers to the bone, then good riddance!" Fortunately, the captain for whom Russell had become cabin boy took an interest in the lad and encouraged him to get back into school and later into the Coast Guard Academy. Mother and son were reconciled and Russell (she always called him "Razz") soon worked his way up the ladder of promotions to become the youngest man to ever receive the rating of Commander at that time.

Aunt Gere had two brothers, Lee and Woods Lucas, and one sister, Camelia Seelamire, who had settled in the Jackson's Hole country. When Gere visited them one summer, she fell in love with the country. She soon returned to stay. Picking out a home site at the foot of the magnificent Grand Teton, she filed her homestead claim in 1912. She hired Paul Imeson to put up her homestead cabin. He did a log job which is still a credit to the log-laying art. Gere did not stint with her own labor in clearing brush, carrying wood and water, and cooking for the carpenters. Soon she was ready for the winter.

The first winter was very simple, with one stove (the cook stove), one bed, the table, and a couple of chairs, all in one room. A kerosene lamp, water by the bucket from Cottonwood Creek, and an outdoor privy completed the setup. It was all standard equipment for the country, but a far cry from a New York apartment.

Gere had an abundance of books, and she busied herself braiding rugs for the bigger cabin to come. She learned to use the webs necessary to get about on the deep snow and visited among the many homesteading neighbors nearby: Jimmy Mangus and his mother; the Brothers Roany and Lew Smith who lived up in Lupine Meadows; the Gabbys; Moritz Locker, who was later to die of a heart attack as he skied over to Kelly and was not discovered until the snow went off in the spring.

The post office for that side of the river was way down at Wilson in those early days. So mail was brought up-country only when someone had the time and energy to ski or web down there and back.

Gere may have had savings, Razz may have helped with money, but her needs were few. Much to the wonderment of the irredeemably nosy folks in the valley, she got along fine with no apparent income from her homestead.

She loved her solitude and independence, but she welcomed the acquaintance of a young girl named Naomi Colwell. At this late date no one seems to know how the acquaintance started, but it developed into a real friendship. Naomi was fascinated with the life Aunt Gere had established, so she filed on the neighboring 160 acre plot and proceeded to build a cabin near their joint property line. They shared the work and mushed around together on their snowshoes. In summer they fenced and did other work to prove up on the claims.

Razz visited the ranch and saw the need for winter transportation. From Alaska, he brought a dogsled, mukluks, parka and a team of Huskies. He brought them overland by train from San Francisco to Victor. Maybe it was on this trip to see his mother, maybe on some other, but the story is that Razz and Naomi fell in love. When Razz left they were engaged. Razz went back to sea; Naomi waited.

Naomi and Gere now rode to the post office (first way down at Wilson; later, only half way, as the post-office of Teton was established near the present location of Teton Village). They also took much longer trips around the neighborhood and brought back more of a load. People *really* took notice when they saw Aunt Gere, togged out in her outlandish cold-weather gear, mushing about the valley with her dogsled. Proof right before their eyes, if they hadn't known for certain before. She certainly *was* a *"character!"*

The dogs were quite a chore to feed and exercise—at one point Gere had fifteen dogs. They had to be tied up in the cottonwood grove pretty constantly, as they were not exactly pets, and the neighbors were afraid of them whenever they did happen to get loose and roam.

Katherine Newlin Burt wrote a novel, titled *Cottonwood Creek*, making the heroine an abused young girl who lived with an old curmudgeon of a woman who made her do all the heavy work and abused her mentally, never letting her out of sight. The characters were so blatantly based upon Naomi and Gere's relationship that there was much comment about it in Jackson's Hole. Aunt Gere was so angry to be cast in such a role. And so hurt, because she had regarded Katherine as a good friend.

Not being the type to take a hurt feeling lying down, Aunt Gere sat herself down and wrote a scurrilous poem about Katherine and mailed off copies to all of Katherine's friends. That was the end of a beautiful friendship.

Just how many years Naomi and Gere were neighbors is not known at this late date, but they completed the necessary occupancy and the work required to prove up on the properties. Razz returned for another visit, but the romance had cooled, at least for him. The engagement was terminated. The record shows that Naomi sold her property to Geraldine Lucas in 1922. Did she leave because of a broken heart? Or for the more mundane reason, the necessity to earn her living?

At first acquaintance, Aunt Gere seemed a rather formidable person. She was below medium height and somewhat stocky. Her expression was sober. But there was a glint of humor and intelligence in her grey-blue eyes. She always wore Levis, cut off, gathered and tightened at the knees at knicker length. She made her own denim or chambray pull-over blouses, used black stockings to the knees and sensible shoes.

Books, magazines and newspapers (and later radio) were her constant companions, so she was a quick and intelligent conversationalist, although a trifle dogmatic. She was a martinet to work for, expecting the work to be done quickly and just so, according to her lights. The wood must be ricked just so, that it might be easy to lift out in the winter. The sleds and dog harness must be stacked just so, to be easier to get out and harness the dogs. But exacting as she was, and free with advice and directions, she was always willing to do her share, and was kind and hospitable. She never used "maybe" or "I think so." Hers was a positive disposition.

Aunt Gere came to view the Grand Teton as her own particular mountain, so it is no wonder that the urge to climb it, to see the view from the top, to conquer it, grew in her. For many years after the Owen-Shives-Spaulding-Peterson party had scaled the peak, there was little interest in the climb. Then suddenly a new type of visitor found the range. People who had climbed in Europe came seeking out the Tetons for climbing pleasure. Being right in the midst of the preparation spot, Aunt Gere became acquainted with Paul Petzoldt, a young climber who had made more than one successful ascent. The party that assisted Aunt Gere on her trip up the Grand included Paul, Allen Budge, Ike Powell, Frank Edmiston and Jack Crawford.

The climb took place August 19, 1924. Gere was fifty-nine years old. She freely admitted that the boys had to pull her and even push her up in some places, but still it was the most exhilarating experience of her life. She wore jodhpurs and field boots for this event, with her usual pull-over blouse, gloves, and a bandanna around her head to keep the perspiration and her short-cropped, grey hair out of her eyes. She posed on the top holding the American flag which she had carried all the way. She had her moment of glory.

Aunt Gere, and the whole valley, thought that she was the first woman to scale the Grand. Since there was no Grand Teton National Park, and records were not kept as they are today, it was years before the general public of this valley knew that a Mrs. Eleanor Davis had climbed the Grand, with her husband and others, just the year before. Aunt Gere never did learn of it and died believing she was the first.

As might be expected, Gere was no proponent of the Yellowstone Park extension, nor of creating a Grand Teton National Park. She said, 'NO!' many times when approached with offers to buy her land. Finally, she told the agent that if he could offer her a stack of silver dollars as high as the peak, she might consider it.

When Park extension was brought up in her presence, she spoke long and forcefully on individual's rights. "Nobody was going to force HER to sell." When most of her neighbors were selling with a lease back agreement, or just taking the money and going to a more favorable climate, Aunt Gere snorted and pooh-poohed. "No guts

❧ *Geraldine Lucas thought she was the first woman to climb the Grand, although later it was learned she was not.* (JHM&HC)

to stay and enjoy the winter," she said, although she knew very well that the poor soil and late springs of the area made farming a losing business. "Well, let them take dudes," was her reasoning. And true enough, those who did remain with their homesteads did just that.

Razz would tease her when she got on this subject, saying. "You know you don't really own that place, don't you? You're on it just at the Government's grace. You're paying them rent, in the form of taxes." Stoking her temper, he'd add, "They could take it away from you any time they want."

"Over my dead body!" Gere would respond. "I'm going to stay right here." And stay she did, her health being remarkably good.

She drove a big Buick touring car in the summers, in winters she used webs to go to the neighbors or out to the highway where she caught a ride to the post office (which was at Jenny Lake during her later years) or to go to Jackson for a few days.

She built a larger, more comfortable cabin on the banks of Cottonwood Creek, calling it Razz's cabin. She had a cesspool dug, but no water system was put in in her lifetime. The creek was her water supply; kerosene or gasoline lamps served for light; a privy still sat out back, screened by bushes. Razz's cabin had a big roomy kitchen with wood burning stove, a large living room with fireplace, and two bedrooms, one of which was full of trunks which were still full of materials she had brought from New York. A wide porch enclosed two sides of the cabin; glass enclosed the south side. One could sit or work there on sunny days of the winter. The side that faced the Grand had large windows for the view.

She had her piano. "All the Lucases could play something," she said, meaning some musical instrument. The living room was surrounded by bookshelves. The tops of the bookcases and occasional tables were covered with exotic things Razz had sent from his travels.

Although Aunt Gere wore her knickers in Jackson and to all functions—even to Dr. Huff's funeral, which shocked some—when she went on a trip outside, she was always beautifully tailored.

The children of Dr. Huff loved to have Aunt Gere come to visit them in town and to go to her cabin at Jenny Lake. She let them crawl in bed with her where she read to them or they recited poems or sang jingles together.

After the dogs became too much for Aunt Gere to keep she disposed of all but one. This one, called old Lum, she brought to town with her when she came in to visit. Most all the children in town got to ride behind old Lum for their first dogsled ride. Finally, Aunt Gere gave old Lum to George Lamb, who had a dog team of his own on his ranch near Snake River Canyon. Since George's dogs were afraid of old Lum, George put them in the lead with him tailing them. Then he'd get a merry, swift ride, with no urging.

Aunt Gere's health gave way in the summer of 1938. She was visiting at the home of Dave and Cornelia Abercrombie when she took sick. She was admitted to St. John's Hospital on August 7 and died August 12. Her ashes were interred under a huge granite boulder on her ranch at the foot of the Grand Teton.

As she said, the Park would get her land only over her dead body. Razz did not sell the place to the Park. Perhaps he respected his mother's stand. However, he did not use the lovely heritage she created for him. Razz's cabins and all the land were sold to Kimball, who had the store and cabins at Jenny Lake. Kimball soon sold the place to the Park.

Aunt Gere would not have liked what then happened to *her* place. The Park furnished it as a summer home for Harold and Josephine Fabian, the Salt Lake lawyer who had handled the legal work for the purchases made by the Snake River Land Company (Rockefeller) for purpose of Park extension. The Fabians used the cabin until 1985. Aunt Gere would much rather it had immediately reverted to nature. Meanwhile, she lies in *her* meadow, at the foot of *her* mountain, the Grand Teton.

$\mathcal{E}$ARLY $\mathcal{P}$RIVATE $\mathcal{E}$LK $\mathcal{H}$ERDS

As the earliest settlers of Jackson's Hole became established—cabins built, fields fenced, little herds of cattle started, and enough hay stacked to winter them—the native elk herds adapted as best they could to the changes in their environment.

When white men first came to Wyoming, the elk summered in the mountains and migrated to the desert plains in winter. Gradually, as their migration routes were settled by homesteaders, the elk ceased to migrate and tried to winter in the mountains. They starved by the thousands and also caused quite a problem by raiding the ranchers' haystacks.

The largest number of elk ranged in the northwest corner of the state and Jackson's Hole was the scene of the greatest problem. Contrary to today's assertions, many residents of Jackson's Hole have always been concerned with "saving the elk herd" and it was through the efforts of local citizens that the first congressional action to appropriate money to feed the elk was instituted.

But there's always someone around who can figure out a way to make a situation work for him instead of against him. With elk constantly getting into private fields, corrals, and haystacks in the winter, it is no wonder that some citizens conceived the idea of a private elk herd. After all, if the beleaguered ranchers hadn't wintered the creatures, albeit unwillingly, the elk would have starved. A return on their hay loss seemed justified. All that was necessary was to feed them in elk-tight enclosures, shut the openings, claim ownership and have an instant elk business.

Two or three ranchers were known to have acquired little herds of elk, held inside elk-tight fences, summer and winter. It was a good deal cheaper to get started in the elk business than the cow

279

business. However, marketing them was a problem. A rancher named Glidden had a little herd which he planned to allow hunters to kill at so much per elk. Others found markets for elk meat by hauling it to the railroad crews in Idaho. This was going on *before* the new state of Wyoming got around to passing strict game laws.

When the state did pass some restrictive game laws and create the Wyoming Game and Fish Commission as an enforcement body, they immediately ran into the sticky problem of these privately owned elk herds. Working on the premise that the state owned the game within its borders, the Game Department decreed that it was impossible to allow private ownership of game to continue. To get the ranchers holding these elk to agree to turn them loose, the Game Department representatives gave each rancher a tally sheet of the number of elk released from his property. In turn the rancher was permitted to kill the same number in or out of game season. The only restrictions were that he had to have a game warden along, and he had to mark the elk he killed off the tally.

The owners weren't too upset about the enforced liberation of their private elk herds. They weren't making any progress domesticating elk anyway. In addition, not too many hunters had evidenced interest in killing a game animal in a pasture. There was no local market since everyone in the valley could go hunt his own elk in season. And just imagine driving a herd of elk to an outside market? Did you ever try to drive an elk? Anywhere?

Pap Carter, living on the place that is now the Cottonwoods Guest Ranch, was one of those who had owned some elk and turned them loose. Since Pap was getting on in years and didn't care to go chasing around to find his elk in order to shoot them, he sold his tally to young Ike Powell. "Let him go fill out the remaining tally of critters." Ike was young and strong and didn't mind hunting elk and hauling them out to the Idaho market.

Ike followed the letter of the agreement and alerted the game wardens that he was going after an elk. This was after the hunting season had closed. Fred Deyo, the local game warden, sent Deputy Game Warden Henry Francis out with Ike. The Cache Creek area was full of elk so this was where Ike headed.

The hunter and warden soon sighted a small bunch of elk, and Ike drew a bead on a nice fat cow. At his shot, the cow dropped. Ike rested his gun against a stump and pulled out his skinnin' knife. As he started toward the fallen animal, she jumped up and ran. Ike swore, picked up his rifle, and the two men took out after the wounded animal. Gut shot! Ike was mad and disgusted; Henry was just disgusted.

They followed the blood trail for a while. In a stand of timber the trail they followed joined the tracks of quite a herd. The bleeding had stopped, soon Ike and Henry lost the blood sign and were on tracks of possibly ten or more elk. There was no telling which were those of the wounded cow. Ike said, "I guess I'll have to let her go and go find another one."

It wasn't long until they found another bunch of elk, and Ike made his kill and marked it off his tally.

"You're gonna mark that other one off too, aren't you?" Henry reminded as Ike started to put the tally book away.

Ike was noted in the country for his violent temper and this question blew his lid.

"Hell no! I'm not gonna mark it off. I didn't get that elk," were the beginning of his remarks—put mildly. Belatedly taking into consideration Henry's official capacity, he later fit in, a little less pugnaciously, "What do you think you can do about it?"

"Well, I think I'm gonna have to arrest you—but not right now." Henry pondered the situation. "I'll get Fred's opinion. Either that's your elk and you mark it off your list, or it's the state's elk and I'll have to arrest you for shooting it out of season, that's the way I see it."

Ike responded with another temper blast. Not speaking any longer they proceeded back to town.

Henry went off to consult with the senior game warden about the legality of his position. "Hell yes, we'll arrest him," Fred Deyo agreed. "We might as well see in court what rights these sonsabitches with those old tallies have."

So, learning that Ike had gone to the movies, they waited around the drugstore and arrested him as he came out. Ike threw another temper fit but they took him along to old Mr. Hoffman, the Justice of the Peace. All Hoffman did that evening was to set a date for trial in Justice Court.

Henry had to present his own case, which worried him considerably. He had nothing to refer to, in law, concerning killing supposedly privately-owned elk. He wrote to the State Game Commission but got no answer. He talked to A. C. McCain, the Forest Supervisor. (In those days the forest rangers were also deputy game wardens during the hunting season.)

McCain promised to come to the trial but had no more knowledge of the legal aspects of the matter than Henry had. The day of the trial dawned with Henry feeling he had no legal basis for his arrest and no help in sight.

The Justice Court convened in the basement of the first courthouse, the Fox building, at the corner of Pearl and Cache Streets. As soon as Justice Hoffman convened the court, Henry asked for a postponement. By this ploy he hoped to have time to get some opinion or advice from the Game Department at Cheyenne.

Jackson didn't have a resident lawyer at the time, but for these little cases brought before the Justice of the Peace many people secured the help of Dick Winger to argue their cases. Dick was regarded by the locals as a mighty sharp cookie who could outsmart many a lawyer. Ike had Winger on hand this day to represent him in court. Dick came over to Henry and asked, "Why get a postponement? Let's get this thing over with."

"I want a postponement until I can find out where I stand," Henry stated. "I'm gonna get an answer back from Cheyenne before I put my case up to the judge."

"I can get this settled in five minutes," Winger replied. "So you don't have to wait for an answer, and we won't have to have another trial date."

"How do you plan to get it settled? If he won't claim the elk, then it is the state's elk, and he didn't have any business out there hunting it." To Henry, the whole thing was pretty well cut and dried, but he sure would have liked to have some legal precedent behind him.

"He *will* claim the elk," Dick said. "He'll mark it off the tally right here. We can all go home with the case closed."

"Well, for Pete's sake. If he'd been that reasonable the day he shot the thing, we wouldn't have had to come here in the first place." Henry was disgusted but mighty relieved.

So Ike marked one more elk off his tally, which was getting pretty short by that time (the early twenties). It must have been just about the last of the privately-owned elk which were loose on the public domain, and the end of the short-lived domestic elk ranch business.

PEARL WILLIAMS: TOWN MARSHALL

IN 1920 WHEN THE TOWN OF Jackson made history by electing
the first all-female slate of town government officials in the
United States, Pearl Williams, a beautiful, petite young lady,
took over as marshall. Pearl was the daughter of Otho Williams,
who did much of the local surveying. Pearl's mother was a sister of
Maggie Simpson. Pearl was in little physical danger as marshall.
Young women were treated with respect in those days. She had no
difficulty in her tenure.

In this interview with a reporter representing an eastern newspaper, Pearl seems to be teasing and stringing the reporter along:

> **Cheyenne, Wyoming May 16**; Folks, meet Pearl
> Williams, the world's champion wild man tamer. Pearl, be
> it known, is the little lady who, as town marshall at Jack-
> son, Wyo., for the past year, has been subduing bad men
> with smiles and in Jackson of all places. For more than
> thirty years Owen Wister and numerous other press
> agents for the west have made Jackson's Hole, of which
> the town of 526 souls is the center, the incarnation of all
> that is wild and woolly and thoroughly western. That is
> they did until Pearl became marshall.
>
> Miss Williams last nite submitted to her first interview.
> You wouldn't call it that back east, but out here in the
> land of magnificent distances it was typical of how things
> are done. Sitting at his desk in the [south]east corner of
> the state, this correspondent tried for 21 hours to get in
> touch with the town marshall. After numberous *[sic]*
> efforts and many calls from Cheyenne to Chicago and

wrong connections, had produced the information that the marshall had no phone at her home that a messenger went there post haste but without results, and that she was not to be found. All day yesterday the calls were repeated but this time they shed the information that Miss Williams had left for the country and would not be back until evening. Last night the lady was landed.

Third-Ha[n]d Interview

The interviewer propounded his questions to the Cheyenne operator, she relayed them to the St. Anthony operator, and she in turn shot them at the lady of Jackson. The answers came back by the same method.

Here is the conversation, reproduced verbatim, between the correspondent and the obliging Cheyenne telephone girl, a few short sentences and many long waits, principally the latter.

Correspondent—"Please ask her for a statement as to how she managed to tame bad men with smiles."

Operator—"She says she can't make any such statements, because she has resigned, and isn't going to be marshall anymore."

Cor—"Why did she resign?"

Op—"She says the town is now so quiet it don't need no marshall anymore (the grammatical error, it was concluded, was the operator's and not the marshall's)."

Cor—"Please ask her if it is not true that the town has no jail and that the county jail is nearly two hundred miles away. Ask her how many arrests she has made during her year's term, and what she did with the men she arrested."

Op—"She says she didn't make any arrests and so she didn't have to go hunt up a jail. She says that a while ago she killed three men and buried them herself and that she hasn't had no trouble with anyone since."

Cor—"All right, please [ask] these questions and then we'll be thru. Would she mind telling the paper how old she is? Is she a native of Jackson, or if not, what town and state is she from? What did she do before she became town marshall, and what is she going to do now that she is about to quit her job?"

Op—"She says she is 22. She says she never lived anywhere but in Jackson. She says she was a soda squirt before she took this job, and that now that she's thru with being town marshall she supposes she'll go back to her old job. She says she's had a-plenty, and doesn't want to be marshall anymore."

So ended the 1000 mile third-hand interview.

Pearl has decided to quit. Her turn in front of the calcium lights is almost finished. Tomorrow the re-elected women's administration will hold the first meeting of its new term. Miss William's resignation will be presented and accepted, and the "city mothers" will then take up the momentous question of whether Mayoress Grace Miller should appoint another woman marshall or let a mere man have the place as in days of old, or, agreeing with the present "police force", that the town has actually become so civilized that it doesn't need any peace-officer, declare the position abolished.

But that isn't quite all. For the benefit of the male readers it might be added that Miss Williams is extremely easy to look upon and that she is winsome and has a lot of good, hard common sense.

A Labor of Love

In making this statement the correspondent admits that he has never seen the lady, anymore than he has had with her a conversation more direct than thru two go-betweens. But last summer he paid a "flying" trip to Jackson, and in the course of his three hours there, he heard all about the woman marshall—how in spite of her comparatively small size, she has not found it necessary to arm herself except on "special occasions"; how, instead of being kept busy running to earth the horse thieves and wild men with which many eastern people think the west is still infested, she has devoted a large share of her efforts to making manly men and womanly women of the future citizens of Jackson; how she has supervised the conduct of the town —.

Pearl Williams may have found that the attention paid her by newspapermen took more of her time than the lawbreakers of Jackson's Hole.

Pearl Williams Hupp lived into her nineties and passed away in Montana in 1994.

JULIANE TANNER:

FIRST COUNTY CLERK & FIRST LIBRARIAN

ONE PIONEER CITIZEN DID MUCH to get the county organized and keep it on the right track through five terms in
office: Juliane A. Tanner, the first county clerk.

In the fall of 1896, Juliane Hammond came into the Jackson
Hole country to teach in the only school in operation at that time,
South Park. She was eighteen. Dave Timmins had been delegated
by the South Park community to meet her in St. Anthony, Idaho,
with a team and wagon. He made the trip count by laying in his
winter supplies.

The old log house which was the schoolhouse still stands on the
Wilfred Nielson property in South Park, probably the oldest house
still standing in the county.

The winter of 1896–97 was the first full winter term of school
held in the valley. Before that, summer sessions were held. One of
Juliane's pupils, Elias Wilson, was a year older than his teacher.
Juliane taught all eight grades and had students in almost every grade.

Juliane was born in Laramie, Wyoming, on November 21, 1878.
Her family moved to Blackfoot, Idaho, when she was very young.

It was there that she was educated through the first year of high
school. Later, she finished high school in Omaha, Nebraska, where
she passed the tests for a teaching diploma.

After the winter in South Park, Juliane taught in Hamsfork,
Wyoming, for two years. While she was in South Park, she had met
and been courted by Frank Tanner. On December 14, 1899, she
and Frank were married. Frank brought Juliane back to his homestead in South Park, near what is now the Rafter J development.

Frank and Juliane proved up on their homestead and lived there
the remainder of their busy lives, except for a two-year period
(1906–1908) when Frank had the contract to carry mail from Victor.

Their ten children, including one set of twins, were born in Jackson.

Juliane played the organ and soon was asked to give lessons. This she did by going to the pupils' homes. Often she rode horseback with one of her little ones behind the saddle and another astride the pommel in front.

When the state legislature passed the bill creating Teton County in 1921, Juliane decided to run for the office of County Clerk. On April 28, 1921, the governor appointed a board of commissioners for the new county: W. P. Redmond, Chairman; P. C. Hansen, and T. R. Wilson, of Alta. Josephine Saunders was appointed clerk for the board. On October 11, 1922, the commissioners held a meeting to proclaim an election.

Juliane was elected County Clerk on November 7, 1922. The geographic area of Teton County had formerly been included in Lincoln County. She spent the rest of that fall and winter traveling to and from Lincoln County's seat at Kemmerer, where she had to transcribe all the records of legal transactions pertaining to Teton County matters.

Since the county had no courthouse (and no money to rent one) Juliane took care of the clerk's business in her own house. During this time, a fire in the Tanner residence destroyed some of the work done with so much labor earlier. The transcribing of some records had to be done over.

Soon, quarters for the county business were rented from Charlie Fox. This was a new house, designed to be a home and built to sell as such. It never served that purpose, except for a few months when Eva Lucas, first County Superintendent of Schools, rented it. When the county became wealthy enough to build a courthouse, the old Fox building became a hotel.

Juliane held the office of county clerk for five consecutive terms, being succeeded by Elmer Moody in 1933. Much of the time she also performed the duties of Clerk of the Court.

In the 1930s, a community effort to acquire a library was sparked by the efforts of Edith Mercill, Stella Weston, and Helen Benson. With donations of books and money from residents of the county, the ladies started a library in the north wing of the American Legion Building.

At first, volunteers took turns keeping the library open and cataloging and arranging the books. Funds were needed, as well as a steady attendant. Funds were raised by community barbecues given by Friends of the Library effort. Some ranchers who helped raise money in this way were Marion Hammond, Margaret Huyler and Jennie DeRahm.

With some funds at their disposal and an enlarged committee, including Hattie Erzinger (then County Superintendent) and Charlie Kratzer (editor of the *Jackson Hole Courier,* now *Jackson Hole Guide*), the library group hired Juliane Tanner as the first official librarian in 1938.

Efforts to make this library a county library were successful. In 1940 the library moved into the log building on King Street. Mrs. Tanner and the original board were still at the helm when this move took place. That new building was built largely with money donated to the Dr. Charles Huff Memorial Fund, started by Edna Huff.

Whenever I think of the practical, but tolerant and humorous attitude, with which Mrs. Tanner faced life, I'm reminded of the night she took her daughter Peg and me to the South Park Community Club party.

Peg was just my age. I was often invited to their ranch to spend a day or two. This particular time I was there, the South Park Community Club was having a party at the Cheney Hall. (The present location of Paul Von Gontardt's ranch.) Peg and I wanted to go. We were possibly twelve or thirteen at that time. We were by no means old enough to have dates but plenty old enough to want to go to a party where there were sure to be boys our age and games and dancing and food.

Mrs. Tanner said we could go. Then it turned out that Mr. Tanner had no interest in going, and neither did the older boys, Bard or Bill.

"All right," Mrs. Tanner said. "We will just go anyway. I'll drive."

We got dolled up and set out. It was raining so we had to put the side curtains up on the Ford. It was only two or three miles down to Cheney (the name of the community). We had gone about one mile when the lights gave out. If we hadn't been in a pair of ruts we might have gone off the grade, a steep little pitch in front of the

George Wilson home. Mrs. Tanner stepped on the brake and considered what she should do. It was a very precarious place to try to turn around without lights. Turning around meant going back home. Peg and I groaned aloud.

"Oh well, we might as well go on to the party, now we're this far," Mrs. Tanner said. She sent Peg in to borrow a lantern from Mr. Wilson.

With the lantern held in front and one of us girls on each front fender to call out the way, and with the upper half of the windshield opened in order for Mrs. Tanner to see at all, we slipped and slid cautiously on to the party. We all got a little damp, but it didn't dampen our spirits. Our party clothes were a bit muddy too, I remember, but we had a wonderful time.

Some mechanically-minded man at the party discovered the loose wire or connection which had deprived us of lights. Mrs. Tanner was able to drive home without our "Statue of Liberty" act. It was just as well. I think Peg and I slept all the way home—even through the stop when she left George Wilson's lantern hanging on his gatepost, and the last stops at the Tanner gate, where Mrs. Tanner got out of the car to open the gate, got back in to drive through, then got out again to close the gate and back in to drive on. She didn't disturb us until we drew up in front of the house.

HIGH JINKS ON THE OPEN RANGE

BACK IN 1920, BEFORE FRED DEYO became a state game warden for Teton County, he was a right good cowboy and bronc stomper, as was Bob Crisp, a fellow who was a mighty good cowboy in Jackson for fifty years. In those days they were both young and full of beans and hard to hold down.

Fred's escapades have become legendary. It seems he was always getting the laugh on someone. Bob was more shy about telling of his adventures.

During the summer of 1920, they worked for the Pederson's AP Quarter-Circle Ranch, the biggest outfit in the valley at the time. Ted Pederson had invented a gunsight, which patent the U.S. Government bought and used on the army rifle. Ted had the biggest investment in ranches and cattle in Jackson up to that time.

The ranch was on the bench and in the river bottom along the Gros Ventre east of the highway where it crosses the river. Ted's brother Chet ran the ranches while Bob and Fred worked with the cattle.

They had taken the cattle to the range as usual that spring. Bob stayed to herd while Fred returned to the ranch. Later in the summer, the crew came back up for roundup. They cut out the steers and then, instead of bringing them to the ranch, Pederson decided to trail them over Union Pass and down to the railroad at Hudson.

Fred went with the steers while Bob stayed with the cows, moving them into Purdy Basin for the last few weeks of the grazing season. When the cowboys got back from the drive to Hudson, Fred rode up the river to help gather the rest of the herd to start them home.

Fred and Bob were sitting on a sage covered slope one day while the cows took a mid-day rest. They were trying out some German Luger pistols they had got in trade from fellows who'd brought them back from World War I. The Luger automatic kept firing as long as you pressed the trigger, quite different from the old Colt. Fred and Bob used everything nearby for a target.

Casting about for a more interesting target, Fred eyed Bob's hat. "Toss your hat up and let's see if this would make a good bird gun."

"Not my hat." Bob settled it more firmly on his head. "I just got this hat this Spring. It ain't hardly broke in."

"Come on," Fred coaxed. "I'll throw mine up and you shoot at it, then you throw yours up and I'll shoot at it. See how many times we can nick 'em before they hit the ground."

Suiting action to words, Fred pulled his old black hat off and sent it spinning in the air above him. "Shoot!" he commanded.

Bob automatically raised his pistol and fired; the fluttering hat settled to the ground. He didn't nick it.

Bob reluctantly took off his ten-gallon, held it in his hand a moment, still undecided.

"Okay, Bob, now don't be a piker." Fred grinned.

Oh, well, Bob shrugged. He hadn't been able to hit Fred's hat, and he sure didn't want to take the razzing for welshing, even if he hadn't exactly agreed in the first place. Maybe Fred would miss the wide brim. Fred shot once or twice, not touching it. Finally it settled gently on the top of a sagebrush. Bob sighed with relief.

Fred went right on shooting—emptied the Luger into it; five or six more shots. A sitting duck....

We won't go into the things Bob called him at the time. Fred just laughed and pointed out that the hat, after all, had not hit the ground. Technically it was still a target.

Bob said that Fred was so full of these tricks that he, Bob, used to lie awake at night, trying to think up retaliations.

He had a start on an idea when he went to visit Harve Burlingham, who was living on the Lemon place at the mouth of Fish Creek.

Harve shot bear in the pay of the cattlemen (strictly on the QT because it was legal only if bear were bothering his cattle, and Harve had none). Harve had several cans of bear grease rendered out, and Bob borrowed some, saying he was out of bacon grease.

Back at the Collier place, which the Pedersons owned at the time and used as a cow-camp, Bob set the bear grease aside and bided his time. Opportunity arrived when Fred was gone on circle without his chaps. Bob fixed them up. They were hairy angora chaps and in good condition—maybe a mite heavy for summer, but warm in the winter. Bob lubricated them liberally (but unnoticably) under the hair and around the belt with the bear grease.

The next time Fred put them on, his horse smelled the bear and wouldn't let him near. Fred had a pretty spooky top horse that he liked a lot. He couldn't figure why the pony went hog wild every time he started up the rope to get a bridle on him. He put up such a fight, Fred couldn't even get the saddle on. Feeling pretty perturbed and a darn sight huffy, Fred finally had to give in and ride an old horse too indifferent to fight.

While all the tussle and cussing was going on, Bob kept assuring Fred that it seemed to be the chaps the horse was afraid of. Fred had to agree. "But," he said, "the son-of-a-bitch has never been afraid of them before!"

The next time Fred went to town, he came back with a new pair of bat-wing leather chaps.

The Collier cabin cow camp had three rooms. The entry room was used for wraps, storage and what not; the middle room for cooking and eating. The partitions were just boards, papered with newspapers and magazines. Bob noted where Fred hung his chaps on the wall of the storage room and another, even better, jobbing-of-Fred idea came to him....

During the course of a long evening, Bob took out and oiled his Luger, and when this was done, he took a practice shot at a knot hole. Fred pulled his gun out and gave it a going over, too. Soon they were shooting out nailheads and some of the pictures of the paper job. Bob was careful to hold his shots to an innocent part of the partition and to urge Fred to shoot this or that picture which he knew happened to be opposite the chaps.

You *know* what Fred said when he found his chaps next morning with both legs full of bullet holes. He knew he had got his comeuppance, with a master's touch. Only thing to do in a case like that is to wait for the next opportunity to pull something on Bob.

You win a few, you lose a few. No need spoiling a good friendship over a little fun.

ELMER MOODY REMEMBERS WHEN

A photocopy of this article, an interview with Elmer Moody on the county's origins which appeared in the Jackson Hole Villager, *was given to the author years ago. The ending appears incomplete, but no originals are known to exist. It is printed here verbatim.*

TETON COUNTY TOOK TIME OUT ON November 9 [1968] for formal dedication of its new court house. A glimpse of the county's past was furnished by Elmer N. Moody who witnessed much of it and had a hand in shaping its development, in the several jobs of county clerk, clerk of court, county treasurer, and county attorney.

When Wyoming became the forty-fourth state of the Union on July 10, 1890, said Moody, every county began at the northern border of the state and extended to the southern border, so each county could tax the Union Pacific Railroad; for as everyone knew in those days, a county could not exist without a railroad to tax.

As new railroads spread throughout the state, new counties were carved, lessening the formidable distances to travel to county seats. Jackson Hole was originally in Uinta County, with the county seat at Evanston, several days' journey to the south. About the time he came to Jackson, said Moody, a justice of the peace sentenced one Beaver Tooth Neal to 30 days in jail for game violation and deputized Frank Williams to take him to Evanston to serve his sentence.

During the journey, Neal managed to steal the papers and on arrival at Evanston tried to surrender Williams as the prisoner. Authorities confined both men until matters could be cleared up.

With Evanston as the nearest land office, it was quite expensive and time-consuming for homesteaders to go there with two witnesses to prove up on their homesteads; so a land office was established in Jackson. Still this did not solve all problems, so when a short-line railroad was built from Ranger Junction and Kemmerer to the northwest, in 1908, Kemmerer became the county seat of the new Lincoln County, comprising all except the southernmost 45 miles of what was formerly Uinta County.

William C. Deloney of Jackson was among the new county's legislators. He did not feel Jackson had ample representation in the state, so in 1921 he introduced a bill into the legislature to create Teton County. His geography wasn't too good, as his bill set the western boundary over into Idaho, and included the Idaho community of Alpine in Teton County.

The governor appointed an organization committee for the new county, comprised of William P. Redmond and Peter C. Hansen of Jackson, and T. Ross Wilson, of Alta. They met on April 28, 1921, and called an election for June 5. The ballot included two questions: Should the new county be created, and if so, should the new county seat be Jackson or Kelly?

The issues created a schism in the county. How could a county survive without a railroad? Others argued that the distance to the county seat warranted a new county, and said it was not fitting that the area with the largest elk herd in the world should have only one vote in the state legislature.

On election night, all ballots were in and counted except seven from Alpine. The voters had decided they did want a new county, and Kelly led Jackson as the new county seat by five votes. However, the next day when the Alpine votes were brought in, all seven went to Jackson, so Jackson was chosen as county seat by two votes.

A provision of the state constitution stated that when a new county was formed, it must have $2 million assessed valuation, and 1,500 inhabitants. The new Teton county had $2,235,000 assessed valuation and 1,620 people.

However, the previous legislature had just passed a new law requiring a county to have $5 million assessed valuation and 3,000 people. Supporters of the new county tried to repeal the new law by adding the customary repealing clause to the bill creating the new county. "All laws and parts of laws in conflict herewith are hereby repealed." The Teton County bill was passed, signed into law, and the legislators at home before it was discovered that some typist had omitted the repealing clause.

The people opposed to the new county hired Robert R. Rose of Kemmerer to represent them. He brought a restraining action to prevent recognition of the new county or turning over of any records or property.

This action pointed out two flaws; that part of the county as proposed by Deloney was in Idaho, and that the new county did not have the assessed valuation or population required by the new law. The suit quickly went to the state supreme court.

The legislature which met in 1923, passed another bill creating Teton County "*nunc pro tunc*," meaning as if it had been passed in 1921, this time omitting Alpine precinct and correcting the western boundary.

A second suit also went to the supreme court, seeking to restrain the state treasurer from giving Teton County any grazing funds which were about to be distributed.

Nobody was paying taxes and the county was broke. County officers were being paid in certificates of indebtedness which nobody would honor. Finally Jackson State Bank cashier Harold Wagner persuaded the board of directors to permit him to cash the certificates. It was a wonderful feeling, said Moody, to be able to eat again.

About this time the Wyoming Supreme Court decided the whole thing was legal from the beginning, and that Teton County could elect one state senator and one state representative. Nothing was ever done about the seven Alpine votes which had made Jackson the county seat.

It was illegal in those days to permit irrigation water to run into the road, where it made mudholes which could prevent travel by early motor vehicles. The county clerk wrote to ranchers, asking them to keep irrigation water out of the roads. Some did and some didn't.

Whenever County Commissioner Peter Hansen met one of the ranchers in town who permitted the water to continue running into roads, he would engage him in conversation and eventually get around to the road problem, saying how difficult it was to hire good help. He would end up by asking the rancher, when he had a slack time on the ranch, to help the county by working on the road for $3 per day for himself and a team of horses. Cash was pretty tight, and usually the rancher was glad to earn the extra money. So the roads were repaired at minimum cost and everybody was happy.

The new county had no money for a court house, so for $80 per month they rented a building from Charlie Fox. There was no jail, but the building did have a basement in which the commissioners placed an iron cage—only to learn that it was illegal to house prisoners below ground.

The cage did once have two inhabitants, however. Art Burlingame asked Moody if he could keep a pair of beavers there until he could sell them. Unfortunately, the animals gave the courthouse an overwhelmingly unpleasant odor, and when sheriff Jim Francis returned from a trip, they were summarily evicted, while Moody and Burlingame trod carefully in Francis' presence for a long time thereafter.

There was no lawyer meeting the county's residence requirements, so Payson W. Spaulding of Evanston was employed. His voting residence was in Uinta County, said Moody, but his fishing residence was in Teton County, and that was the one which counted. Moody said he kept the county from making a lot of mistakes and covered up a lot which were made, for which the county owes him a debt of gratitude.

In January, 1924, county commissioners accepted the offer of Teton Forest Supervisor A.C. McCain to build a road over Teton Pass, if the county would maintain it forever after.

In 1929, the county hired Charlie Fox to build the county's first court house, which served from then until the fall of 1968. The cost was around $13,000.

When Jackson Lake Dam was built in 1912, by the federal government, a number of irrigation companies decided to add another twelve feet in height, and it was agreed that they owned the additional impounded water.

The new county, looking for tax revenue, decided that the upper twelve feet of water was taxable, and valued it at $1,500,000. The irrigation companies claimed all the water was federal property and could not be taxed. The federal court agreed with the irrigation companies. Still, said Moody, if you should go swimming in Jackson Lake, it might be well to stay twelve feet under so you'll know you are not trespassing on private property.

*L*ANDSLIDE ON THE *L*OWER *G*ROS *V*ENTRE

"WHAT MAKES THAT LONG BARE SCAR on the mountain to the east? There where it looks like the timber and dirt was scooped off down to bedrock?"

These questions are still asked by visitors to the valley, just as the natives asked each other when they first noticed the scar which appeared on June 23, 1925.

When the north shoulder of Sheep Mountain slid, jamming earth, trees and rocks into the narrow valley of the Gros Ventre River to a depth of 225 feet, in a swath a half mile wide, the cataclysmic event was not without forewarning. William Bierer, known affectionately throughout the valley as "Uncle Billie," had predicted that the mountain would slide some day. Uncle Billie had homesteaded at the mouth of Bierer's Creek, where the slide came to rest. Before the slide ran, he had sold his claim to the Guil Huffs and had gone east to live with a daughter. But while he lived in the valley, he'd said:

"Anywhere on that slope, if I lay my ear to the ground, I can hear water tricklin' and runnin' underneath. It's runnin' between strata. And some day, if we have a wet enough spring, that whole mountain is gonna let loose and slide."

Uncle Billie wasn't a geologist, but he could see that the heavier rocky strata overlaying the bentonitic clays (he and the rest of the natives call it "gumbo") on the steep sides of the mountains would slide when conditions were right. Evidence of such happenings is found all along the Gros Ventre River. A "slow" slide had run in 1911–1912, damming the river and creating Upper Slide Lake. Other slides come into the river periodically and are washed down without damming at the big bend downstream from the Darwin

300

place. Note how Bierer's prediction fits the factual statements of geologists who studied the area after the event. The following is taken from the Eleventh Annual Wyoming Geological Association Guidebook:

"The slide occurred about 4:30 P.M., on June 23, 1925. The uppermost part of the slide broke loose 2000 feet above the river on the south side of the narrow valley. The mass roared down the mountain, jammed the bottom of the valley full, and the momentum carried debris 400 feet up the slopes of the north side. This blocked the Gros Ventre and soon created a lake about four or five miles long. The engineers estimated the volume of rock to be 50 million cubic yards.

"The slide was caused by the resistant Tensleep sandstone sliding down dip on the water saturated shale of the underlying Amsden formation. Several other factors set the stage for the slide: (1) the dip of the beds is about 20 feet north and the valley side is essentially parallel to the dip; (2) a relief of approximately 2100 feet between the top of the slide and the river level in the horizontal distance of one mile; (3) the river had eroded completely through the Tensleep sandstone, thereby increasing slide potential by producing one free side to the rockmass; and (4) there had been a prolonged period of extra heavy precipitation."

As Uncle Billie said, "Give it a wet enough year and all that rocky strata will just slide right down on that gumbo like a beaver's slickery slide."

Guil Huff had just built a lovely home on the bench overlooking the river. It was built of log, but was lath and plastered inside. Guil had worked as a cabinet maker, so the inside was tastefully finished and had modern conveniences, unusual even in the town of Jackson in 1925. Guil and his wife had put all their savings and work into the ranch and home. They had a start of cattle, enough hay meadow to feed them in winter and forest range all around them for summer. They were happy living on their ranch with their five-year-old daughter Dorothy.

The day of the flood, three homesteaders occupied in cowboying chores had stopped to chat across the river from the Huff place. Forney Cole had just driven some strayed cows out of Guil's meadow across the bridge back to the road. Leonard Peterson was bringing some cattle along the road, and Boyd Charter had just caught up with them. He was taking the cavvy [horse herd] up to the Fish Creek cow camp. Bob Seaton had passed Boyd at the Devil's Elbow switchback—Bob going downstream, Boyd up. Ned Budge was up on Turpin Creek hunting horses. Mrs. Huff was in the house. All of these people saw the slide, or parts of it, or heard it.

Mrs. Huff happened to look out the window and could see only the top of the slide as it started.

"Trees started moving and tipping. Dust rose above them. I wondered for a minute, then I realized what it was. I called Dorothy, who was playing nearby. 'Come look out the window, a slide is running up on the mountain.' She didn't stop playing, and I couldn't see the lower part of it, so I didn't know how close it was coming."

Ned said he saw the top of the slide start moving and slipping down hill. Dust rising over there had first caught his attention. He could hear a loud hissing sound at first, then a big rumble that grew to a roar. He lit out for home, forgetting about horse hunting.

Boyd, Forney and Leonard heard rocks rolling and looked up to see weird spirals of dust and heard an increasing noise which quickly grew into a roar and a heavy dust cloud. The mountainside seemed to be moving and spreading out. Their horses became spooked and jumpy. "It's a slide," they shouted to each other as they were mounting up. "I wonder if it will get over this far? Do you suppose it will get Huff's house?"

Boyd said he would go tell Dibble, the ranger at the Horsetail Creek Station about a mile up the road. He had to catch up with the remuda; the horses had spooked and were running up the road. Forney and Leonard went to the Huffs to help if they were needed.

Bob Seaton was on the Turpin Creek slope, so he did not see the slide, but he heard it. The rumble and the shaking of the earth scared both lad and horse so badly they tore down the road without stopping to investigate the cause.

Guil was plowing in the lower field with four head of horses. He heard boulders rolling and saw some dust spirals. He quit early to ride up on the slope to see what was happening. He saddled a horse and was riding up the hillside when increasing noise and dust caused him to look further up the heavily forested mountainside towering above him.

A brown mist rose from a stand of lodgepole pine, swirling and drifting in the rays of the sun. To his horror he saw the trees begin to move, to twist and lean, to toss and to leave their rooted place and start toward him. The rumble grew to a roar and the earth began to move. Guil knew the only avenue of escape was the trail back down to the ranch, although it seemed to be directly in the path of a moving mass of the mountain.

His horse needed no spurs, he had whirled and started home while Guil was taking in the situation. They streaked down the trail. Guil said he wasn't sure if he opened the gate to the field, if the slide had moved posts enough to break it open, or if the horse jumped it, but when the crest of the slide thundered into the riverbed it had missed them. They had outrun it.

But then came another peril. The vast mass of debris, upon hitting bottom and hitting against the nearly perpendicular opposing wall of the north side of the narrow valley, split. The upstream part of this mass, under incalculable momentum, curled off to the right, spreading across Guil's field. It followed him so closely as he raced for home that huge boulders even shot past him, and tumbling trees, whipping about like willows, seemed about to outrun the straining horse. The slide eventually came to rest; the horse and Guil charged on, finally outrunning the danger almost in his own yard.

Supper was almost ready but was never eaten. The family felt they had to get out of there. There was no telling if that slide might touch off something more. In addition, they could soon see that the slide had dammed the river. Much had to be done to save what could be saved from the rising water.

The William Card place was just above the Huff's on the same side of the river. The Cards were alerted and the two families, with the help of Forney, Leonard and Ranger Dibble, worked far into the night getting their possessions hauled by wagonloads across the river to higher ground. Mrs. Huff reports that about 4 or 5 A.M., the family trooped to the ranger station.

There the Huffs slept on a mattress on the floor of the office cabin. The next morning, after breakfast, they returned to the ranch to see what more could be done. The water was already about eighteen inches deep in the house.

The Forest Service and Dr. Huff, brother of Guil, had been told of the slide by telephone. Supervisor A.C. McCain, Ranger Felix Buckenroth, Dr. Huff, Dick Winger and newsman-author Donald Hough came in two cars. They drove to the downstream edge of the other side, then climbed the mountain side on the north face of the canyon to get up to the Guil Huff place. The Guil Huffs returned with these men to town, climbing back up around the slide, the men carrying Dorothy most of the way.

Knowing the water would continue to rise, Guil could not wait for a road to be built to get their necessary household items from the ranger station where they had been hauled the fateful night. He started packing them out on pack horses. Henry Francis tells of helping him pack out a mattress on one of Guil's work teams. He says it was the hardest pack to throw a diamond hitch on he ever tried.

That day they wound up packing all the horses but one saddle horse. Henry says they agreed to ride and tie. (A process where one man rides ahead, dismounts and ties the horse, and walks on. The second man walks to the tied horse, mounts and rides past the walking man for a distance, then ties the horse and walks ahead.) But Guil must have forgotten to tie. So Henry had to walk all the way from the ranger station to the lower end of the slide, climbing up around it afoot. Not much of a jaunt if you are hunting, but terrible if you are a packer with a pack outfit.

The Horsetail Ranger Station seemed to the Dibbles to be safe enough—unless the water should back that far. They decided to stay on as long as possible. However, on the night of June 29, they were awakened by a roaring rumble. Remembering the slide, they jumped out of bed and streaked out into a pouring rain in their nightclothes. To get to high ground they had to go through a barbed wire fence. Charlie said bits of nightclothes and some hide were left on the barbs on the way out.

They ran until the roaring ceased, then after a wait in the pouring rain, Charlie Dibble and his wife Cap braved the cabin long enough to get dry and dressed. They climbed into their Model T

Ford and drove to higher ground. There they pitched a small tent in which to spend the remainder of the night.

The mountain did not slide that time, it only settled and made large terraces down the side of the mountain. The settling was impressive enough to cause waves to wash against the ranger station. The Dibbles moved the next morning and three days later the cabin floated away.

Those directly involved in escaping the slide and the resultant lake were too shaken and busy recovering from the events to have much time to take it all in. But the slide made news throughout the country. People came from far and near to see the huge avalanche and the new lake it had made.

Jackson had always had dudes who came to stay awhile. This was the first big summer of "tourists."

Roads were not so good in those days. The main valley road went east of town through the Dry Hollow Hills to Kelly then on north, with a branch going up the Gros Ventre. It was just a pair of tracks, not even graded and graveled.

People walked and climbed around in the debris and marveled at the size and scope of the landslide. They looked at the long earth fill in the river, so deep and thick, and thought it could never wash out. Water seeping through the dam coming out the south end kept the river below the dam at normal flow. Everything seemed back to normal.

Engineers who came to look at it thought that a safe channel would eventually be cut along the path of the seepage and that the river would continue down its bed as before. Residents of Kelly were not so sure. They suspected the whole thing might collapse sometime and turn the flood of the lake down upon them.

Despite the opinion of many engineers who came in to view the dam, it was not safe. On May 17, 1927—after another winter of heavy snow and a wet spring—the angry swirling waters which had backed up behind the dam softened the long earthen fill until it gave way. Water, rocks, trees, and trash gouged through the canyon below the dam and burst like a bulldozer blade through the town of Kelly. Six people were drowned and many head of livestock and game were lost. However, the flood could have taken everyone in the town if the break had occurred in the night, or if there had not been a slim margin of warning. *[See Albert T. Nelson chapter.]*

ᘒ

The Huffs moved to a timber claim near Wilson shortly after the slide and have been only occasional visitors since that time. I was very pleased to come upon Guil by chance, in 1960, as I stood at the slide overlook, explaining the history of the slide for the Student Conservation Program youngsters. Guil had come to do a little private remembering and to see how the valley had recovered. He kindly told the students his story and answered their questions.

ᘒ

Today Slide Lake is one of the attractions of the valley, offering good fishing and boating. The Verland Taylors have rebuilt the William Card place into a profitable cow ranch, while Florence Lamb has a private hunting and fishing lodge on the George Card place. Only three acres of the Guil Huff land are arable. The Glen Taylors bought this land and built a home there.

*L*IFE IS FOR *L*IVING

THE INTERVIEW STARTED WITH A SPIRITED discussion of chalcedony from Dunoir Creek, turretella from south of Wamsutter, petrified algae from the South Pass area, and petrified palm wood from the Eden area, as Ida Chambers showed us samples from her rock collection.

Being a rock hound is just one of the hobbies Ida pursues. She is so full of enthusiasms and interests that the word "bored" is not part of her vocabulary, unless referring to some poor soul who doesn't know what life is for.

"Life is for living" fits Ida, and she lives it gaily.

Once, as she was masterfully threading her way through rush hour traffic on the Phoenix streets, she said, "I wish they would quit broadcasting how many cars are wrecked on the streets each day and start bragging on how many get home safely. That is the marvel of this city driving." Ida believes in positive thinking. "Putting it the other way is depressing."

When Ida came to Kelly to stay, in 1917, she says she was "coming home." Her step-mother and father, Anna and Milton Henry Kneedy, came to Kelly to homestead in 1910, but Mr. Kneedy would not let his children, John and Ida, come until they finished high school. Ida lived with her sister Clara Gentry at Valley Forge, Kansas.

The Kneedys' homestead was north of Kelly on Antelope Flat near the present Shadow Mountain homes. Milton had started a sawmill there which he later moved to Kelly.

Ida liked to be out of doors and where the action was, and her first summer in Wyoming was spent helping her brother John get out poles, build bucks and make fence. Her first winter, she taught at the

Grovont grade school. She boarded with Hannas and Margaret Hartshorn on the "Row" (Mormon Row), and some of her pupils were Ted and Nellie Woodward; Lester, Leland and Clifton May; Jim, Charlie and Ida Lou Smith; and Gordon and Pauline Riniker.

Ida taught at Moran one year also, having the Feuz, Ford, Lozier, Steingrabor and Heninger children for students. But that was after she had been married a year.

Andy Chambers, as full of life and fun as Ida, claimed the young school teacher for his bride in 1918.

They started ranching on Andy's homestead on Mormon Row. (This two-mile lane in the Kelly district of Jackson's Hole was so named because almost every homesteader along the stretch was of the L.D.S. faith, and the only church in the neighborhood was of that denomination.) The next few years were full and busy ones for Ida and Andy.

Ida had no more time for teaching as her little brood came along: Vera, Roy, Reese, Cora, Inez, Glen and "Peach" (Anita). A houseful of kiddies was as natural as the sunlight to Andy and Ida, who filled their lives with the proper blend of love, fun and work. Ida taught each one, and most of the neighbors' kids, to swim in the pond Andy scooped out in the field. The days were never long enough for all they liked to do.

Sometime in their young married life, Andy and Ida even took up poaching beaver. Andy had found a dam under construction, so he borrowed a trap, listened to a little advice, and acquired some beaver castor for bait. Andy had never trapped for beaver before; Ida, of course, was full of enthusiasm, though she knew nothing about trapping. They set the trap and managed to catch the beaver, but since this was the first one, they didn't know the hide should be stretched flat and round. They stretched it on a coyote-hide type of board.

The next set Andy made, he managed to get his fingers caught in the trap. He was out at the stream alone, so he had quite a struggle trying to step on both levers of the trap at once to free his hand. Later he talked it over with Ida, and they decided it was easier to farm than to trap.

For a good many years Andy had the mail contract to haul the mail from Jackson to Moran. In the summer, Ida often drove the route with the pickup. But in the winter, Andy always drove with the teams and the covered sleigh.

One day the postmaster at Moran said, "Andy, I've got a passenger for you. It's a lady."

"All right," Andy answered. "So long as she's good lookin'."

Avoiding commenting on the lady's appearance, the postmaster said, "You'll have to help me put her in," and led the way to where a female corpse lay. A visitor to the valley who had died suddenly, she was just wrapped in sheets as she was and was being sent to Jackson to the undertaker.

Andy put the corpse at the rear end of the sleigh—outside the canvas cover—to keep her cool. He took a nip from a bottle because it was the first time he had "gone out" with a dead lady, and started down the road.

Arriving at Mormon Row, he remembered how Margaret Hartshorn loved to ride to town whenever she got a chance, so he stopped there.

"Margaret," he said, "I've got a lady passenger to take to town. How about you coming along for a chaperone?"

Margaret knew Andy was teasing in some way, but she was ready for a trip to town.

"Just let me get my hat," she answered.

Andy escorted her to the sled and helped her climb into the covered front end.

"But where is the lady friend?" Margaret wondered.

"Here she is!" and Andy threw back the canvas and blankets. Margaret screeched in proper shock. But the fright didn't make her give up the trip to town.

Andy took another swig from his bottle, and they trotted off to give a shock to Aunt Nan Budge at the Grovont Post Office.

After two or three more stops so Andy could shock various friends with his "lady friend," and subsequent nips to cap the fun, Margaret finished the trip to town driving the team.

⁂

Ida lost her father, mother and adopted brother in the Kelly flood.

Mr. Kneedy, with the help of Albert Nelson, Sr., had just finished taking the saws from the mill to the house, thinking they would be safe there. Mrs. Kneedy had been helping, too, getting so grimy that she felt she had to change her clothes.

Little Joe was in the house trying to get his parents to come away when the huge, inverted V-shaped mass of water, rock, trees and debris hit Kelly and swept it away.

Of the six people drowned in the flood three were Ida's family.

Ida, Andy, and the children put their lives back together and lived on the homestead until Andy died prematurely. Then Ida spent the winters in Jackson so the children could attend school. When they were all through school, or married, Ida spent her winters in Arizona. She and her long time neighbor, Chloe May, traveled in a camper and explored much of Arizona hunting semiprecious rocks.

When in their eighties Henry Francis and Ida were married. These two old timers who had watched the development of Jackson Hole through the years spent their golden years migrating from Arizona winters to Jackson Hole summers. Both are gone now but each felt life worth living to the hilt.

LOST FIRE WARDEN

A s HENRY FRANCIS TELLS THE STORY, he starts with his first knowledge of the hunt for Forest Service Fire Warden Copenhaver. The search was started a few days after the man was reported missing in the late autumn of 1929. Henry was working at Roy VanVleck's Jackson Hole Mercantile at the time but also, on occasion, served as deputy sheriff.

On this day he recalls A.C. McCain, Teton Forest Supervisor, came into the store for some purchases. During the course of his stay, McCain told about Forest Guard Copenhaver being lost.

"I sure wish I could get a few men to go up and help in the search," the supervisor said. "I've got every man from my force up there searching now."

Fred Perkins, an uncle of John and Jess Wort, was in the store and volunteered. Roy volunteered Henry's service, saying, "Why don't you go up and help too, Hank?"

Henry was agreeable and even offered the services of Dewey Van Winkle. Dewey was boarding at the Bluebird Cafe, run by Henry and Hazel Francis. The autumn jobs were about finished, and Dewey was out of work until winter stock feeding commenced.

McCain told Henry that the search camp was located at the Arizona Creek Ranger Station. Henry gathered up Dewey, Fred, their bedrolls, and Hank's dog Pal, a big German Shepherd, and loaded them all into the Francis's new Dodge Victory Six sedan. They headed north. When they reached the Forest Service camp, only the cook, Phil Korrall, was in. He filled them in on what had transpired at the search camp until that morning.

Copenhaver had been a fire guard at the Berry Creek station all summer. When the hunting season began, he went on as an

311

auxiliary game warden, a customary practice at the time.

Copenhaver had been across Jackson Lake at the Berry Creek cabin until it was time for him to move his camp and horses out. He was not missed, nor was anyone concerned, until his horses came in alone. They appeared in the Reclamation Service camp where men were cleaning up the lakeshore debris. This camp was at Lizard Creek on the east side of the river. Copenhaver was supposed to be at Berry Creek on the west side.

The reclamation workers notified the Forest Service men, and a search was begun.

Every man in the area who could be spared was involved. Copenhaver's big-boxed powerful old-time Philco radio had been found on a ridge above the lakeshore on the east side. It was left where it was, and searchers fanned out from there. Others walked the river and lake shores on both sides, and as far north as the Yellowstone boundary and west to the Idaho line. It was generally feared that Copenhaver had caught some poachers and had then been overwhelmed by them.

"We found out from Phil about where the radio was found, and we decided to mosey up there and look around," Henry continues. "It had been found on a ridge near the lakeshore, north from Arizona Creek. When we got near there, we fanned out. I was nearest to the lake, while Dewey and Fred worked along the ridge through the timber. We could see each other most of the time. I came out on a place that was free of the tall timber; it was willowy and a little swampy. I stopped to have a good look with my field glasses.

"Up on the ridge I saw a stump where some birds seemed active. They would light, then fly away, then fly back again. They weren't crows. I think they might have been camp robbers. Pal went up there and started sniffing around the stump. I hollered at the others to get up to the top of the ridge and take a look. Pretty soon they yelled down, 'Here he is!'

"When I got up there, I could see that part of the stump was Old Copey all right. He was sittin' agin' it, slumped over. His rifle was braced between his knees. A bullet had gone into his face, or below his chin, and had blown the whole top of his head off.

"Well, the first thing we did was to decide that Dewey should go back to camp to give the word, him being the youngest and maybe the fastest. Fred and I would stay at the spot until the law officers came to make the examination. I guess that may have been around one o'clock or so. We had had lunch with Phil.

"We didn't touch or move anything, but we looked around the location. Snow had fallen after he was dead. But it was softening up, and you could see that he had come on horseback, where he had tied his horses and unpacked them and turned them loose. The halters and bridle and all the saddles and equipment were piled neatly and a tarp thrown over them.

"The whole pile was covered with new snow. His Smith and Wesson .38 was by his side. He had evidently shot up all the ammunition he had for it. Pal was sniffing around in the snow uncovering spent shells all around the body.

"I started to lift the tarp a little, and Fred said, 'Oh, don't touch anything. Better wait for the law to arrive.' But I peeked anyhow. Right on top of the saddles was a note. I don't remember the exact words, but it said, 'I've cut my arm and I'm bleeding pretty bad,' and something about, 'the radio is about a hundred yards north of here.'

"I put the note back under the tarp and shook out the water that had formed a puddle in a depression on the top, so it wouldn't leak through and get it wet. Then old Pal and me started walking in the direction of the radio. As we walked along, Pal was sniffin' along, so I kicked aside some snow and found he was following a blood trail. Pal followed it right to the radio.

"The radio was wrapped up in a tarp and all tied up with a lightweight rope which had been cut in one place. Man tracks under the fresh snow led to the lake shore. Just across the lake was the shortest distance to the Berry Creek ranger station. There were horse tracks around the spot too, under the new snow, as well as new tracks made by the men who had found the radio.

"I went back to where Fred waited with the dead man. We sat around and backtracked Copey in our minds while we waited for the men to come.

"We knew they kept a boat over at the Berry Creek station. Copey must have brought that awkward old radio across in the boat to keep from packing it on a horse all the way. Then he must have gone back to the cabin and packed up his outfit and ridden up the west side of the river until he found a ford, crossed over and came back down this side. On this side, he tied up his outfit while he rode around to find the place where he had left the radio.

"We never did figure out why he would want to cut the wrappings off the radio, but there was the rope cut through, and old Copey had a deep gash in his left arm near the elbow on the inside. It must have been bleeding pretty bad because Copey didn't use good judgment from then on. He must have panicked.

"He knew where the Reclamation Camp was. He could have held his wound with the other hand and walked or ridden to it in twenty minutes. He was a nut about caring for his horses, maybe he couldn't stand to leave them out there tied up.

"But there again, he had the knife he cut himself with, he could have cut all the halter ropes and let them come along in on their own. Instead he went back where they were, unpacked and unsaddled them, piled all the stuff and covered it. That took more work with the arm than would have been needed to mount his saddle horse and ride out. Then he sat down and shot into the air, expecting someone to hear and find him.

"I didn't investigate the case and I don't remember if I heard whether he had shot up all his rifle ammunition or not. Fred and I figured he didn't intend to kill himself, just got weak and the gun wobbled, or he did, as he pulled the trigger that last time.

"While we was sittin' there figurin' and waitin', Captain Felix Buchenroth [at that time Chief Ranger for the Teton Forest] came along. We heard him coming through the timber and called him over. When he discovered that we had found Copey, he said, 'Vy in hell didn't you shoot?'

"'Shoot?' we said. 'What've we got to shoot at? Looks to us like too much shooting has already been done.' He said the searchers had agreed to shoot several times in the air when any of them found anything. So he shot into the air to signal them in.

"Buck waited with us until the sheriff's party arrived with Dewey. Dewey had waited at the camp until Slim Pendergraft [the sheriff] and Bill Grant [the coroner] arrived from town. I guess he had called them from Moran. It was about four o'clock by that time. Some more searchers came in with them. They had brought along a little ladder, poles for sides, and one-by-fours for rungs. We strapped Copey onto that and took turns packing him out to the highway.

"Back at the camp, more of the searchers were coming in. One of them, Mr. W. Louis Johnson, of the Sargent place, said, 'Here we have been wading around in this snow for days and along comes these town dudes and he finds Copey in half an hour.'

"By that time I was wishing Johnson, or anybody else, had found Copenhaver. He was a pretty bad find, and the worst of the day was still to come. When we got him back to town I had to lay him out for burial." Roy VanVleck was the town undertaker, and another of Henry's part-time jobs was the undertaker's assistant.

"He was buried up here in the Jackson cemetery. I can't remember if he had any folks anyone notified or not. I didn't take care of that end of the undertaking business."

COWBOYING THE WILD ONES

ON A LATE-WINTER EARLY-SPRING DAY in 1933, many of the
natives of Jackson could be seen with their heads tipped
back watching the skyline of the East Gros Ventre Butte,
looming above the village to the west.

Some were pointing; others, seeing this, followed their gaze and
motions, until soon everyone who happened to be outside was "lifting his eyes to the mountain" to see a uniquely Jackson's Hole scene.

From the high southern point of the butte, over the crown and
on for about a mile to the north, a band of elk was strung out, possibly two or three thousand head. The leaders were just starting
down into Allen Draw. To the rear two tiny human figures could be
seen, some hundred yards apart and a like distance from the rear of
the drags.

John Hoagland and Otto Nelson, on snowshoes, were moving
the part of the herd which had been fed at the Charlie Wilson
ranch, just southwest of town, onto the Government Ranch where
they would be fed the remainder of the winter. The hay which the
Wyoming Game and Fish Department had bought from Charlie
Wilson had been fed out.

It is possible to drive elk, to get them where you want them to
go, if you are wise in their ways, if you want them to go where they
happen to want to go, and if you have a few advantages, like webs
or a well-fed horse in winter—or, in these modern days, a snowmobile or snow plane.

Of course, all the cowboys in the valley couldn't drive them
through town, or down wind. But two long-winded young men on
webs could move them from one feed ground to another by a route
the elk *wanted* to travel.

By 1933 the elk feeding program was well under way, with the Government Ranch (which was comprised of the Miller ranch and several other ranches which the government had purchased along Flat Creek) furnishing most of the hay. However, the Wyoming Game and Fish Department had to buy supplemental hay.

Since they did not, at that time, own the South Park feed ground, the hay there was fed on the fields where it grew. Very few balers had made the Jackson scene by then, and transporting loose hay any distance was an uneconomical thing to do. It was much easier to bring the animal to the hay.

So these elk were moved to a new supply of hay so they would not scatter out over South Park ranches and raid private haystacks.

To get the herd started that morning, the feeders drove a rack full of hay across the highway and up on the shoulder of the butte as high as they could break out a track with the team, continuously stringing a little hay as they climbed. With the lead elk eagerly following the hayrack, it was not too hard for the men on webs to urge on the drags.

When the dab of hay was slicked up by the lead elk, the herders made a racket and waved their coats. The wise old leaders started right up the hill, the natural thing for an elk to do. They were soon slowed down by the deep snow, so the herders had no trouble keeping up with and encouraging the weaker ones in the drag.

The men knew the herd would head for the top of the hill, the only problem was how to keep the leaders from coming off the butte on the western, or Spring Gulch, slope.

Leaving John to bring up the rear, Otto climbed steadily, keeping a little west of the leaders, always visible to them when they stopped to look back. The elk went up the wind-swept side of the little draws and broke through the drifted places. When they topped the butte they were well on the eastern side.

The crown of elk gracing the brow of the butte slipped crazily down off the north slope into the Allen draw. From there they slanted northward and down to the valley floor.

Fred Deyo, game warden of Teton County, had been patrolling the valley by car, watching to see how the drive went and to be in the right place if needed. Everything was going so well he scarcely needed to get out of the car. When the leads came off the butte near the Ward's dance hall, at about the Elk Refuge Motel, he was on hand to turn them to join the Government Ranch herd across the Flat Creek meadows. No tall fence was there then. The Winegar place and the Crawford place were still under private ownership.

Seeing that everything was under control, Fred went back near the Flat Creek bridge where he could watch the herders. He spotted them nearing the top of the Allen grade coming down from the draw. When John and Otto caught sight of him and waved, he got out of the car and started frantically motioning them to proceed up the next shoulder of the butte. They looked at him in wonderment.

"What d'ya suppose he wants?" John wondered.

"I dunno," Otto answered, "but I think he just wants to see us squirrel up to the top again. I ain't agonna do it. This bunch is goin' on the refuge all right. If there's any more up on top they can wait 'til another day."

So down they came. If Fred had one of his famous pranks in mind, he had met his match.

This move was only one of the many times some portion of the herd has had to be "cowboyed" for one reason or another. The most common reason for driving the elk was to keep them out of the haystacks of the private ranchers.

❧

"The first time I went out to chase elk was the winter before the Kelly flood—1927, I guess it was. We weren't drivin' them that time, we were really only countin' them."

Otto Nelson was reminiscing in 1973 about the elk-cowboying days in Jackson's Hole when the elk management program sometimes required herding elk. Sometimes done on horseback, sometimes afoot on webs if the snow was deep, these trips required stamina and great familiarity with game habits.

"The elk feeding program was goin' good on the Government Ranch by then. More elk was bein' fed hay on the ranch then, than they ever have there now. The count was in the twenty thousands there for several years. There was still a lot of elk tryin' to winter out up the Gros Ventre watershed. The Game Department kept gettin' reports of elk starvin' up there. I guess they wanted to do somethin' to try to save them and started out by tryin' to get a count on what was wintering there.

"Fred Deyo and Slim Pendergraft was the game wardens here then. They hired me and Arley Hersey. Almer Nelson went along for the Government Ranch, and Charlie Dibble to represent the Forest Service. The six of us snowshoed all over the Gros Ventre drainage. We got a count of six thousand plus.

"Old Delta Wiese, representing the Izaak Walton League, didn't believe there was that many elk on the Gros Ventre, so another count was organized. This time, the older Jimmy Chambers went along, representing the League. There was only Fred, Arley Hersey and me, Jim Chambers and Steve Callahan, who hauled us up the river with a team and a sleigh.

"It was in the middle of a cold snap when we started up that second time. I remember Jimmy Chambers gettin' off the sleigh to walk along behind in the ruts to get warmed up.

"Fred and Steve had brought along a gallon of moonshine which they was keepin' under wraps in the sleigh, treatin' themselves now and then along the way. I guess they thought Arley and I was too young to have any, and Old Jim was back there on his horse, trottin' along behind. Arley got a hold of it when we was unpackin' and took it and hid it.... He and I finished off the rest of it. Steve and Fred had an idea who got it but they wouldn't let on they missed it.

"We counted over seven thousand head just on the Gros Ventre drainage that trip. They was dyin' by that time, for sure. We found dead elk on every area we covered. I'll bet fifteen hundred or two thousand elk died just on the Gros Ventre that winter. When Albert [Otto's brother] and I went up the Gros Ventre to work for the Forest Service that next summer, we found winter-killed elk everywhere we rode.

"The Game Department hadn't made any effort to feed the elk that were trying to winter out before that. Soon after that count they put some tin storage sheds up on Alkali Creek and started feeding cottonseed cake whenever the winter was bad enough that the elk needed it.

"Later they built bigger sheds there and at the Dew place and stored and fed hay, as well as cake, on feed grounds up the Gros

Ventre. Now, of course, they have the Collier place for a feed ground if they need it.

"Charlie and Albert [Nelson brothers] were hired by the Game Department to build storage sheds on the Greys River and Green River headwaters for elk that were trying to winter out in those areas.

"Now the size of the herd is cut down so much, and they've got the habit of comin' in to the Government Ranch to winter, so not too many elk try to winter on the Gros Ventre any more."

Of all the big game animals, the elk is the most like cattle in living habits. They are gregarious and live and graze in small herds upon the same type of forage cattle prefer. It is to be expected, then, that when the elk come down to the valleys in the wintertime they will raid the haystacks of the ranchers, a handy well-preserved supply of their natural feed. Getting them off the rancher's fields and onto the Government Ranch feedground or the Wyoming Game and Fish Department's feedgrounds is a cowboying job very much the same as for domestic cows.

To understand why a wild game animal should be getting fed hay at all, a quick résumé of the habits of game animals of Wyoming since the advent of the white man may make it clear.

One might suppose that the settlement of Jackson's Hole robbed the elk of their natural winter pasture. Not so. From the earliest records and diaries of the fur trappers, it is apparent that the elk was a plains animal, migrating to the high mountains in the summer, as did the bison and antelope, and returning to the plains during the winter months.

Something upset the migrating pattern of the elk herds to the plains. Various reasons have been advanced, principally that the settlement of ranches intruded on the migration route. It was more likely many things: the competition of cattle and sheep on the plains; hunting pressure in the open country driving elk back to the hills; the severe winters that swept the plains at the end of the eighties could have taken a severe toll of the herds that migrated onto the desert, while not impacting so severely the elk which wintered on the wind-swept ridges of the mountains.

Sometime around the turn of the century the elk stopped migrating to the plains and tried wintering in the mountain valleys.

In open winters they did all right, but in severe winters they starved by the thousands.

(About this same time the antelope quit migrating into Jackson's Hole in the summer time. For fifty years a wild antelope was not seen in Jackson's Hole. Then in the 1960s, a few little bands showed up on the Gros Ventre drainage, and the small herds have been increasing each summer since.)

Due to pressure originating from Jackson, Congress allocated money to buy hay for the elk and later to buy ranches along Flat Creek.

By the thirties, the elk had adapted well to feeding on the Government Ranch along Flat Creek. The only difficulty was that many of the elk still didn't care whether it was Government Ranch hay or valley rancher's hay they ate, since it all tasted the same to them, and they continued to breach fences at will wherever they came across a likely supply.

Since the game animals of Wyoming are wards of the state, it was the duty of the game wardens to overcome this trespass. Fred Deyo and Slim Pendergraft, the permanent wardens for the area, hired a crew of deputy wardens to cowboy the wild bunches into the Government Ranch.

When Fred had a call that elk were bothering, he called up his crew and made plans for a ride. Many of the fellows lived in town and rode out from there in the early morning cold. At other times Fred hired some ranchers from the area he wanted cleared, and they would start from home. No one carried a lunch.

It was usually forenoon by the time the elk were gathered and started, and from then on there was no stopping to eat. When the herd had been delivered to the Flat Creek flats (or lost along the way), the rider could ride home and get supper. It was usually after dark.

Otto Nelson recalls the groups he worked with as including Boyd Charter, Henry Francis, Glen Ricks, Charlie Erzinger and Carl Roice. Albert Nelson and Olin Emery rode out from their ranches in Spring Gulch many times, and other crews that started out from the Kelly area included Ned Budge, Jess Wilson, Bill Wells and probably many others that Otto didn't get to see.

"One time Ned Budge and Jess and Lester May and Slim Pendergraft and maybe some others had started a herd down from the

Mormon Row ranches," Otto began one incident. "We had to kill one old bull that got down in a drift and was too weak to get up. Slim told me to go get his teeth after he had shot him. They was a good set. I got twelve dollars for 'em later on. It was a big herd and we was bringin' 'em along in good shape, gettin' near the Gros Ventre, when the wind changed."

"Them elk turned and came right back over us. You couldn't no more turn them than nothin'. You could have reached out and slapped them in the face and it wouldn't have fazed them. They were determined to travel into the wind, even if it did have our scent in it. They knew what we were, but they weren't goin' to travel downwind into something they couldn't tell about. They were just goin' back where they'd come from—and they did.... We never did get that bunch in that day.

"When we rode the Spring Gulch area we'd start up on the West Gros Ventre Butte and get 'em down onto the fields, then they would usually go right up over the top of the East Butte and we'd have to go right up after them. There was hardly a day when somebody didn't have a horse fall with him. Olin Emery had a bronc fall on a steep place and catch Olin's foot in the stirrup under him. Olin held that bronc's head up with one rein until he could get his pocket knife out and cut the cinch strap. That was lucky. I'd hated to been drug offa that hill.

"We rode the Zenith area from the Liz McCabe place down through Prentice Gray's, Curtises', Nephi Moulton's, Seelamire's and the upper Hansen place and brought them out over the Barber Boys' places [now the golf course]. We drove them across the Glidden and Nichols' places [Warm Springs Ranch] and shoved them off the bench onto Flat Creek. Fred made Glen Ricks ride nightherd from the Botcher Hill to the Gros Ventre bridge for a few nights to scare them back if they tried to sneak back up toward the Zenith area."

One morning when the cowboy crew was riding out, bunched close enough together to do a little gabbing, they got to arguing about the merits of their clothing.

"This old sheepskin Mackinaw is the warmest thing you can wear. Even if it is heavy, I'm warm," Carl stated.

"Yah, and it will wear you and your horse both out," Henry Francis rejoined. "Now, the thing I use is two wool sweaters and a wind breaker. That way I can shed a layer at a time as I warm up."

"Angora chaps are too heavy."

"Leather chaps are too cold."

"You can't do much in mittens."

"Fur-lined gloves can freeze your hands."

"What's the matter with sittin' on them?"

Otto ended the discussion with the flat statement, "It ain't the clothes that's warm or cold, it's the god-damned weather." At ten below zero everyone had to agree.

Otto continued recounting some of his trips with Fred. "Once we went up to Hoback Basin with Fred in his car. We had webs along and was goin' to bring some elk off some of those ranches down to the South Park feedground. We never did find the elk so we came back to the Hoback junction and went down to Dog Creek. We drove back slow, countin' the deer with field glasses. Fred said we could use an easy day and he'd been wondering how many deer were in that area. We counted eight hundred head between the Dog Creek area and town. I don't believe there's that many there now.

"Fred was the best game warden we ever had," Otto continued. "He thought nothin' of throwin' packs on a couple of horses and ridin' to the head of the Buffalo or Gros Ventre or Crystal or the Hoback. He kept track of where the game was and how they were doin'.

"Found a lot of poachers that way, too," he added. Otto grinned and I knew he had remembered one more incident.

"On one drive he got bucked off a bronc five times when he was bringin' some elk off that little butte south of the Y. The horse could buck him off on the side hill, but he managed to keep a hold of the reins and get back on. When they got down on the flat, Fred rodeoed that bronc 'til he decided he was a good broke horse and behaved himself the rest of the day."

Sometime in the mid or late thirties the Government Ranch purchased the remaining ranches in the Flat Creek flats and strung the tall woven-wire fence along the west side. This kept the wild bunch from drifting off their feedground once they were down for the winter. It cut the cowboying job to practically nothing.

❧ *In the 1920s the Sportsman Association of Washington obtained elk from the Jackson feed ground to stock the Blue Mountains. They were carried part of the way in cribs holding two elk each, mounted on sleighs. When they arrived in Dayton, Washington, the elk jumped out of the stockyards and headed for the mountains.* (JHM&HC)

❧

A wild bunch of elk precipitated one difficulty between Fred Deyo and Ike Powell in 1934. A band of elk had been hanging out along the Snake River bottoms in the Zenith area, raiding the stack yards of the ranchers each night, especially the Seelamire ranch. The Game Department was notified, and Deyo said he would come move them the next day. Fred arrived at the Seelamire ranch accompanied by game warden Slim Pendergraft and deputy warden Boyd Charter. Will Seelamire sent his hired man, eighteen year old Weldon Richardson, along on the drive, as Weldon knew where the little herd was hiding out in the riverbottom. They found the herd and carefully worked them across the fields, across the highway near the Gros Ventre bridge, and were crossing a portion of Ike Powell's fields when Ike appeared on his hayrack, having just finished feeding his cattle.

Ike's dog was trained to keep elk away from the cattle feed ground, so he immediately chased after the herd. The riders were strung out, keeping the elk calmly moving without pushing them. Fred was nearest the dog, which had caught one elk by the nose and hung on. The elk whirled around, lifting the dog off his feet. Fred drew his pistol and rode at the animals, shouting and shooting into the ground, trying to scare the dog loose. He succeeded by riding practically on top of the dog, which then let loose and ran for the hayrack. Meantime, Ike shouted imprecations and reached for a gun which hung in a scabbard on the center post of the rack.

"Don't you shoot my dog! I'll shoot all you sons-a-bitches!"

Having chased the dog as he ran back to his master, Fred was pretty close to the hayrack. Ike tried again to pull his gun from the scabbard. Fred shot. (He said he aimed at Ike's hands. That may be the case, because he clipped a thumb off.) Ike still struggled to pull the gun from the scabbard but, with the team jumping around, he had trouble keeping his balance. Fred shot again, this time clipping Ike's mustache. Ike still tried desperately to get his rifle into position to shoot, but Fred's next shot caught him again. Ike was bent over, partially falling, so the bullet entered a hip, traveled up through fleshy parts of his trunk and just nicked his lung. He fell off the sleigh onto the snow.

Sudden quiet filled the valley as the shooting stopped. The other riders came up and gathered around the hayrack. The team still nervously treaded about, but the lines wrapped about the center post held them. Ike flopped around in the snow, partially conscious. Fred said something like, "My God, what do we do now?"

Weldon, the youngster, said, "We better get him up out of the snow." So they did. They put some hay under him and wrapped him warmly in their coats against the minus-ten-degree weather.

Slim said, "I'll ride down to Billy Francis's and telephone the doctor. We'll have to take him almost to town on the sleigh. Don't think they can get very far up the highway with a car." Slim rode off at a gallop. It was about two miles to the Francis place. The others started to town, leaving the herd of elk to find their way any which way they wanted.

Fred drove the team, Olin Emery held and supported Ike, Weldon and Boyd rode and lead Fred's horse. Ike drifted in and out of consciousness.

Once, on seeing Fred up front driving, he swore and said, "What is that son-of-a-bitch doing driving my team?"

Fred said, "I don't think he likes me very much. Weldon, why don't you drive?" So they changed places. They made the best time they could down the road.

At the Ward Dance Hall, Dr. Huff and Sheriff Jim Francis were waiting. They transferred Ike to the car as gently as possible. Fred handed his gun to Jim saying, "I guess you want this?" Jim took it with some embarrassment, hating to have to arrest a fellow officer and friend.

Weldon was given the sad job of returning the team to the Powell place and breaking the news to Mrs. Powell. This he did, telling her only that there had been a bad accident and that Ike had been taken to the hospital and was under the care of Dr. Huff. He also told her that Bill Francis would be over shortly to take her to town.

Patched up by Dr. Huff, Powell recovered satisfactorily in the St. John's Hospital and was released by the doctor with the warning to do no strenuous work for the rest of the winter.

Ike brought charges of felonious assault against Fred, the hearing took place in Jackson, February 19, 1935. Deyo's attorney, Arthur E. Oeland from Sublette County, called no witnesses, but he closely questioned the witnesses called by Wilfred Neilson, the County and Prosecuting Attorney. Ike's testimony about the shooting follows:

> "I was riding on a hayrack, reading a newspaper when the team hesitated. I looked up and saw a band of elk in the road. About the same time, I saw Deyo, about a hundred yards north, shooting at my dog. I yelled, 'Don't shoot that dog!' At the same time, I raised the rifle in the scabbard, which was hanging on the center post of the hayrack." Powell said that Deyo then rode to the hayrack and asked if he sicced his dog on those elk and that he replied, "No. I didn't even see the elk until you started shooting." The rancher then said that Deyo brought "his gun down and shot, the first bullet missing. I thought he must have blank shells. The team jumped and I reached for the lines. The second shot cut across my thumb and across my upper lip. Then I jumped from the rack, and as I did he fired the third shot."

It was testified by Powell and other witnesses that the third bullet entered just above the hip bone and emerged from the upper part of the chest. Powell said that he was in a crouched position, jumping from the rack to seek cover.

Powell made the statement, "He shot me in cold blood," several times.

The case was bound over to district court from this preliminary hearing. Later in February, Judge Christmas sat on the bench as the case was tried in Jackson. The State Game and Fish Department supplied the defense lawyer for Fred—a man named Mechan, of Cheyenne. The courthouse was packed. Weldon remembers that he sat beside Jim Francis and behind County and Prosecuting Attorney Wilfred Nielson. Jim nudged Weldon and grinned his little pinched up closed-mouth smile as he pointed out how Wilfred's posterior hung out over the edge of his chair.

Witnesses were called and the story was presented, much as it had been told at the hearing. Sometime during the dull parts of lawyer exchange, Jim dozed off. His head tipped forward with a little jerk and his false teeth cascaded out onto the floor. Not too many people noticed. There was no pause in the presentations. The verdict was pronounced self defense.

It would be better if there were no epilogue to this story....

Doctor Huff told Ike to go home but to take it easy, lie around. He didn't give stern enough orders for the kind of man his patient was. Ike just could not take it easy. In April when the heavy Spring work always comes, he was out feeding, calving and branding. About mid-May he was taking cattle from his place on the Gros Ventre up to his range. His horse roughed him up some, according to local tale. It started some inner trouble which brought him to the hospital again. After several days' treatment, Doctor Huff decided he needed exploratory surgery and sent him to the Idaho Falls hospital.

He was flown out by Bennett. He was perhaps Jackson's first hospital patient to be flown out to another hospital. Ike died there May 22, 1935, age thirty-three.

Now-a-days the elk seem to stay put better, but if they do bother the rancher's stacks, the game wardens go out and chase them around with snow machines. This works pretty well except that occasionally the man on the machine doesn't gauge the endurance of the elk and runs them down. If he had to get back on webs or a horse, he would soon learn to enjoy a breather whenever the herd would pause.

THE DUDE RANCH AND THE CON ARTIST

THIS ALL HAPPENED A LONG TIME ago, when the west was young and trusting and naive, when the ranch doors were always unlocked, when a man's word was a contract, and when a dude ranch in Jackson's Hole was just trying to get itself started and a dude by the name of Jackson decided to cut himself in.

The ranch lay in the Turpin Meadows at the foot of Togwotee Pass, the eastern entrance to Jackson's Hole. The Turpin Meadows were named for an old trapper, Dick Turpin, who came to the valley in the 1880s. He built trapping cabins here and there on his trap lines and thus got Turpin Creek and Turpin Meadows named after him.

The Buffalo River tumbles out of the mountains to the east, hits the flats and slows, to meander through the grassy, willowy meadow until it joins the Snake some miles to the west. On the western horizon the mighty Tetons rear their saw-toothed wall.

A man named Dutch Henry was probably the first to try a business at the foot of Togwotee Pass when the highway was completed in the early twenties. Dutch had a store, a cabin or two and a gas pump—forerunner of the modern motel. Jimmy Simpson and his son-in-law, Lester Leek, acquired the buildings and lease and were shaping it up into something more, aiming at dude ranch/hunting lodge accommodations.

Jimmy Simpson was one of the early settlers of Jackson's Hole. He sold his homestead, the Red Rocks Ranch on the Gros Ventre, to his sister and her husband, the Redmonds. He operated a drugstore in the town's first public building, the Clubhouse. Early in 1932 he decided to concentrate on his favorite line of work—the big game outfitting business—to be operated in conjunction with dude ranching from the Turpin Meadows Ranch.

Jimmy's son-in-law, Lester, born in the valley to the rancher, big game guide and photographer, Stephen Leek, was a young man totally familiar with the valley and how to entertain the valley's visitors. Lester and his wife Helen were also the leaders of Jackson's orchestra—Helen at the piano, Lester with the fiddle. Guests of a dude ranch run by Simpson and Leek would be well cared for, guided and entertained.

They added cabins, enlarged the dining-room and remodeled in various ways. They were well on their way to dude ranch status; all they needed was a good supply of summer guests.

As it was too early to do much spring work at the Turpin Meadows place, the Leeks and Jimmy were at their homes in Jackson when an old friend, Fred Lovejoy, called on them. Fred had been owner/operator of the Jackson Telephone Company until he had sold out a short time before. He had wintered outside, so the Leeks hadn't seen him for awhile. They were glad to see him and to learn what he had been doing with his new retirement. Fred was accompanied by a friend he introduced as Mr. Frank B. Jackson.

It didn't take long for Mr. Jackson to make known that he was interested in finding a ranch which could accommodate a group of guests he would recruit from the teachers in the Chicago area. This was the very solution the ranch in Turpin Meadows needed. Soon plans were being formulated and verbal agreements reached. Jackson went off back east to recruit guests, and the Simpson/Leek partners renewed their efforts to make the Turpin Meadows Ranch ready.

Letters flew back and forth. Mr. Jackson reported success in signing up guests. Plans for entertainment were exchanged and approved. A rodeo was scheduled for the day of arrival. The big event was to be a six-week pack trip into the Thoroughfare and Yellowstone country. It was to be a whole summer of horseback sight-seeing.

With such a sudden influx of guests expected, the cabins proved inadequate and tent frames with tents were set up. They hired kitchen, dining-room and cabin help. Jimmy hired wranglers, trying to find boys who had some horses of their own which could be hired as well. They contracted for rodeo stock and built a bucking chute and additional corrals. They stockpiled supplies for the long, long pack trip. Expenses piled up.

At last, the big day arrived. Busses brought the guests from the railroad at Lander, escorted by Mr. Jackson. A flurry of introductions took place in the ranch office/dining-room/lounge. Mr. Jackson collected the fees as each guest checked in. Guests were allotted their cabins, refreshed themselves, had their lunch, then hurried down to the corrals to the excitement of the real ranch rodeo.

Mr. Jackson was there, too, collecting entrance fees at a convenient gate from guests and natives alike. There was a goodly crowd. The rodeo had been advertised around the area and quite a group of tie-hacks from the Dubois side of Togwotee were on hand. Cowboys who furnished the stock for the event were on hand. Cowboys who intended to ride in the events milled around, some of them paying their entrance fees to Mr. Jackson. Whiskey was available to anyone with a thirst.

The judges called the first events and the rodeo got underway. It was a real Western Day.

The rodeo stock had been gathered up from outlaw horses owned by ranches around in the valley. The rodeo "hands" were the ranch help plus any volunteers who offered. Sometimes a pick-up man rescued the bronc rider after the whistle blew. More often, he just had to ride the horse out or fall off.

Sometimes the race horses suddenly decided they were bucking horses and a jockey unexpectedly turned bronc buster to finish the ride. Teachers and natives sat on the top rails of the fences, cheering everything.

Fights erupted here and there around the grounds. Some were caused by tie-hacks jeering cowboy efforts, but mostly they were caused by whiskey. One report said a gang fight between tie-hacks and cowboys was broken up by mounted cowboys wielding doubled up ropes, whipping into and around the melee.

When the last race and ride had been run the crowd started to disperse. The riders gravitated toward the judges stand to collect prize money. The results were pretty well tabulated and the judges were prepared to announce the winners. But where was the prize money? Everyone thought Lester or Jimmy should have it. But neither of them had the cash box. Where was Mr. Jackson? He had the cash box, the last anyone knew.

First some unconcerned questions. "Where is Jackson?" "Have you seen Mr. Jackson around?" This was followed by frantic searching, looking in rooms and everywhere. "Have you seen Jackson since the start of the show?"

Finally an awful suspicion started to rise. "Could he have absconded with the money?" The thought was unacceptable. He must have gone to town to put it in safekeeping—perhaps the bank? There must be some explanation. He had worked so long and faithfully with them on this whole business venture.

Simpson and Leeks tried to delicately explain to the rodeo riders that their prize money was not available but that didn't quite work. Lester was nearly roughed up by some of the disgruntled riders and might have been hurt if some of the cowboys who were his good friends hadn't intervened. The event winners left without their winnings.

The "Real Western Day" ended with a western-sized worry.

For two or three days the Simpson/Leek partners waited. Maybe the man would show up, with a perfectly good explanation. Maybe the sheriff would get a line on the guy. The telegraph lines were busy. Finally the ranchers had to accept the fact—they had been "had."

Something had to be done with all these teachers! Something had to be done about all these plans! All of these horses and help! All of these supplies!

The ranchers felt they must honor their commitment to the teachers who had spent all their money on this once-in-a-lifetime trip. The guests offered to reduce the time of the trip to three weeks; the wranglers agreed to go out on the chance of being paid if, and when, Jackson was caught. The pack trip got underway.

We will not go into the details of the pack trip, as this story isn't about that—just a few sidelights by the way. This was such a big party that the Forest Service, to protect the wilds, sent along a ranger to assure that the horses didn't overgraze or the party litter. Also, some of the rented horses were not well-broke dude-wise nags, and some of the teachers got treated to a bronc ride. No one was badly hurt so it added to the sense of adventure.

Some of the teachers turned into big game hunters of a romantic sort and tried to "bag" a wrangler. At least one came in with a trophy—the forest ranger! This was probably the most memorable vacation any of them ever had.

Jimmy Simpson and Lester and Helen Leek sold everything—horses, outfitting equipment, the ranch, the works—but still could not cover all the debts. One of the wranglers who had his own pay coming, plus two dollars per day per head for ten head of horses, said, "No, I never did get paid… Except, I did get my board while I was on the trip. Oh, and one of the girls did give me a pack of cigarettes."

Without even a six-gun, Mr. Jackson made the biggest hold-up ever recorded in Jackson's Hole history.

The article from the *Jackson Hole Courier* and letter quoted below give a glimpse into the breadth of his chicanery.

Postmistress Found Guilty, Embezzlement
Elk Postmistress Victim of Swindler; $900 Shortage

Mrs. Dave Eldridge, postmistress at Elk for the past several years was indicted on charges of shortage of accounts and last week found guilty by the jury at Cheyenne. Her sentence is being held in abeyance for several days by the federal judge.

An unexpected visit by a postal inspector in early September caught Mrs. Eldridge before she could make up the shortage of $900 which she fully intended to replace. The charge of shortage of funds was brought against her by the inspector and her position as postmistress was replaced by another.

Victim of Grafter

Mrs. Eldridge is another innocent person who has fallen victim to the grafter, known here as Frank B. Jackson and by other names in various places where he has done his racketeering.

Last summer she accepted Jackson as a bona-fide promoter of Jackson Hole tourist travel and when he became interested with Lester Leek in the Turpin Meadow Lodge and planned to accommodate a large dude contingent, the postmistress was even more convinced that this man Jackson was ok.

Gaining her confidence, he managed to cash many checks at the post office stating he needed the money for his dudes. For a week or more, Jackson kept the post office and store stripped of cash for which he gave his checks. When Jackson finally skipped, leaving Lester Leek with a busload of stranded dudes to take care of, Mrs. Eldridge found he had about $900 in cash of her money and in lieu thereof were valueless checks.

Promotes Fake College

A recent issue of the Courier told how Jackson, under the name of Gordon Blake had also promoted a fake college in the mountains near Sheridan which led to his indictment.

Since leaving Sheridan he is said to have pulled off a $900 deal in California and succeeded in getting away.

※

Billings, Montana
July 28th, 1932

Miss Muriel Schrage
332 Linden Ave.
Oak Park, Ill.

Miss Esther Bulwan
4113 Tonawanda Drive
Des Moines, Iowa

Dear Miss Schrage and Bulwan,

Referring to our visit in Jackson, Wyoming and the talk we had on Mr. Frank Jackson. I hope that you had a pleasant and interesting trip on the short pack trip you were to have as the guests of Lester Leek and the cowboys who were hired by Jackson to take you on the long and well planned trip through the two National Parks and the Jackson Hole.

As you know the Lions Club of Jackson have become interested in this deal, as has the several other organizations affected by the operation of this promoter, and as far as we are concerned we have our files nearly completed and only awaiting the contracts and especially the confidential letters of instructions that Jackson wrote to the counselors, and the other things you were going to send to me, this I hope you will do as soon as possible.

From my conversation with you I know this deal did not spoil your desire to come west to ranches in the future, and the next time if you are having any trouble checking up on a place please remember that the services of this association are at your disposal, without charge, also at the disposal of anyone that wants to check up on any of the dude ranches in the west, hoping to hear from you soon, and that your trip home via Yellowstone was pleasant, interesting and enjoyable, I am,

   Yours very truly,

     AL CROONQUIST
     EXECUTIVE SECRETARY

Forney Cole's
Bare-Handed Battle With a Bear

IN 1944, THE U.S. WAS JUST EASING up from the war effort. Albert and I had been "unfrozen" from our wartime jobs in order to come home to Jackson and help in our own labor-short bailiwick. We were doing some shopping in Jackson when we happened to meet Forney Cole near the drugstore corner. Albert greeted Forney with more than his usual gusto because Forney was the hero of the hour.

With all the mortal combat happening in faraway places, Forney was a hero of note because, right here in this peaceful valley, he had been jumped by an enraged mother bear and had come out the victor in bare-handed man-to-bear combat.

"I'm glad to see you around, Forney, after that battle with the bear. How are your wounds feeling by now? What happened, anyway?" Albert knew a long account would ensue. "Tell me about it."

"By Dod, Abert, I thought I was a goner."

Then followed the full story—I suppose. Forney had a speech impediment which made it impossible for him to pronounce the "n's," "m's," hard "g's," the "l's" and "k's." He lost me with his first sentence. Being much better acquainted with Forney, Albert was able to understand, and thoroughly enjoy, the whole tale.

Forney began his story with the day he had the fight with the bear, but I'll go back years earlier, so you can enjoy a slight acquaintance with Forney.

Born in Nebraska, probably in the early 1880s, Forney was twelve when his family moved to Montana. They camped in Wyoming the first night and it was the last night he ever spent with them. He was a heavy sleeper and hard to roust out in the mornings. When he didn't roll out on order, his dad doused him with a bucket of cold water. Without a word, Forney crawled out of his wet bed, went to catch and saddle his horse, got on him and rode away, still without a word of good-bye. There were no communications between them for years.

During those years, Forney worked as a cowboy on ranches in the north central part of Wyoming. He had a "way" with horses, loved them and got their best work out of them without the usual rough handling common at the time. He told once how he and a partner got a contract to break sixty head of green colts for the U.S. Cavalry. They had to deliver them, gentled, in thirty days. They were riding those broncs day and night to make the deadline. But they delivered on time.

An incident of far more serious note during those years was Forney's reported involvement in the Johnson County War. His gun, a .35 Remington, was used to kill two sheepherders who were then chucked into their wagon and the wagon burned. The rifle was later found buried in an irrigation ditch. Forney was exonerated by testimony of cowboy friends who were with him elsewhere when the deed was done. The court decided that his gun had been stolen by the assassins hired to clear the range of sheepmen and nesters.

In 1917, Forney drifted into Jackson to work. At that time he was a man in his mid-thirties, of medium height with powerful shoulders and frame. He worked on various ranches around the valley and as a cowboy on the range in summer. He had an agreeable personality but a reputation, gained from somewhere, of being a pretty tough hombre, if riled. But then folks soon found he was pretty hard to "get riled."

Forney and Bob Crisp were herding on the Gros Ventre one year when they fell into a disagreement which almost led to blows. Bob was hopping mad and ready to fight, but Forney wouldn't fight him. With a few well-chosen cuss words, Bob wanted to know, "Why?"

"You're too Dod-dabbed liddle," Forney explained. "I cud taj your nej betweed by thub ad fijjer and pich your Dod-dabbed head off."

When the Gros Ventre slide ran in 1925, Forney and Boyd Charter had just driven the Fish Creek cavvy across I.W.W. Creek when the rumbling started. The horses spooked and ran. When the fellows looked back over their shoulders, they couldn't believe their eyes. Under a cloud of dust, boulders and trees bounded up the opposite hillside, then folded back down into the canyon. The two fellows felt as shaken as the firmament. They slowed their horses and considered what they should do. Nearby, the Guil Huff ranch buildings were almost hit by the landslide. Charter went for help while Forney helped the Huff family move their possessions. Although they didn't know it at the time, they were two of only three people to actually see the slide. [See Chapter: *Lower Gros Ventre Slide*]

In 1927, Forney was working a four-horse team on a fresno, digging the McBride ditch through the Dry Hollow draw. There he met Cal Carrington, the foreman of the Countess Gazika's Flat Creek Ranch. Eleanor (Cissy) Patterson, heiress to the Patterson newspaper chain, was Countess Gazika when she acquired the ranch. Ever since it has been known as the Countess place, even though she changed names herself.

In the beautiful setting up in Flat Creek canyon, the Countess was building a summer retreat. Cal hired Forney to help with the ranch work. The Flat Creek Ranch became Forney's home until 1946. When Cal died, Forney became foreman.

As a hired man, Forney was dependable and able; as a bachelor housekeeper, he would have to be graded low-low. In personal appearance he would have to be termed unclean. Although when he went to town he scrubbed and bathed until he smelled of Lysol, around the ranch the top of his longjohns was his only shirt and it looked about the color of his overalls. Except when eating, he always had his pipe in his mouth, lighted or not.

The ranch boasted electricity from a water-powered generator which Mel Ennis, manager of Benson's power plant downstream a couple of miles, had helped to install for the Flat Creek Ranch. This generator also turned a wood saw for Forney. He also had a Maytag washer which he used faithfully, but alas with fairly negative results. Observing his wash out on the line, you'd be hard pressed to tell the difference in color between overalls, blankets, underwear or dishtowels. He probably just washed them all together.

One fine sunny day, Forney started up the Maytag with a load, then decided to ride on down to Ennises to hear the latest news. At Ennises, he forgot all about his wash and rode on in to town. There he had a few drinks and stayed two or three days. Finally, when he did get back to the ranch the faithful old Maytag was still chugging away. But, as he said, "All dat was deft was buttods ad strijs."

Besides the five or six horses, which behaved like horses, Forney lived with a dog, two cats and two pigs. Dog, cats and pigs followed him about the ranch, in and out of the house and enjoyed all the privileges of regular folks.

As soon as Forney crawled out of bed in the morning, the dog crawled in, laid his head on the pillow and stuck his four paws up in the air. The cats sat on the table as Forney cut the bacon or elk steaks, expecting a small bite before the cooking started.

When he stirred up the sourdoughs, he tossed in any leftovers that happened to be around. Two guests were surprised to find spinach in their hotcakes one morning.

Eddie Schultz arrived at the cabin one evening to find Forney sitting exhausted and battered at the cabin door. His undershirt and overalls were shredded, and scratches covered his arms and face.

"What goes on around here, Forney?" Ed greeted.

"Oh," Forney sighed. "I shot a Dod-dabbed choyote."

"You got a coyote, eh?" People tended to repeat key words in Forney's explanations, probably to make sure they were tracking with him. "Is it a good hide? Let's see it."

"I didn't jit jib. He was over at the edge of the tibber. I shot ad he fell, so I wedt over with by skiddid dife. I left by jun here. He jubbed up and rud idto the dowd tibber. I rud after hib. The Dod-dabbed bardin dods and the dweelin hods, ad even the chat was yowlin and ruddid aroud. That choyote was so chared he rud udder every dowd loj in the Dod-dabbed forest and tried to chatch hib. I tried to dab hib but I dever jot chose."

Forney shook his head at the sorry scene he remembered, and Eddie shook all over with suppressed laughter.

Rose Crabtree was the Countess's great friend in Jackson and acted as her contact with Forney. In doing the writing for Forney, Rose became interested in making contact between him and his long neglected family. When she did get in touch with them, one brother came from Mort, Montana, to visit Forney. Rose called Ed Schultz to ask if he would drive the brother up to the Countess's place.

On the way to the ranch Ed hatched a scheme. He would introduce the brother as Mr. Cole, a hunter from Texas. (Ed had brought some Texas hunters up to the Flat Creek Ranch just the week before.)

After arriving at the ranch and with introductions over, Ed said aside to Forney, "I hope this Texan isn't as big a pain as the last ones were." The brother also had a speech impediment, and this along with the family resemblance, Ed thought, would tip Forney off. Forney did look brightly at the brother every time he spoke but seemed unsuspicious of the similar name and looks. Finally Ed could stand it no longer and turned to Forney. "You old coot. Don't you recognize your own brother?"

The brothers then had a good time visiting. Forney's brother had brought pictures of the relatives and news of all they had been doing. From that time on, Forney always had some contact with his family.

But to get back to the fight with the bear.

The visits of Eleanor Patterson (Countess Gazika; by now Eleanor Schlesinger) to her mountain retreat had become very rare in the 1940s. Forney Cole, foreman and caretaker of the Flat Creek Ranch, lived in almost unrelieved loneliness with his dog, pet pigs and cats.

He had neighbors. Mel and Irene Ennis lived at Benson's electricity-generating plant a few miles down the canyon, and friends often stopped with him a few days—especially during hunting season. Most of the time, though, he lived alone. He irrigated a small pasture, put up enough hay to feed his horses, ran a trap line in the winter, and kept the buildings in repair.

There were beaver ponds all up and down Flat Creek; in fact, keeping the beaver from damming up his irrigation ditches was a never-ending job. The Countess enjoyed having them around, so Forney was not to trap them—just try to keep from doing damage.

Forney had made a start on his haying when he noticed the upper end of the meadow was getting wet. He went to investigate the small beaver-cut channels to see if a new dam was flooding the meadow.

He was bent double, pulling sticks out of the channel, when he was suddenly flattened by a terrific blow to his head and shoulders. The weight of the enraged bear held him pinned as she clawed and chewed at her victim.

🐾 *Forney Cole, on right with his ever-present pipe, shows Bob Brown the club he picked up and used to clobber the bear.* (JHM&HC)

Out of the confusion of thoughts that swirled in his head, Forney grasped, "It's a bear. All I can do is play dead." He went limp. He never knew why she quit fighting and raised up. Maybe she saw his dog? He didn't know.

When the bear finally got off, Forney struggled to his feet with the only thing at hand, a hefty beaver-chewed quaking-aspen branch. He turned and brought it down on her head with such force it laid her out. In telling about it later, he said he then "Drajjed her to the edge of the tibber." He never knew why she jumped him. He thought she might have had a cub around, and he had come, accidentally, between them.

Still pretty dazed, he went to the cabin. His scratches and bites were bleeding so badly he decided he had better go to town to be sewed up. Getting in his old Model A pickup, he drove down to the light plant. Mel drove him into town from there. Dr. MacLeod sewed up the bites and scratches on his head, shoulders, ribs and thighs. Dr. MacLeod released Forney to stay with friends Slim and Edna Linville until danger of infection was past.

News of his exploit spread around the country. Friends of Forney, Bob Brown and Ed Schultz, went up to the ranch but could find neither bear nor the club Forney used. When Forney got home later, he retrieved the stick. He had tossed it into the brush near the creek. It now is an object of interest in the Jackson Museum.

The *Jackson's Hole Courier* of August 15, 1944, carried a short two-paragraph account of the incident, with no details. Not so with the bigger newspapers. Forney's prowess was headlined by the *Chicago Tribune* and other papers as the "Man Who Killed the Bear with a Stick." Forney received a pile of congratulatory letters and many proposals of marriage. Forney was never one to pursue women, nor was he a correspondent. The letters went unanswered and were given finally to the Schultzes' daughter Frances. Soon Forney, with Ed Schultz to help him, went back to the ranch to get his interrupted haying done.

Forney was sixty years old when he had the encounter with the bear. It slowed him not at all. The few days in town waiting to be released to go back to work were spent visiting and telling and retelling his experience.

The accident which really laid Forney up happened a year or so later. Forney had one horse which was afraid of going through the barn door. She always made a jump through. One evening Forney was lighting his pipe as he led her in, and she pinned him against the door frame as she jumped. His rib cage was crushed, with broken ribs on each side. The pain was such that he passed out.

Forney came to with the morning sun shining on his face. He dragged himself to his Jeep, got in somehow and drove down the road, his body draped over the steering wheel and the horn blaring. Near the gate, some young people were camped, fishing. They went to the car to see what was the matter, one of them drove him on to the light plant. Mel once more took him in to the hospital. Dr. MacLeod despaired of saving his life that time, but Forney was too tough to knuckle under to punctured lungs, broken ribs and torn up innards. He made it out of the hospital. But this time it took a long recovery period.

The Countess died while Forney was recuperating from that mishap. The estate lawyers felt they needed someone on the property, so Andy Sonek became the caretaker of the Flat Creek Ranch.

Although Forney took a long time to recover from that accident, his misadventures were by no means over. When he was able to work, he was given an easy job at the light plant under Mel. Later, he went to work for Ben Goe as caretaker and helper at Counts' Hot Springs.

Ben Goe had improved the natural hot springs by scooping out a pool roughly forty by sixty feet with steeply sloping dirt sides. He planned to concrete it, but meantime he had piped the hot spring water to it and charged for swims.

Jim Brown, Drew Jensen and Kenny Neal were swimming there one day. Ben and Hilda were nearby, and Forney was fussing about with some chore at the pool. His Jeep was parked on the side of the embankment. When he finished the job, he said, "Well, have a jood tibe boys." With that he climbed in his Jeep, his dog jumped in too, and Forney started the motor. He engaged the gears and the Jeep backed slowly and deliberately into the pool. Forney was puffing at his pipe, staring straight ahead through the windshield, steering like he was going forward instead of backwards.

Of course, the boys were flabbergasted to watch the Jeep chug lower and lower into the eight foot depth and settle completely submerged to the bottom. As nothing else happened, except bubbles coming to the top, they dove down and wrenched open the door. Forney was still sitting in the driver's seat, gripping the wheel. They pulled him out, up to the top and over to the side.

When he could quit coughing and sputtering, he pushed them aside and said, "Dod dabbit boys, my dod's dowd there." So the boys dove down again and got the door open. Some air was still captured near the top of the Jeep, and the dog sat on the seat, his nose up in the air bubble. They hauled him topside by the scruff of his neck. Then remained only the job of rescuing the Jeep.

When Bruce Porter bought the hot springs and started construction of the modern plunge and baths, renamed "Astoria," Forney finally moved into town. Still independent, he had his own trailer house which he parked in the Schultz yard. When the census taker wondered who lived in the trailer, Ed told her, and Forney got mad, looking on it as some sort of betrayal. She asked him a lot of

"Dod-dabbed twestions," so he moved his outfit out to Ed Lloyd's.

While living at Lloyd's, Forney had a couple of serious accidents which seemed to indicate he was slipping. He was wandering around outside in the middle of the night and fell into Cache Creek. No one knows how many hours he was in the almost freezing water. When he was discovered and rushed to the hospital, his body temperature was so low they couldn't even get a reading on a rectal thermometer. He recovered in spite of a bout with pneumonia.

Out and about again, Forney suffered a broken leg. The leg was set, but as soon as he got into a walking cast, Forney took off in pursuit of his usual interests, which included walking all over in the corral. The manure softened the cast (as well as stinking up his bed and trailer), so it had to be replaced.

What with one thing and another, Forney's friends and doctors thought he would be safer and better cared for in the geriatric ward of the hospital. Forney died at St. John's hospital in December of 1963, just short of eighty years of age—but not before giving the nurses two or three years of excitement trying to keep him out of harm's way. Forney figured anyone who had chased up and down the almost impossible road to the Flat Creek Ranch for a quarter century, had driven his Jeep up and down the slopes of the most rugged part of the Gros Ventre Range, and had tramped all over the peaks of the Sheep Mountain afoot and horseback, should know how, and more importantly, be allowed, to drive his own wheelchair.

The last time I saw Forney, his wheelchair was chained to a post to keep him from running it down the ramp of the solarium and tipping it over in the yard.

"Da Dod-dabbed durses wodt even let be jo to da toidet alode!"

Today, whenever anyone speaks of Forney, he is remembered as the man who won the fight with the bear, bare-handed.

*J*ACKSON *V*IGILANTES

*P*IRATE *H*IGHWAY *E*QUIPMENT

WE ARE CONSTANTLY REMINDED THAT the West was settled by rugged individualists. Because of winter isolation, Jackson's Hole settlers had to be more rugged than most. An ingrained sense of what was right and lawful kept human relationships on a reasonably livable keel. When the sense of what was right and lawful became outraged, the citizens usually talked it over, formed a committee, and acted.

This self-sufficient attitude was in evidence as early as the "Indian troubles" in 1895 and lasted through the blithe assumption in 1954 that Jackson should have open gambling even though gambling was illegal in the state, because not only were the needs of the county great, but they were unique within the state's infrastructure and not being met. Collectively the Jackson citizenry was as self-willed as each of its rugged individualists.

The need to keep the Teton Pass lifeline to the railroad functioning in the winter of 1940 awakened this collective spirit and led the Jackson citizenry to an act they considered reasonable. But it was illegal.

The 1920s saw the changeover from entirely horse-drawn equipment, to horse-drawn sleighs in winter and motor cars and trucks in summer. The 1930s saw the introduction of snow-removal equipment for the roads. In 1937, for the first time, the road over Teton Pass was kept open to car traffic all winter.

Roads through Hoback Canyon and over Togwotee Pass were also routinely cleared. Although this permitted rail connections 167 miles away at Lander or 187 miles at Rock Springs, the favored route was still the twenty-three miles over Teton Pass to the Oregon Shortline Railroad at Victor.

❧ *These plows were part of the equipment highjacked by a committee of citizens to open the road in 1940.* (JHM&HC)

Jacksonites soon depended upon motorized winter travel over the pass. Freighters used their teams and sleighs for other business during the winter months. A few of them freighted over the Pass with trucks.

The State Highway Department suddenly decided that there was not enough money in its budget to keep the Teton Pass road open all winter. District Highway Engineer William Sutton, of Rock Springs, sent the order. Plowing ended as of January 1940.

But the fact was that Jackson was not prepared to give up motorized travel over the pass during the severe winter months.

Mayor Harry Clissold and the county representatives wrote and telephoned appeals to State Highway Engineer R. J. Templeton and to Governor Nels H. Smith. The verdict was not altered.

Word was passed around, and on January 9, 1940, some two hundred Jackson citizens met to assess the situation. The consensus was, "By god, if the State Highway Department ain't gonna plow the road, we'll do it ourselves. We'll just use their equipment. It belongs to us anyway. It's just here to plow the roads of Jackson's Hole."

In force, the Jacksonites went to the Highway Department equipment yards where they demanded that the night watchman open up to "save yourself some trouble." The watchman complied and the regular snowplow crews manned their machines, "to assure that they were not damaged." The force, with a greatly swelled "voluntary crew," drove off to Teton Pass where the night was spent clearing the accumulated snow.

This happened on a Tuesday. Salt Lake City and Idaho Falls newspapers carried the story on Wednesday. The *Jackson Courier* covered it in its weekly Thursday issue. Snow plowing on Teton Pass was a hot topic.

Communications flew back and forth between Jackson and the State Engineer's office, and between Jackson and Governor Smith.

As a matter of law, Jackson citizens should have been strongly reprimanded and made to understand that they could not pirate state equipment. However, throughout the rest of the state and even outside, public sentiment was so strongly with the Jacksonites that the state authorities hesitated to take punitive action. The order stopping snow removal on Teton Pass was rescinded and a new order given to continue snow removal as long as it could be done with the "light" plows.

Maybe the snows were light enough to require no more than the "light" plows the remainder of that winter, or maybe the crews just used their own judgment about "light" snow. The pass was kept plowed the rest of that winter.

The Teton Pass road has been closed at times since that winter of 1940, but it has always been by an act of God—snow slides or *heavy* snows—and not because the State Highway Department refused to spend the money necessary to keep it open.

TOP OF THE WORLD

THE RANCH FURTHEST "UP THE RIVER" in Teton County, Wyoming, is the Darwin place. The river is the Gros Ventre, a large tributary of the South Fork of the Snake River.

Early trappers may have named the river the Gros Ventre after a tribe of Indians, or they may have named it for the fact of the big bend it takes on its journey from its headwaters to its mouth at the Snake River. The word Gros Ventre can mean big bend or big belly. It is also thought the French trappers might have named the Indians Gros Ventres because of their bellies.

The river flows easterly some ten miles from its source and then makes an almost right-angle turn to flow northerly to its confluence with Fish Creek. The basin on that first bend of the Gros Ventre is just big enough for one ranch.

The original homesteader, Fred Darwin, probably first picked out the spot when hunting in the area. His friend, Teddy Roosevelt, with whom he had served in the Rough Riders, apparently gave him the land by "presidential decree." This might explain the isolated (some might think choice) location away from other deeded land.

It commands a perfect area for wilderness living. It is entirely surrounded by Forest Service land. Wild animals are in abundance. The scenery is gorgeous—and the roads are atrocious. There is no danger of an influx of travelers.

Years before, a good wagon road had meandered up the Gros Ventre, over the divide at Kinky Creek and down the Green River to connect up Pinedale and Jackson. Many early homesteaders used that route to enter the valley. Intermittent, unpredictable land slides on the Gros Ventre side below the Darwin place eventually took out the road. It's about sixty miles from Jackson to the Darwin place. A horseback trail serves the traveler on the last leg of the journey. Residents at the Darwin place must use Pinedale (some fifty miles away) for their source of supply.

Locally, Darwin was considered a cranky old cuss, and he was generally avoided by the other settlers up the Gros Ventre. He had, at different times, partners on the ranch. He ran them off. Gossip spread that he would keep them on until he had exhausted their money and physical help in building up the place, then he'd become so obnoxious that they would leave.

He did not develop a cattle herd, so the only income from the place was as a hunting camp. He sold to Ray and Winnifred Black in 1917. Jackson's Holers have no record of where he went when he left.

Ray Black is the same man who later came to Jackson and built the Meadowbrook Motel. During the time he owned the Darwin place, it was used as a private hunting lodge. While he may have had some paying guests, it was not developed as a dude ranch, nor even as a big game outfitting/hunting camp. He sold to K.M. (Milton, called Mitt) and Lulu Robinson in 1923.

"Mitt" Robinson turned the place over to his nephew, Bob Robinson, who, with his wife Waife, and his son Bill, ran it as a dude ranch/hunting and fishing lodge for the next sixteen years. The Robinsons built a lodge cabin, other cabins, and outbuildings. When they sold in 1939 to go back east to live, young Billy decided he would rather stay with his uncles, Butch and Eddie Robinson, who lived down the river about ten miles.

(Later, Bob and Waife established a fishing and hunting lodge near Butch and Eddie, where Fish Creek joins the Gros Ventre. This place they only operated in the summer. When his parents and uncles died in the course of time, Billie Robinson inherited their places and still uses them as headquarters for his hunting, fishing and outfitting business.)

Edward C. Severence (called Cassie) bought the Darwin place from the Robinsons. A railroader from the Laramie, Wyoming, area, he did not develop the holding commercially, but used it for a private get-a-way and hunting lodge. He sold, in 1946, to Phillip and Lalita Norton.

With the advent of the Nortons, the Darwin place took on an interesting and exciting aspect, at least in the eyes of struggling locals. Phil and Lalita really did qualify as Westerners; Lalita having been raised on a big ranch in southern New Mexico, Phil having grown up somewhere in Wyoming. But their brand of *western* was entirely foreign to the native's way of thinkin'. Long-time locals had to call them Western dudes — they had money to cushion their upbringing and lifestyle.... And what a lifestyle.

Phil was educated to the business world and gravitated to the real-estate business in southern California. Lalita, the child of wealthy land owners of Mexican descent, grew up knowing all about horses and riding, ranching and domestic life, but she had always had servants to do all the physical work. They met in California and joined in the social whirl of the booming twenties.

Phil was important enough politically to be invited into the consular service and served the State Department in various European countries, chiefly Russia. Upon retiring from that service, the couple decided to retire also from the fast lane of society. They scouted out the most remote place they ever heard of — eventually bought the Darwin place, and set off to "rough it."

Phil and Lalita loved their ranch. With just a short ride up Kinky Creek, they could go from the Gros Ventre watershed onto the Green River watershed. With a little longer ride, they could be across the Bacon Creek ridge and onto the headwater streams of the Wind River. They really were at the top-of-the-world! — the headwaters of the three major rivers that drain the western part of the United States. This was their retreat; their place to get away from the rat-race of modern society; their chance to "rough it."

But there was no point in roughing it in discomfort. The Nortons built a lovely new cabin for their use. They installed an electric generator and automatic pump to make the place modern. Comfortable, although rustic, furniture filled the rooms. Navajo rugs covered the polished wood floors; exotic mementos from their travels filled the rooms. In the old lodge, they installed a couple who were willing and anxious to share the isolation and help with the work. They brought their horses from California. Old timers watched and listened.

For summer travel, they had a four-wheel-drive vehicle, and for winter they procured a sled and dog team. Not just any team of dogs—this team was entirely made up of descendants of Admiral Byrd's lead dog, who had accompanied Byrd on his expeditions to the Poles. The Nortons kept one beautiful white husky at the house for a house pet, the others had to stay out at the edge of the timber on chains—all ten or twelve of them.

At first the dogs were allowed some freedom, but soon complaints from neighbors fifteen or twenty miles away came back to them. The dogs had been seen in the cattle herd. Someone's child had been frightened upon seeing one of the dogs as she was out hiking. "She thought it was a wolf." Since the dogs wouldn't stay close to home, they had to be tied up.

The first year or two, Phil bought old horses (called bear bait locally) for dog food. They were butchered as needed during the year. He found it hard to find a hired man who would stay on when he found that was part of the job. Norton solved that problem by ordering a train-car load of dog food delivered to Rock Springs, then trucked on up to the ranch and stored in a shed. All that just for dogs? He had no trouble keeping a hired couple from then on.

He just about lost the good help of a neighbor, though, and through no fault of his own.

Snooks Moore lived down the Green River side of the pass about seven miles. Snooks was a Jackson's Hole kind of westerner —one who had all-around ranching skills and he wasn't above using them. Anything that needed doing on a mountain ranch, Snooks could do. The Nortons found it very convenient to hire Snooks whenever Snooks had time enough from his own work to lend a hand.

He always came from home to work and went back home at night. Mrs. Norton thought it would save time and gas if he would just stay at the Darwin place for a few days. Snooks gave no heed to the idea, saying he had to go home to take care of things.

One day Lalita happened to be talking to Snook's wife Evelyn. She broached the plan to Evelyn, saying it would be so much more practical—and Evelyn didn't mind staying alone a night or two, did she?

❧ *In Jackson's Hole, it's common for snow slides to bring travel to a halt. Here a snowslide on the Hoback Canyon Road is shoveled out by hand in 1934–1935.* (JHM&HC)

Evelyn told her that she wouldn't mind, but Snooks wouldn't stand for it.

Lalita teasingly said, "Why don't you feed him some salt-peter? Maybe then he could stand to be away a night or two."

Evelyn was not amused and couldn't think of a quick rejoinder, but after thinking it over she did see a little humor in it, so she repeated it to Snooks.

He blew his top. "Why that dirty-minded old biddy," he snorted. "That's the last time they'll get me to trot up there to do their work."

That wasn't all Snooks said, and it took a long time for Evelyn to cool him down—pointing out that the crowd the Nortons associated with in California was a loose-talking crowd, and that maybe Lalita didn't mean any real harm

Later on, Snooks really had his straight-laced morals shocked when the Nortons' regular hired man whispered around that he had gone up to the main house to wish the Nortons a Happy New Year, and as he passed the window he happened to glance in—and there were the Nortons, acting high as a kite. They were dancing nude to the tunes on the radio.... He thought he had better let them have their own private Happy New Year.

The Nortons entertained relatives and very close friends at the ranch, but they did not encourage their hosts of California friends to come. This was not a dude ranch. The fast crowd was what they were trying to leave behind.

Phil ran a trap line in the winter. His catches of martin, mink, and coyotes, with one or two lynx, were tanned and proudly hung on the walls of the lodge. He really didn't consider it a job to make a living at; rather it was a romantic proof of his ability. After all, Phil was retirement age. Sometimes the hired man went along on the trapping trips, sometimes Phil traveled alone, and sometimes Lalita accompanied him.

One day when she was preparing to go along, Phil was packing the sled when something excited the dogs. They made a tremendous lunge which caught Phil off balance. (He was holding the lead dog.) They jerked the sled against Lalita and toppled her across it in such a way that it injured her back. She was helped into the house and relaxed on the bed.

Phil wanted to take her immediately on the dog sled to Kendall, then by team on to Pinedale, where she could be taken by car to Rock Springs or Jackson to the hospital. Lalita wouldn't hear of it.

"Just give me a hot water bottle, a shot of brandy and a few days to rest my back. I'll be all right."

After a few days Lalita did seem to be all right, but the back problem did not go away.

Lalita loved her horses. In summer the rides up all the streams, and along Sportsman's Ridge or Bacon Creek Ridge, or following the old road used by earlier settlers to enter Jackson Hole were her main delight. She insisted her pet horse, a beautiful Palomino, kept his eye alert to overhanging tree limbs or other obstructions which might hit her and took care to avoid them.

It was a major tragedy, then, when her pet horse took sick and died in spite of all the veterinarian could do. Phil was alarmed for the safety of the rest of the ponies, as well as wishing to know just what had been the cause of death, so he had the vet perform an autopsy. They found a few inches of bailing wire in the horse's stomach.

That would have been the end of the matter for most any rancher in the country, but Phil still couldn't stand to have Lalita lose her good top horse forever. He quickly thought of something that might comfort her.

He had the hired man take off the hide, then asked the vet to deliver it to the taxidermist to be tanned.

When the hide came back with a beautiful soft job of tanning, Phil then couldn't make up his mind if Lalita would be pleased or repulsed. He asked a lady friend for advice. She told him that for herself she would rather remember the horse with the hide on him.

Poor Phil, he wanted so badly to ease Lalita's pain. I never learned what became of the hide.

In the early days of settlement, homesteads were taken up all along the valley of the Green River—about to the mouth of Tosi Creek. There the post office of Kendall was established.

Across the divide on the Gros Ventre, settlement came a little later, but soon ranches were strung along up the river to the Lafferty place. The next six-mile stretch of river flows between rugged buttes—almost a canyon. Then the basin containing the Darwin place opens up. Because Kendall, just over the divide, was much nearer than Jackson, the residents of the upper Gros Ventre went to Kendall for their mail.

In 1905, the upper Gros Ventre folks acquired their own post office; they named it Brooks. Billy Lafferty carried the mail over the divide from Kendall once a week. In summer he rode horseback, in winter he made the trip on snowshoes—a round trip of approximately twenty-five or thirty miles.

The Brooks Post Office was abandoned in 1912, so the residents of the Darwin place had always used Kendall for their mail service. Phil and Lalita did too.

In the winter it was an exhilarating ride down to Kendall and back with the dog team, but after Lalita's sled accident, they were a bit concerned about that mode of travel. They thought of a better way.

Price Milward had his flying service in operation at that time so Phil got in touch with him and arranged an airmail delivery right at the ranch.

Norton placed two long poles in the yard with a wire and pulley system stretched between them. Outgoing mail would be placed in a pouch and strung between the poles. Price would fly past dragging a long line with a hook attached. He would hook Norton's line and mail sack and reel it in; exchange the outgoing mail for the incoming mail, drop the line and pouch in the yard and fly off. Private airmail service! In stormy weather they might have to wait a few days. It didn't take long for news of the Norton's latest extravagance to make the rounds.

Aging (I'm sure Lalita wouldn't appreciate the term, but what else is there?) brings problems, whether in the city or on an isolated ranch. Usually the problems can be dealt with easier in the crowded city. Lalita's back continued to give her periods of great pain. They made trips to consult with doctors. The doctors diagnosed a ruptured disk in the spine and recommended surgery. Lalita still refused this option.

They imported a contour chair; she tried back braces of various kinds. Finally, one winter after they agreed to dispense with the dogs, she awakened in so much pain that she couldn't move. Phil snow-shoed to Kendall to telephone to the Forest Service office in Jackson for emergency rescue. He knew that the Forest Service had been using an oversnow machine (a Thiacol) for some of their winter work.

It was the quickest method he could think of to get Lalita to a hospital. The Forest Service responded, not without misgivings. "Might this lead to calls from everyone in trouble?"

At the hospital, Lalita was put in traction. She still refused spinal surgery. After a rest period in California she again returned to the ranch.

One Christmas day the Robinson family, who lived down river on the Gros Ventre about eight miles and were just sitting down to a Christmas dinner with family and neighbors, were amazed to have Phil Norton arrive at the door. He had troubles. His hired man, Al Pheiffer, had died that morning, apparently of a heart attack.

The snow was too deep for cars but not too deep for horses. Phil thought that if someone could help him bring Pheiffer's wife Lee and the body this far on a toboggan, that a team and sleigh could be used to haul them on down to Jackson. Of course the neighbors were willing and anxious to help.

Glen Taylor and Billie Green, being the two youngest and most free of responsibilities, were delegated to return to the Darwin Place with Phil and bring the body out. Al's widow, Lee, rode out with the boys when they brought the body on the toboggan, then went on into Jackson with the sleigh. After the funeral, Lee rode back up the river, returned to the Darwin place, and stayed the rest of the winter.

Phil and Lalita lived at the Darwin place from 1946 until 1958. I'm sure they enjoyed their life there, getting back to the basics. The immediate reason for their giving up that life was Lalita's back problem. After another emergency call to the Forest Service for Lalita's evacuation, the Forest Service personnel told them that they would come this time but that they could not respond to another call. It was setting a precedent that they could not follow.

Forest Service personnel strongly recommended that the Nortons get out of the ranch in the winter. Faced with what amounted to an ultimatum, the Norton's regretfully made the decision to leave. They sold the Darwin Place to A. H. McIntyre and returned to California, where their son had been conducting the family real estate business. The last word Jacksonites heard from Phil and Lalita, they were running the Casa Blanca Resort Hotel in Palm Springs, California.

Under the ownership of McIntyre, and the ownership in 1960 of Mr. and Mrs. Gene Chapman, the Darwin Place didn't make news waves. It was next acquired by Charles B. Woodman and his wife in 1964. Since then it has been used as a summer guest ranch.

In 1972, Charles B. Woodman deeded it to Charles Loring Woodman. A landing strip was smoothed out where the Kinky Creek meadows make a fine big flat near the divide between Kinky Creek and Tosi.

Now us old-timers figure it's a sign things are getting pretty modern when one can fly to one's doorstep. Especially when that doorstep happens to be Norton's "Top-of-the-World!.... The headwaters of the three major rivers that drain the western part of the United States...."

Just a few years back—along about 1985—the Woodmans allowed winter snowmobile accommodations at the ranch. Something must have gone awry because now the ranch is posted, bluntly warning *Snowmobiles KEEP OUT*.

BIBLIOGRAPHICAL NOTES

The author is indebted to many friends and acquaintances who have shared their histories and their memories over the years. The passing down of stories has been a respected ritual for centuries, and this book would not exist without those valued chroniclers of early life in Jackson's Hole.

The author acknowledges that this book is just a beginning. There are many more stories in the valley which are equally interesting and deserve to be recorded. She hopes the omissions in this book will inspire someone to compile additional pioneer stories of the area.

Many of these chapters appeared in an earlier form under the author's byline in the *Jackson Hole Guide,* primarily in the early 1970s. Much of the information comes from first-hand accounts by long-time Jackson Hole residents and their descendants given to the author during interviews she conducted while researching the newspaper articles.

Jackson newspapers and courthouse records have been used extensively in the research for this book.

THE FIRST HOMESTEADERS. Jackson Hole historian Elizabeth Hayden interviewed the relatives of Carnes and Holland, as well as many other old-timers, in the 1930s. Hayden's remarkable collection of articles and notes are now in the archives of the Jackson Hole Museum and Historical Center. Other information came from records on water rights and other legal documents.

A WINTER ADVENTURE. The source for this story was Homer Richards, grandson of Albert Richards.

THE WILSONS OF JACKSON'S HOLE. The history of the Wilson family is easily confused because of the number of family members who pioneered in Jackson's Hole. Joyce Imeson Lucas granted permission to use her well-researched history of the family. Imeson with Judy Rosbrook Anderson is the author of *The First Families into Jackson Hole*, a compilation of Wilson family biographies.

STEPHEN LEEK: THE MAN WHO SAVED THE ELK. The Stephen Leek collection is housed at the Western Heritage Center at the University of Wyoming.

THE SIMPSONS GAVE JACKSON ITS NAME. Dorothy Redmond Hubbard, daughter of Bill and Ida Simpson Redmond, provided Maggie Simpson's diary, as well as much of the other information in the story.

MAGGIE McBRIDE'S DIARY. Maggie McBride's diary appeared in the *Jackson Hole Courier* on July 27, 1950 and is used with permission.

ED HARRINGTON, ALIAS TRAFTON: HIGHWAYMAN. Sources for this story include Buster Estes's reminiscences to the author and information provided by John Markham. Ben Goe surmised often that Harrington murdered Goodwin.

TOO BIG A DREAM. The life of John Sargent has been well-documented by several sources including Grand Teton National Park archivists. Other information was gained from newspaper reports, from an interview with Mary Sargent Cunningham Sears, from legal documents loaned by the Sargent's daughter Adelaide to the Park Service, and from local sources including Maria Allen and Slim Lawrence, long-time caretaker of the Sargent place.

THE DELONEY REMINISCENCES. Family data and Jackson Hole happenings came from interviews with Frances Deloney Clark and Jim Deloney. Quoted documents were provided by Frances Deloney Clark.

FROM NOTHING TO NOW. Pearl Nelson Deyo and Almer Nelson provided information during an interview in 1972.

THE SHEFFIELDS OF MORAN. Benjamin Sheffield, Jr., provided information for the Sheffield chapter.

J.R. JONES: WINNING A BET WITH UNCLE SAM. Ellen Jones Dornan, daughter of J.R. Jones, supplied much of the information for this chapter. Also J.R. Jones's biography and many of his stories were compiled by his granddaughter-in-law, Reade Dornan, in a book titled *Preserving the Game,* released in 1990 by Hemingway Western Studies, Boise State University Center Press. Information from this source is used by permission of the author.

SNOW SLIDE BURIED ELIAS WILSON. Jim Imeson's story of the snowslide is in the Sylvester Wilson Family Collection and is used by permission of Joyce Imeson Lucas.

HE'S MEAN, BUT I'M MENOR. Frances Judge's delightful article on the Menors which appeared in the *Jackson Hole Courier* on July 12, 1945, provided information for this story. The information on the car swept off the ferry was found in a news clipping in the Sylvester Wilson Family Collection and is used with permission of Joyce Imeson Lucas.

THE DUDE RANCH AND THE CON ARTIST. This story, co-authored by Fern K. Nelson and Ed Loyd, first appeared in an article in the *Dude Rancher Magazine* in the Fall/Winter issue of 1982.

*J*NDEX

FERN KNUTSEN NELSON CAME into the Jackson Hole Valley in the autumn of 1911 carried in her mother's arms over Teton Pass. Dorothy Knutsen did not trust that the wagons would not tip over on the steep trail. Fern's father, Lou Knutsen, had just contracted to carry mail from the railroad end at Victor, Idaho to Jackson, Wyoming; some twenty-six miles over the rugged Teton Range. He was moving his family from Driggs, Idaho, to Jackson where they would make a new home. Fern's earliest memories are of ranch life in South Park, an area just south of the town of Jackson. She grew up with two brothers and three sisters; plenty of animals and wildlife, and lots of elbow room.

With her family, and later with husband Albert Nelson, Fern has participated in most of the growth activities of the valley. She has been homesteader, rancher; helped her sister at her restaurant and motel operation; and helped her husband with his carpentry contracting business and his dude ranch and big game outfitting business.

She knows the mountain and valley terrain from riding the range with cattle or dudes until retiring in 1961.

Albert and Fern raised three children, a boy and two girls, who have given them eleven grandchildren. All are grown now with homes in separate towns in Wyoming.

Upon retiring Albert took up artistic painting; something he had always wanted to do. Fern wrote for the local newspaper. Albert encouraged her to paint also, which she did. They had many congenial lessons and expeditions before Albert's untimely death in 1970. Since then Fern has pursued writing and some desultory painting. Her memories of life as it was in Jackson Hole are authentic.